Table of Contents

Introduction

Basic Math Skills is based on current NCTM standards and is designed to support any math curriculum that you may be using in your classroom. The standard strands (Number and Operations, Algebra, Geometry, Measurement, and Data Analysis and Probability) and skills within the strand are listed on the overview page for each section of the book. The skill is also shown at the bottom of each reproducible page.

Opportunities to practice the process standards (Problem Solving, Reasoning and Proof, Communication, Connections, and Representation) are also provided as students complete the various types of activities in this resource book.

Basic Math Skills may be used as a resource providing practice of skills already introduced to students. Any page may be used with an individual child, as homework, with a small group, or by the whole class.

Skill Practice

Each skill is covered in a set of six reproducible pages that include the following:

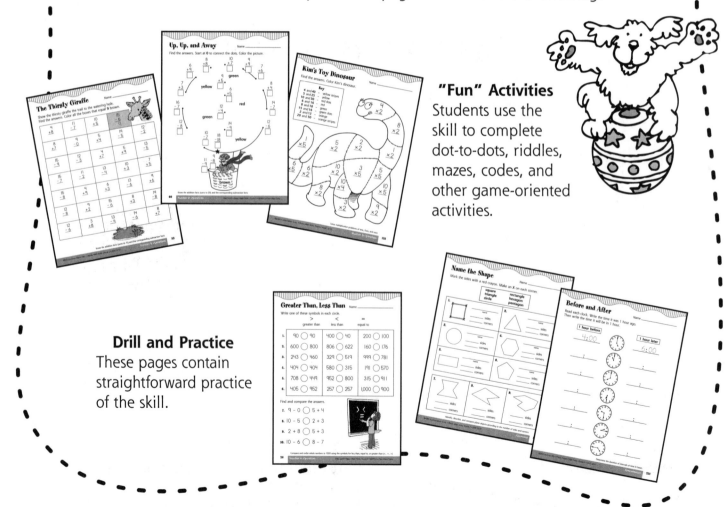

"Fun" Activities

Students use the skill to complete dot-to-dots, riddles, mazes, codes, and other game-oriented activities.

Drill and Practice

These pages contain straightforward practice of the skill.

EMC 3015 • *Basic Math Skills, Grade 2* • ©2003 by Evan-Moor Corp.

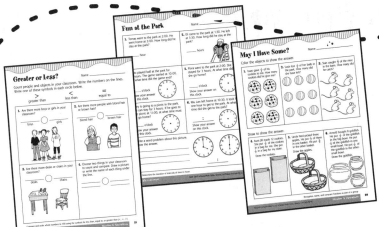

Application/Word Problem Activities

Students use the skill to problem solve and explore real-life situations.

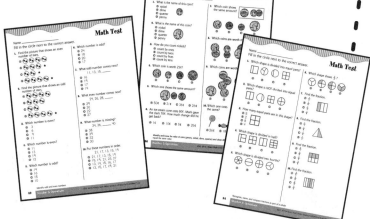

Math Test

A test in standardized format is provided for each skill.

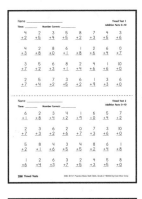

Additional Resources

The following additional resources are also provided:

- Timed math tests
- Class record sheet
- Test answer form
- Awards
- Reproducible practice cards for addition (teens), subtraction (teens), and multiplication (2s, 5s, 10s) facts

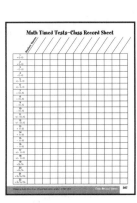

Awards

Number and Operations

100 Puzzle

Name _____

You will need a sheet of paper and a glue stick or paste.
Cut out the puzzle pieces and glue them in order from **1** to **100**.

7	8	9	10
17	18	19	20
27	28	29	30

31	32	33
41	42	43
51	52	53
61	62	63

71	72	73
81	82	83
91	92	93

77	78	79	80
87	88	89	90
97	98	99	100

1	2	3
11	12	13
21	22	23

34	35	36
44	45	46
54	55	56

4	5	6
14	15	16
24	25	26

37	38	39	40
47	48	49	50
57	58	59	60
67	68	69	70

64	65	66
74	75	76
84	85	86
94	95	96

Count, read, and write whole numbers to 100

Number & Operations

What Am I?

Connect the dots from **50** to **100** to find the animal.

I am a _____.

Count, read, and write whole numbers to 100

What Is the Missing Number?

Name _____

Write the missing numbers.

In between	After	Before
50 _51_ 52	37 _38_	_66_ 67
26 ____ 28	69 ____	____ 37
82 ____ 84	56 ____	____ 54
37 ____ 39	30 ____	____ 49
29 ____ 31	49 ____	____ 19
42 ____ 44	57 ____	____ 70
39 ____ 41	70 ____	____ 88
68 ____ 70	89 ____	____ 69
59 ____ 61	53 ____	____ 20
92 ____ 94	19 ____	____ 100

Count, read, and write whole numbers to 100

Number & Operations

Unscramble the Numbers

Write the numbers in order in the boxes.

Name _____

1.

12 14
13   16
15   11

| 11 | 12 | | | | |

2.

40
80   70
60
50   30

| 30 | | | | | |

3.

77   82
81
80
78   79

| 77 | | | | | |

4.

55   56
53   54
52   57

| 52 | | | | | |

5.

68   59
35
16
27   44

| 16 | | | | | |

6.

57   98
63
82
76   100

| 57 | | | | | |

Count, read, and write whole numbers to 100

Number & Operations   EMC 3015 • Basic Math Skills, Grade 2 • ©2003 by Evan-Moor Corp.

Classroom Count

Name _____

1. Help Miyeko count the paper clips.

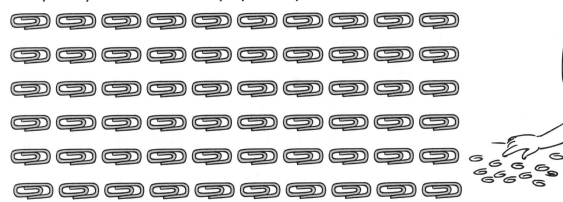

_____ paper clips

2. Help Roscoe count the crayons.

_____ crayons

3. Find something in your classroom to count. Draw one here.

[ ]

Write its name here. _____

How many did you count? _____

Count read and write whole numbers to 100

Number & Operations

Name _____

Math Test

Fill in the circle next to the correct answer.

1. What number comes next?

56, 57, 58, 59, _____

Ⓐ 50
Ⓑ 40
Ⓒ 30
Ⓓ 60

2. What number is missing?

34, 35, _____, 37, 38

Ⓐ 33
Ⓑ 36
Ⓒ 35
Ⓓ 39

3. What number is missing?

_____, 41, 42, 43, 44

Ⓐ 45
Ⓑ 43
Ⓒ 50
Ⓓ 40

4. Find the numbers that are NOT in order.

Ⓐ 36, 37, 38, 39, 40
Ⓑ 55, 56, 57, 58, 59
Ⓒ 42, 41, 40, 43, 44
Ⓓ 46, 47, 48, 49, 50

5. Which number is 1 more than 60?

Ⓐ 55
Ⓑ 59
Ⓒ 49
Ⓓ 61

6. Which number is 1 less than 40?

Ⓐ 39
Ⓑ 55
Ⓒ 41
Ⓓ 47

7. Find the number that is 1 more than 31.

Ⓐ 40
Ⓑ 30
Ⓒ 33
Ⓓ 32

8. Find the number that is 1 less than 71.

Ⓐ 70
Ⓑ 72
Ⓒ 60
Ⓓ 7

9. Find the number that is 10 less than 100.

Ⓐ 70
Ⓑ 90
Ⓒ 80
Ⓓ 99

10. Find the number that is 10 less than 50.

Ⓐ 51
Ⓑ 60
Ⓒ 40
Ⓓ 49

Count, read, and write whole numbers to 100

EMC 3015 • Basic Math Skills, Grade 2 • ©2003 by Evan-Moor Corp.

How Many Elephants Can You Find?

Name _____

Color boxes to find the elephants.

Less than 50 – **blue**

Greater than 50 – **brown**

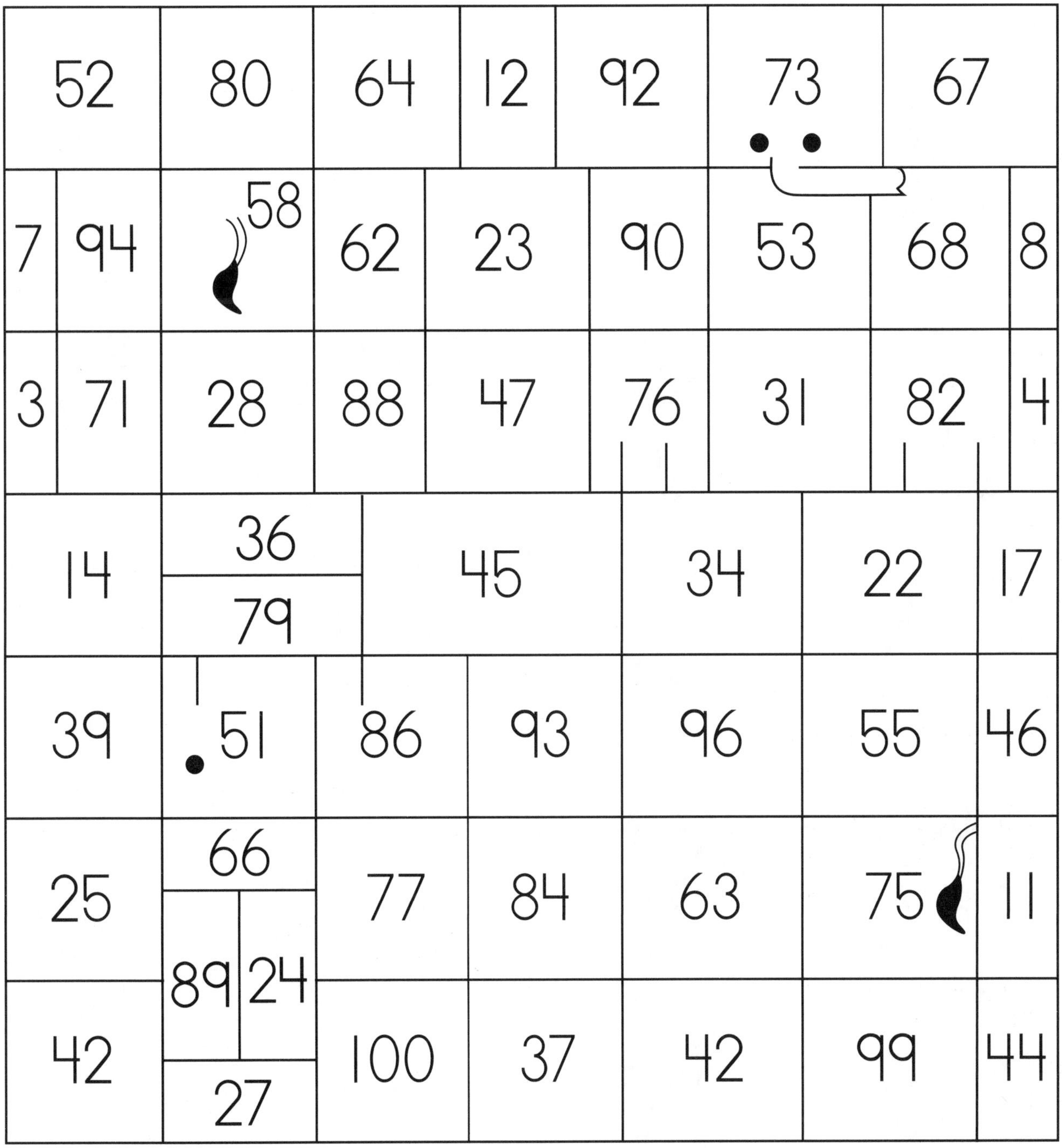

52	80	64	12	92	73	67
7	94	58	62	23	90	53	68	8
3	71	28	88	47	76	31	82	4
14	36 / 79	45	34	22	17
39	51	86	93	96	55	46
25	66	77	84	63	75	11
42	89	24 / 27	100	37	42	99	44

I found _____ elephants.

Compare and order whole numbers to 100 using the symbols for less than, equal to, or greater than (<, =, >)

Number & Operations

11

Carl, the Cookie-Loving Bear

Name _____

Carl loves cookies. He always takes the sack with more cookies. Write one of the symbols in each circle below to show which sacks Carl would take.

>	<	=
greater than	less than	equal to

1. Cookies 12 ◯ Cookies 8

2. Cookies 15 ◯ Cookies 10

3. Cookies 36 ◯ Cookies 29

4. Cookies 27 ◯ Cookies 75

5. Cookies 30 ◯ Cookies 30

6. Cookies 41 ◯ Cookies 26

7. Cookies 74 ◯ Cookies 75

8. Cookies 88 ◯ Cookies 59

9. Cookies 65 ◯ Cookies 95

10. Cookies 46 ◯ Cookies 32

Compare and order whole numbers to 100 using the symbols for less than, equal to, or greater than (<, =, >)

Number & Operations   EMC 3015 • Basic Math Skills, Grade 2 • ©2003 by Evan-Moor Corp.

Crazy About Cars

Name _____

Jamal and his friends collect model cars. Use the graph to compare the number of model cars the children have.

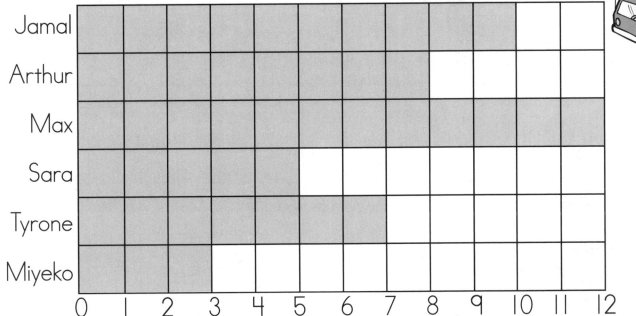

	0	1	2	3	4	5	6	7	8	9	10	11	12
Jamal													
Arthur													
Max													
Sara													
Tyrone													
Miyeko													

Write one of these symbols in each circle below.

> greater than   < less than   = equal to

1. Jamal ◯ Tyrone

2. Arthur ◯ Max

3. Sara ◯ Miyeko

4. Sara + Miyeko ◯ Max

5. Tyrone ◯ Miyeko + Arthur

6. Miyeko + Tyrone ◯ Arthur

Compare and order whole numbers to 100 using the symbols for less than, equal to, or greater than (<, =, >)

Number & Operations

Greater Than, Less Than, or Equal?

Name _____

3 is **greater than** 1	2 is **less than** 4	5 is **equal to** 5
3 > 1	2 < 4	5 = 5

Write one of these symbols in each circle below.

>	<	=
greater than	less than	equal to

1.	3 ◯ 8	9 ◯ 4	7 ◯ 5
2.	40 ◯ 20	50 ◯ 20	60 ◯ 30
3.	46 ◯ 26	62 ◯ 32	28 ◯ 18
4.	63 ◯ 68	49 ◯ 49	32 ◯ 37
5.	59 ◯ 61	27 ◯ 32	44 ◯ 63
6.	95 ◯ 67	83 ◯ 69	72 ◯ 91

Write these numbers in order from the smallest to the largest.

68   72   59   41

_____   _____   _____   _____
smallest   largest

Compare and order whole numbers to 100 using the symbols for less than, equal to, or greater than (<, =, >)

EMC 3015 • Basic Math Skills, Grade 2 • ©2003 by Evan-Moor Corp.

Greater or Less?

Count people and objects in your classroom. Write the numbers on the lines. Write one of these symbols in each circle below.

>	**<**	**=**
greater than	less than	equal to

---

1. Are there more boys or girls in your classroom?

_____ ◯ _____
boys 　　　　　　 girls

2. Are there more people with blond hair or brown hair?

_____ ◯ _____
blond hair 　　　　 brown hair

3. Are there more desks or chairs in your classroom?

_____ ◯ _____
desks 　　　　　　 chairs

4. Choose two things in your classroom to count and compare. Draw a picture or write the name of each thing under the line.

_____ ◯ _____

Compare and order whole numbers to 100 using the symbols for less than, equal to, or greater than (<, =, >)

Number & Operations

Name _____

Fill in the circle next to the correct answer.

1. Which number is greater than 68?
   - Ⓐ 66
   - Ⓑ 67
   - Ⓒ 68
   - Ⓓ 69

2. Which number is greater than 85?
   - Ⓐ 82
   - Ⓑ 65
   - Ⓒ 80
   - Ⓓ 90

3. Which number is less than 44?
   - Ⓐ 50
   - Ⓑ 48
   - Ⓒ 39
   - Ⓓ 53

4. Which number is less than 30?
   - Ⓐ 30
   - Ⓑ 29
   - Ⓒ 51
   - Ⓓ 48

5. Find the missing sign.
   66 ◯ 74
   - Ⓐ <
   - Ⓒ >
   - Ⓒ =

6. Find the missing sign.
   59 ◯ 21
   - Ⓐ <
   - Ⓑ >
   - Ⓒ =

7. Which number is missing?
   40 < _____
   - Ⓐ 35
   - Ⓑ 31
   - Ⓒ 47
   - Ⓓ 32

8. Which number is missing?
   15 = _____
   - Ⓐ 18
   - Ⓑ 51
   - Ⓒ 10
   - Ⓓ 15

9. Tammy has 25 animal stickers. She has 23 plant stickers. Which one tells about her stickers?
   - Ⓐ 25 animal stickers > 23 plant stickers
   - Ⓑ 25 animal stickers < 23 plant stickers
   - Ⓒ 25 animal stickers = 23 plant stickers
   - Ⓓ 23 plant stickers > 25 animal stickers

10. Mark has 62 pennies. Jakob has 79 pennies. Which one tells about the pennies?
    - Ⓐ 62 pennies > 79 pennies
    - Ⓑ 62 pennies = 79 pennies
    - Ⓒ 62 pennies < 79 pennies
    - Ⓓ 79 pennies < 62 pennies

Compare and order whole numbers to 100 using the symbols for less than, equal to, or greater than (<, =, >)

EMC 3015 • Basic Math Skills, Grade 2 • ©2003 by Evan-Moor Corp.

3, 2, 1, Blast Off!

Start at **279**.
Connect the dots in order.

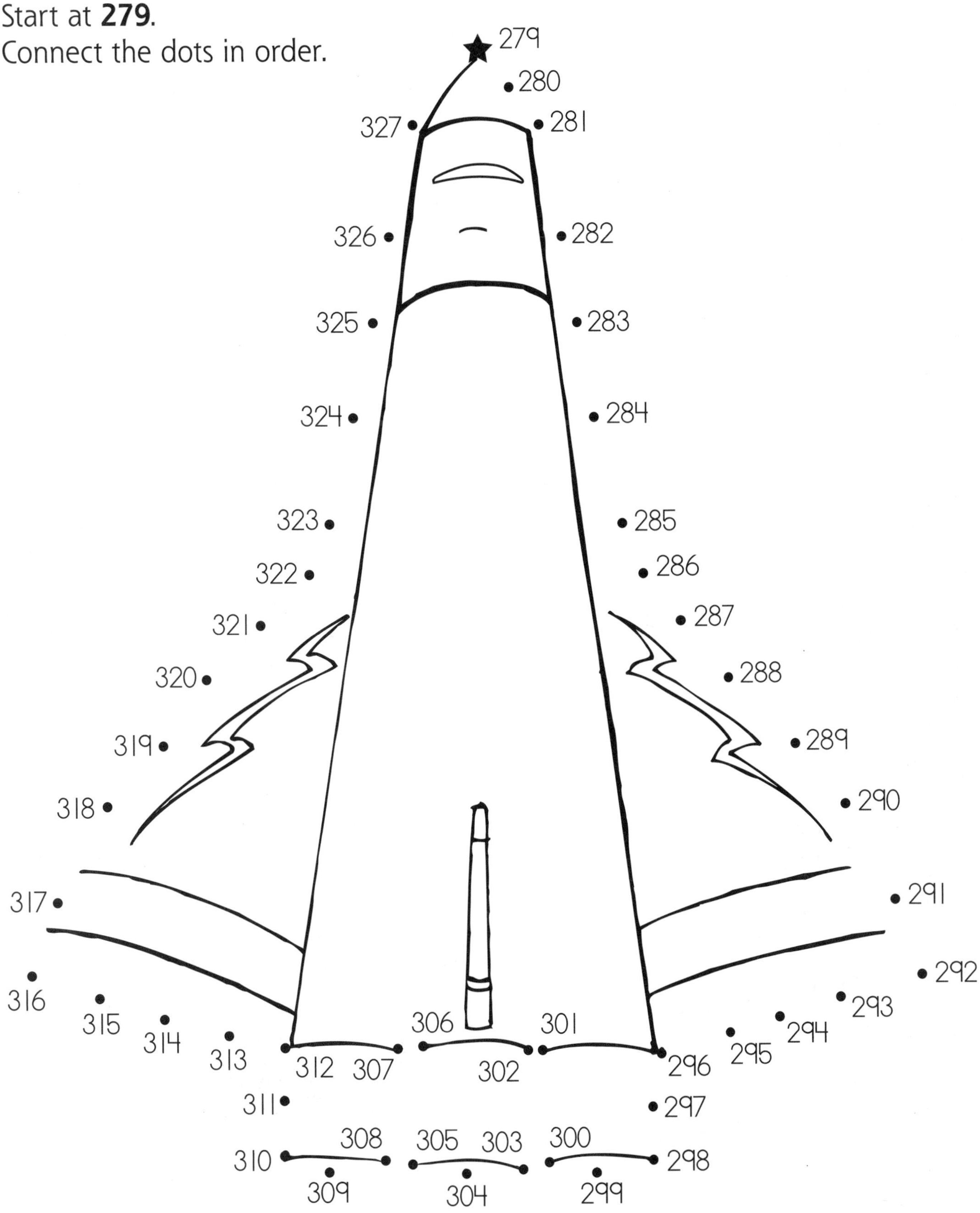

279
280
281
327
326 282
325 283
324 284
323 285
322 286
321 287
320 288
319 289
318 290
317 291
316 292
315 293
314 294
313 306 301 295
312 307 302 296
311 297
310 308 305 303 300 298
309 304 299

Count, read, and write whole numbers to 1000

Road Race

Count by 100s to win the race.

100   ____   ____

____   ____   ____

____   ____   ____   1,000

Fill in the missing numbers to show what comes next.

100   *200*   300   _____

700   _____   900   _____

400   _____   500   _____

200   _____   800   _____

600   _____

Count, read, and write whole numbers to 1000

Number & Operations

EMC 3015 • Basic Math Skills, Grade 2 • ©2003 by Evan-Moor Corp.

100 to 1,000

Name _____

Count by 10s.

100 <u>110</u> <u>120</u> ___ ___ ___ ___ ___ ___

200 ___ ___ ___ ___ ___ ___ ___ ___

300 ___ ___ ___ ___ ___ ___ ___ ___

400 ___ ___ ___ ___ ___ ___ ___ ___

500 ___ ___ ___ ___ ___ ___ ___ ___

600 ___ ___ ___ ___ ___ ___ ___ ___

700 ___ ___ ___ ___ ___ ___ ___ ___

800 ___ ___ ___ ___ ___ ___ ___ ___

900 ___ ___ ___ ___ ___ ___ ___ ___

1,000

Fill the missing numbers.

200 201 ___ ___ ___ ___ ___ ___

450 451 ___ ___ ___ ___ ___ ___

893 894 ___ ___ ___ ___ ___ ___

Count, read, and write whole numbers to 1000

Number & Operations

What Number Comes In-between?

Name _____

Write the missing numbers.

1. 134 __135__ 136

2. 301 _____ 303

3. 645 _____ 647

4. 578 _____ 580

5. 832 _____ 834

6. 327 _____ 329

7. 161 _____ 163

8. 929 _____ 931

9. 499 _____ 501

10. 800 _____ 802

11. 515 _____ 517

12. 222 _____ 224

13. 715 _____ 717

14. 600 _____ 602

15. 256 _____ 258

16. 483 _____ 485

17. 720 _____ 722

18. 900 _____ 902

19. 199 _____ 201

20. 998 _____ 1,000

Count, read, and write whole numbers to 1000

Number & Operations

EMC 3015 • Basic Math Skills, Grade 2 • ©2003 by Evan-Moor Corp.

Help Uncle Fred

Name _____

Uncle Fred numbered his flowerpots. Now he is putting them in neat rows.
Can you help him put them in order on the plant rack?
Cut out the pots. Glue them in the correct order.

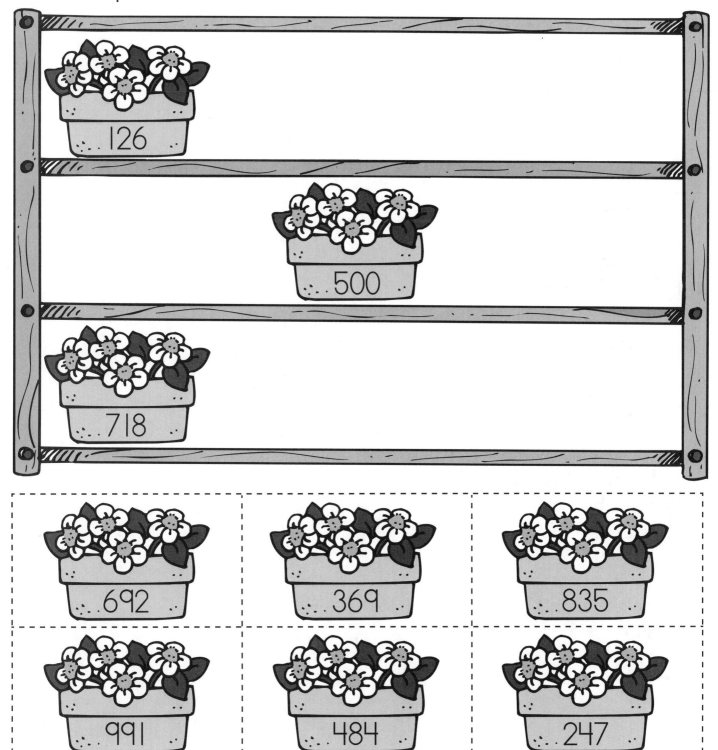

Count, read, and write whole numbers to 1000

Number & Operations

Math Test

Fill in the circle next to the correct answer.

1. What number comes next?

356, 357, 358, 359, _____

- Ⓐ 350
- Ⓑ 340
- Ⓒ 330
- Ⓓ 360

2. Find the missing number.

834, 835, _____, 837, 838

- Ⓐ 833
- Ⓑ 836
- Ⓒ 835
- Ⓓ 839

3. Find the missing number.

_____, 441, 442, 443, 444

- Ⓐ 445
- Ⓑ 443
- Ⓒ 450
- Ⓓ 440

4. Find the numbers that are NOT in order.

- Ⓐ 236, 237, 238, 239, 240
- Ⓑ 355, 356, 357, 358, 359
- Ⓒ 742, 741, 740, 743, 744
- Ⓓ 546, 547, 548, 549, 550

5. Which number is 1 more than 600?

- Ⓐ 555
- Ⓑ 590
- Ⓒ 499
- Ⓓ 601

6. Which number is 1 less than 400?

- Ⓐ 399
- Ⓑ 550
- Ⓒ 410
- Ⓓ 437

7. Which number is 1 more than 311?

- Ⓐ 401
- Ⓑ 312
- Ⓒ 335
- Ⓓ 300

8. Which number is 1 less than 171?

- Ⓐ 170
- Ⓑ 172
- Ⓒ 160
- Ⓓ 17

9. Which number is 100 more than 900?

- Ⓐ 810
- Ⓑ 910
- Ⓒ 800
- Ⓓ 1,000

10. Which number is 100 less than 500?

- Ⓐ 510
- Ⓑ 600
- Ⓒ 400
- Ⓓ 490

300

720

410

Count, read, and write whole numbers to 1000

Who Is Hiding Here?

Name _____

Color the spaces to find the animal hiding here.

more than 500 – **brown**   less than 500 – **blue**

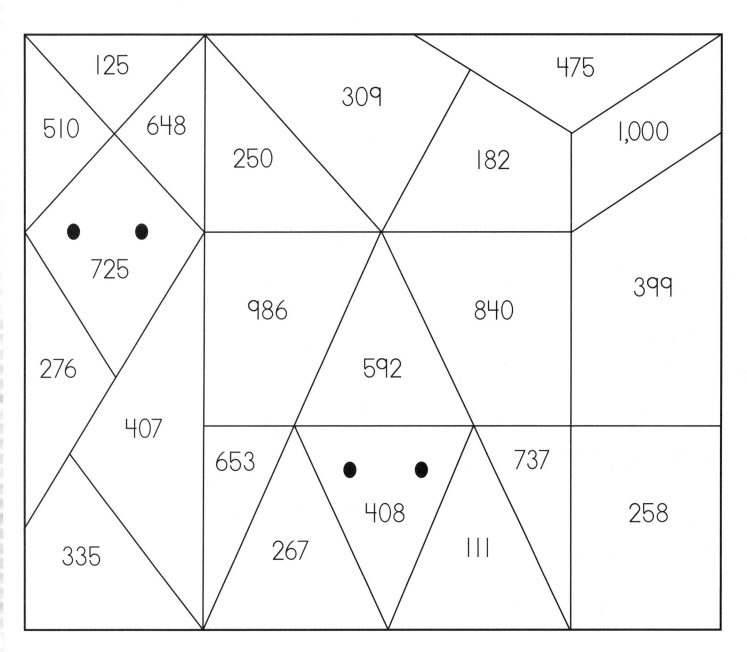

Circle the animal you found.

rabbit   hamster   fox

Compare and order whole numbers to 1000 using the symbols for less than, equal to, or greater than (<, =, >)

©2003 by Evan-Moor Corp. • Basic Math Skills, Grade 2 • EMC 3015

Number & Operations   **23**

Berry-Picking Time

Name _____

Draw a line from each number to the correct box.

78

550

180

624

709

269

333

832

452

> 500

(greater than)

< 500

(less than)

97

250

971

1,000

106

573

647

325

840

Compare and order whole numbers to 1000 using the symbols for less than, equal to, or greater than (<, =, >)

Compare the Numbers

Write one of these symbols in each circle.

> **>**
> greater than

> **<**
> less than

1. 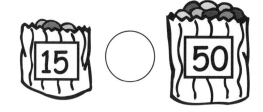 15 ◯ 50

2.  100 ◯ 20

3.  96 CRAYONS ◯  250 CRAYONS

4. 419 ◯ 82

5. 76 ◯ 79   100 ◯ 80   112 ◯ 115

6. 99 ◯ 100   200 ◯ 201   190 ◯ 180

7. 342 ◯ 399   410 ◯ 400   777 ◯ 766

8. 450 ◯ 449   305 ◯ 315   942 ◯ 952

9. 700 ◯ 800   580 ◯ 570   191 ◯ 911

Compare and order whole numbers to 1000 using the symbols for less than, equal to, or greater than (<, =, >)

Greater Than, Less Than

Name _____

Write one of these symbols in each circle.

>   <   =

greater than   less than   equal to

1. 90 ◯ 90	400 ◯ 40	200 ◯ 100
2. 600 ◯ 800	806 ◯ 622	160 ◯ 176
3. 243 ◯ 460	329 ◯ 519	999 ◯ 781
4. 404 ◯ 404	580 ◯ 315	191 ◯ 570
5. 708 ◯ 449	952 ◯ 800	315 ◯ 911
6. 405 ◯ 952	257 ◯ 257	1,000 ◯ 900

Find and compare the answers.

7. $9 - 0$ ◯ $5 + 4$

8. $10 - 5$ ◯ $2 + 3$

9. $2 + 8$ ◯ $5 + 3$

10. $10 - 6$ ◯ $8 - 7$

Compare and order whole numbers to 1000 using the symbols for less than, equal to, or greater than (<, =, >).

Number & Operations   EMC 3015 • Basic Math Skills, Grade 2 • ©2003 by Evan-Moor Corp.

Recycling

Name _____

Compare the numbers to find the answer. Use < = > symbols.

1. Mina collected 125 glass bottles and jars. Hamid collected 195 glass bottles and jars. Who collected more?

125 ◯ 195

_____ collected more

2. Carmen and Hector collected 150 cans. Kimiko and Yoshi collected 190 cans. Who collected more?

150 ◯ 190

_____ and _____ collected more

3. Scott and Bill were in a contest. They wanted to see who could collect more magazines to recycle. Scott collected 298 magazines. Bill collected 295 magazines. Who collected more?

298 ◯ 295

_____ collected more

4. Washington School collected 895 cans and bottles. Elm Street School collected 999 cans and bottles. Which school collected more?

999 ◯ 895

_____ collected more

5. Mr. Brown collected two large boxes of cans. One box held 315 cans. One box held 453 cans. Which box held more cans?

Write a symbol to show your answer.

315 ◯ 453

6. Cory collected 247 cans. He collected 247 bottles and jars.

Write a symbol to compare the numbers.

247 ◯ 247

7. Write a word problem about this picture. Show the answer.

798   769

_____

_____

_____

_____

Compare and order whole numbers to 1000 using the symbols for less than, equal to, or greater than (<, =, >)

Number & Operations

Name _____

Fill in the circle next to the correct answer.

1. Which number is greater than 218?

Ⓐ 216
Ⓑ 217
Ⓒ 218
Ⓓ 219

2. Which number is greater than 175?

Ⓐ 172
Ⓑ 155
Ⓒ 180
Ⓓ 170

3. Which number is less than 120?

Ⓐ 130
Ⓑ 118
Ⓒ 190
Ⓓ 123

4. Which number is less than 500?

Ⓐ 530
Ⓑ 529
Ⓒ 515
Ⓓ 458

5. Find the missing sign.

116 ◯ 124

Ⓐ <
Ⓑ >
Ⓒ =

6. Find the missing sign.

169 ◯ 131

Ⓐ <
Ⓑ >
Ⓒ =

7. Which number is missing?

420 < _____

Ⓐ 415
Ⓑ 411
Ⓒ 427
Ⓓ 412

8. Which number is missing?

159 = _____

Ⓐ 118
Ⓑ 151
Ⓒ 15
Ⓓ 159

9. Marcus collects sports cards. He has 195 baseball cards. He has 189 soccer cards. Which one tells about his cards?

Ⓐ 195 baseball cards > 189 soccer cards
Ⓑ 195 baseball cards < 189 soccer cards
Ⓒ 195 baseball cards = 189 soccer cards
Ⓓ 189 soccer cards > 195 baseball cards

10. A swarm of ladybugs flew into the garden. The same number of ladybugs landed on the ground as on the flowers. Which one tells about the ladybugs?

Ⓐ 200 on the ground > 200 on the flowers
Ⓑ 200 on the ground = 200 on the flowers
Ⓒ 200 on the ground < 250 on the flowers
Ⓓ 250 on the ground < 200 on the flowers

Compare and order whole numbers to 1000 using the symbols for less than, equal to, or greater than (<, =, >).

Count the Chickens

Name _____

1. __100__ + __20__ + __6__ = __126__ chickens
   hundreds   tens   ones

2. _____ + _____ + _____ = _____ chickens
   hundreds   tens   one

3. _____ + _____ + _____ = _____ chickens
   hundreds   tens   ones

4. _____ + _____ + _____ = _____ chickens
   hundreds   tens   ones

Count and group objects in hundreds, tens, and ones

   Number & Operations

Hundreds, Tens, and Ones

Name _____

Color the blocks.

1. 4 hundreds
   2 tens
   6 ones

   Write the
   number
   you colored. _____

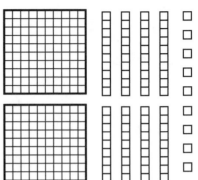

2. 5 hundreds
   6 tens
   3 ones

   Write the
   number
   you colored. _____

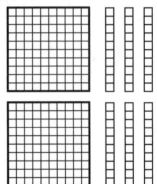

3. 2 tens
   3 hundreds
   6 ones

   Write the
   number
   you colored. _____

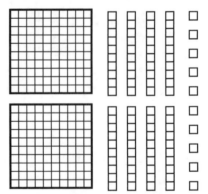

4. 6 ones
   2 tens
   3 hundreds

   Write the
   number
   you colored. _____

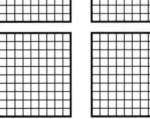

Count and group objects in hundreds, tens, and ones

EMC 3015 • Basic Math Skills, Grade 2 • ©2003 by Evan-Moor Corp.

Count the Blocks

 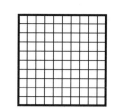

Name _____

Count how many hundreds, tens, and ones there are.
Write how many blocks in all.

   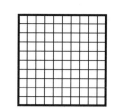

Each block is one.
Here are **3 ones**.

Each stack has 10 blocks.
This is **1 ten**.

Each square has 100 blocks.
This is **1 hundred**.

1.

_____ hundred   _____ tens   _____ ones   = _____

2.

_____ hundreds   _____ tens _____ ones = _____

3.

_____ hundreds   _____ ten _____ ones   = _____

4.

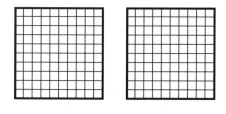

_____ hundreds   _____ tens _____ ones = _____

Count and group objects in hundreds, tens, and ones

How Many Are There?

Name _____

Count how many hundreds, tens, and ones there are.
Write how many blocks in all.

1.

hundreds	tens	ones	in all

2.

hundreds	tens	ones	in all

3.

hundreds	tens	ones	in all

4.

hundreds	tens	ones	in all

5.

hundreds	tens	ones	in all

6.

hundreds	tens	ones	in all

Count and group objects in hundreds, tens, and ones

EMC 3015 • Basic Math Skills, Grade 2 • ©2003 by Evan-Moor Corp.

Sticker Collections

Yoshi and his friends have a huge sticker collection. They want to count every single sticker. Show how many stickers each person has.

Yoshi 2 hundreds   3 tens   9 ones   = _____

Alice 1 hundred   8 tens   3 ones   = _____

Jacob 3 hundreds   0 tens   5 ones   = _____

Tanisha 2 hundreds   5 tens   1 one   = _____

Domingo 3 hundreds   3 tens   0 ones   = _____

Write the names in order from the person with the **most** stickers to the one with the **fewest** stickers.

1. _____   4. _____

2. _____   5. _____

3. _____

Count and group objects in hundreds, tens, and ones

Math Test

Fill in the circle next to the correct answer.

1. How many ones are there?

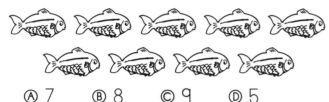

Ⓐ 7　　Ⓑ 8　　Ⓒ 9　　Ⓓ 5

2. How many tens are there?

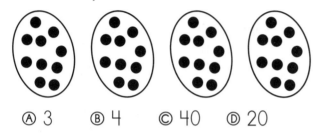

Ⓐ 3　　Ⓑ 4　　Ⓒ 40　　Ⓓ 20

3. How many hundreds are there?

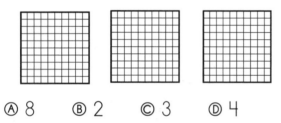

Ⓐ 8　　Ⓑ 2　　Ⓒ 3　　Ⓓ 4

4. How many tens are there?

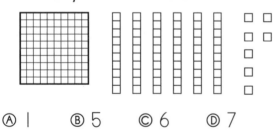

Ⓐ 1　　Ⓑ 5　　Ⓒ 6　　Ⓓ 7

5. Which number is 4 tens and 8 ones?

Ⓐ 18
Ⓑ 84
Ⓒ 12
Ⓓ 48

6. Which number is 3 hundreds, 6 tens, and 0 ones?

Ⓐ 610
Ⓑ 360
Ⓒ 63
Ⓓ 306

7. How many tens and ones are in 57?

Ⓐ 5 ones and 7 tens
Ⓑ 5 tens and 7 ones
Ⓒ 5 tens and 7 tens
Ⓓ 7 ones and 5 ones

8. How many hundreds are in 597?

Ⓐ 7 hundreds
Ⓑ 9 hundreds
Ⓒ 5 hundreds
Ⓓ 0 hundreds

9. Find the number for this picture.

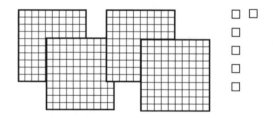

Ⓐ 406　　Ⓑ 460　　Ⓒ 46　　Ⓓ 604

10. Find the number for this picture.

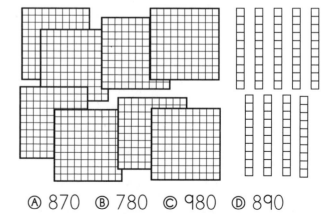

Ⓐ 870　　Ⓑ 780　　Ⓒ 980　　Ⓓ 890

Count and group objects in hundreds, tens, and ones

Odd or Even?

none left over – **even**

1 left over – **odd**

Circle two at a time. Write **odd** or **even**.

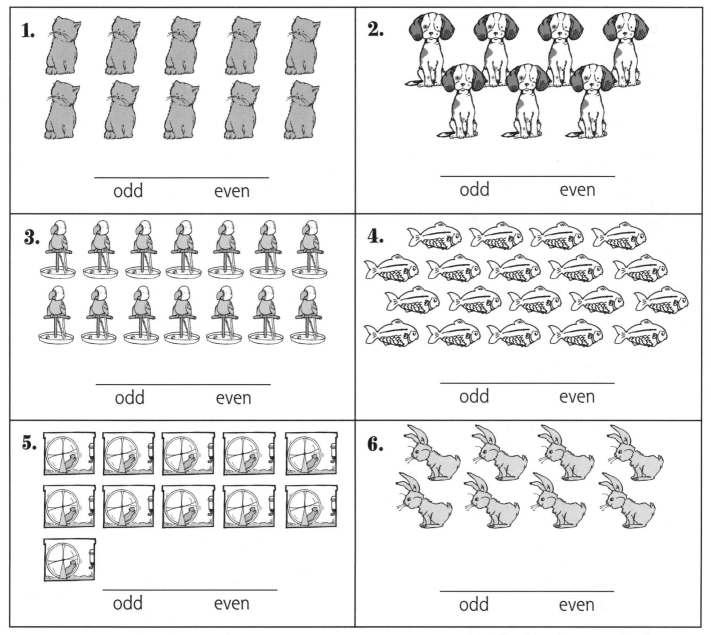

1.

_____
odd   even

2.

_____
odd   even

3.

_____
odd   even

4.

_____
odd   even

5.

_____
odd   even

6.

_____
odd   even

Identify odd and even numbers

Number & Operations

What Is Hiding Here?

Name _____

Color **odd** numbers **green**.

   1, 3, 5, 7, and 9 are some of the odd numbers.

Color **even** numbers **blue**.

   2, 4, 6, 8, and 10 are some of the even numbers.

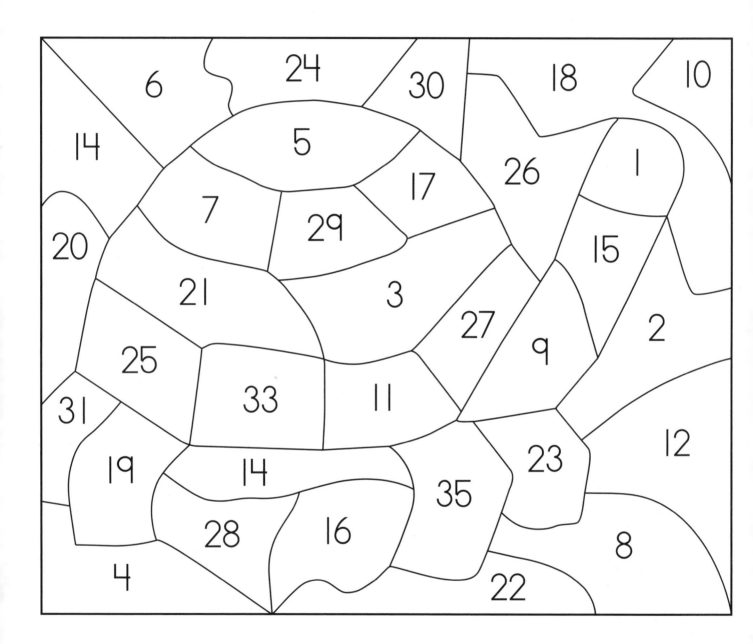

What animal did you find? _____

Identify odd and even numbers

Number & Operations

EMC 3015 • Basic Math Skills, Grade 2 • ©2003 by Evan-Moor Corp.

Count On

Draw a **box** around the even numbers and a **circle** around the odd numbers.

even	odd

0 1 2 3 4 5 6

7 8 9 10 11 12

Count on. Write **even** numbers from **0** to **30**.

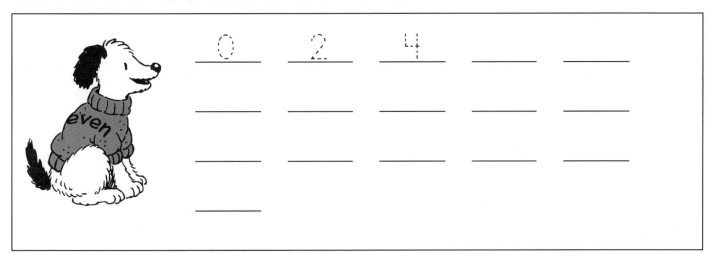

0 2 4 ___ ___

___ ___ ___ ___ ___

___ ___ ___ ___ ___

___

Count on. Write **odd** numbers from **1** to **29.**

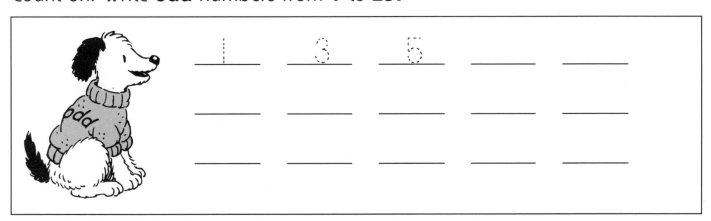

1 3 5 ___ ___

___ ___ ___ ___ ___

___ ___ ___ ___ ___

Identify odd and even numbers

Odd and Even

Draw a ☐ around the **even** numbers.

Make a ◯ around the **odd** numbers.

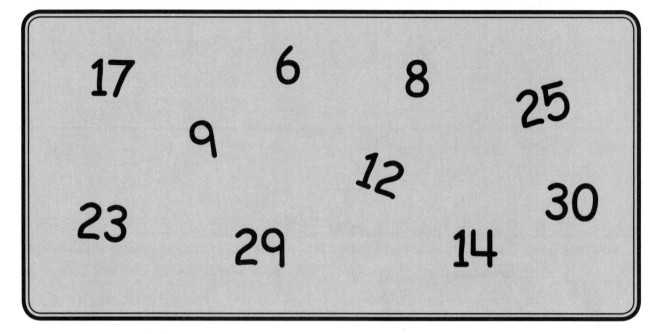

Count on. Write **even** numbers to finish each row.

50   5▢   ___   ___   ___   ___

66   6▢   ___   ___   ___   ___

Count on. Write ___ finish each row.

79   81   ___   ___   ___   ___

51   53   ___   ___   ___   ___

This could be fun — Math for after the calendar

Identify odd and even numbers

The Name Game

Ask 10 people to write their name on your list.

Count the number of letters in each name.

Write if the number is **odd** or **even**.

Name	Number of letters	Odd or Even?
Christopher	11	odd
1.		
2.		
3.		
4.		
5.		
6.		
7.		
8.		
9.		
10.		

Identify odd and even numbers

Number & Operations

Name _____

Fill in the circle next to the correct answer.

1. Find the picture that shows an even number of stars.

   Ⓐ ★★ ★★ ★★ ★★
   Ⓑ ★★ ★★ ★★ ★
   Ⓒ ★★ ★★ ★
   Ⓓ ★★ ★★ ★★ ★★ ★

2. Find the picture that shows an odd number of stars.

   Ⓐ ★★ ★★ ★★ ★★
   Ⓑ ★★ ★★ ★★
   Ⓒ ★★ ★★
   Ⓓ ★★ ★★ ★★ ★★ ★

3. Which number is even?
   Ⓐ 3
   Ⓑ 6
   Ⓒ 9
   Ⓓ 11

4. Which number is even?
   Ⓐ 11
   Ⓑ 13
   Ⓒ 19
   Ⓓ 12

5. Which number is odd?
   Ⓐ 14
   Ⓑ 16
   Ⓒ 15
   Ⓓ 10

6. Which number is odd?
   Ⓐ 24
   Ⓑ 18
   Ⓒ 20
   Ⓓ 17

7. What odd number comes next?

   11, 13, 15, _____
   Ⓐ 16
   Ⓑ 19
   Ⓒ 17
   Ⓓ 14

8. What even number comes next?

   24, 26, 28, _____
   Ⓐ 29
   Ⓑ 30
   Ⓒ 22
   Ⓓ 27

9. What number is missing?

   34, 36, _____, 40
   Ⓐ 38
   Ⓑ 39
   Ⓒ 32
   Ⓓ 30

10. Put these numbers in order.

    21, 17, 13, 15, 19
    Ⓐ 21, 17, 13, 15, 19
    Ⓑ 15, 19, 21, 23, 27
    Ⓒ 13, 14, 15, 16, 17
    Ⓓ 13, 15, 17, 19, 21

Identify odd and even numbers

Friends from the Farm

Name _____

Write the number words in order next to each barnyard animal.

Words

second	eighth
seventh	fifth
sixth	first
tenth	fourth
third	ninth

first

Number & Operations

We Live in an Apartment House

Name _____

FRIENDLY APARTMENTS

Read the number words to find where each child lives.

Draw a line from each child to the correct floor in the apartment house.

Start counting at the first floor.

- Kim – ninth

- Ali – seventh

- Otis – eighth

- Walter – fourth

- Angela – tenth

- Orlando – third

- Tina – second

- Bob – sixth

- Lisa – fifth

First Floor

Use ordinal numbers to sequence objects

Name My Place in the Garden

Name _____

Look at the row of flowers.

| first | second | third | fourth | fifth | sixth | seventh | eighth | ninth | tenth |
| 1st | 2nd | 3rd | 4th | 5th | 6th | 7th | 8th | 9th | 10th |

Circle the answer.

1. Which flower is first?

2. Which flower is last?

3. Which one is between the 4th and 6th flowers?

Write the order.

4. The is _____ in line.

5. The  is _____ in line.

6. The is _____ in line.

7. The is _____ in line.

Write the number for the word.

third _____   fourth _____   ninth _____

seventh _____   second _____   first _____

Use ordinal numbers to sequence objects

Number & Operations

Laundry Day

Mother needs help with the laundry.
You can help by hanging the shirts on the line in order.

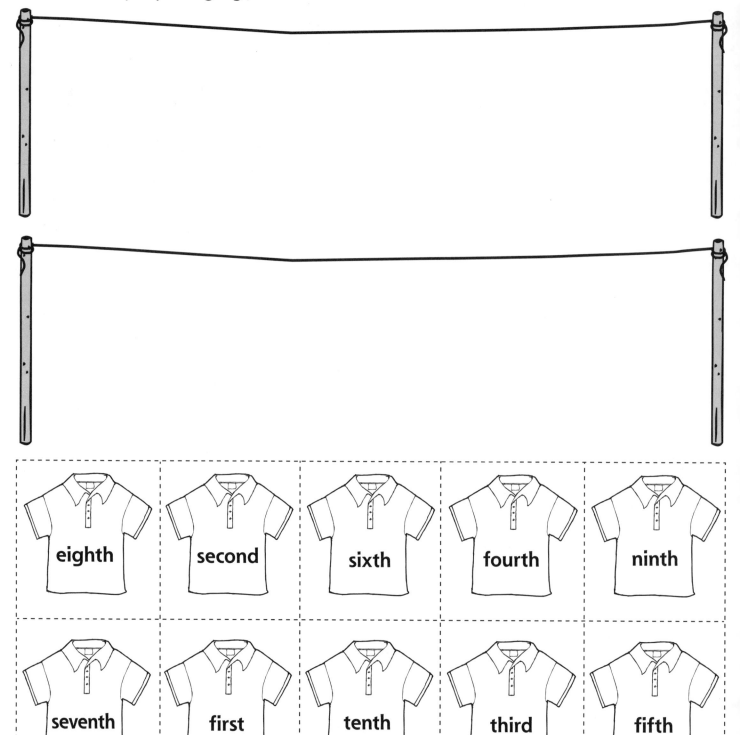

eighth   second   sixth   fourth   ninth

seventh   first   tenth   third   fifth

Use ordinal numbers to sequence objects

Hats in a Row

Color any five of the hats.
Use different colors or patterns.
Then tell about each of the five hats.
Use number words like **first** and **tenth**.

I made the **second** hat green with yellow dots.

1. _____

2. _____

3. _____

4. _____

5. _____

first	second	third	fourth	fifth
sixth	seventh	eighth	ninth	tenth

Use ordinal numbers to sequence objects

Math Test

Fill in the circle next to the correct answer.

1. Who is fourth?

   Ⓐ   Ⓑ   Ⓒ   Ⓓ

2. Which shape is sixth?

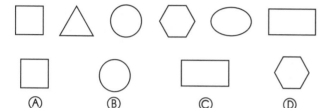

  Ⓐ   Ⓑ   Ⓒ   Ⓓ

3. Where is the circle?

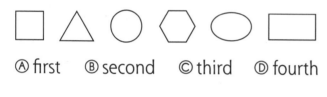

Ⓐ first   Ⓑ second   Ⓒ third   Ⓓ fourth

4. Where is the square?

Ⓐ first   Ⓑ second   Ⓒ third   Ⓓ fourth

5. Find the missing number word.

    seventh, eighth, _____, tenth

Ⓐ fifth
Ⓑ ninth
Ⓒ fourth
Ⓓ sixth

6. Find the missing number word.

    ninth, tenth, _____, twelfth

Ⓐ seventh
Ⓑ second
Ⓒ eleventh
Ⓓ eighth

7. Where is Raul?

Bob Jill Ann Tom Raul Ken

Ⓐ first
Ⓑ fifth
Ⓒ fourth
Ⓓ sixth

8. Find the seventh hat.

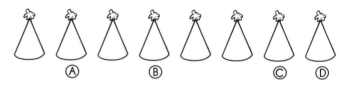

    Ⓐ   Ⓑ   Ⓒ Ⓓ

9. Find the third hat.

  Ⓐ   Ⓑ   Ⓒ   Ⓓ

10. Which words are in order?

Ⓐ first, second, seventh
Ⓑ fifth, fourth, first
Ⓒ fourth, fifth, sixth
Ⓓ ninth, eleventh, twelfth

Use ordinal numbers to sequence objects

Riddle Fun

Name _____

Color the spaces with the answer **10 yellow**.
Color the spaces with the answer **9 green**.
Color the spaces with the answer **8 orange**.

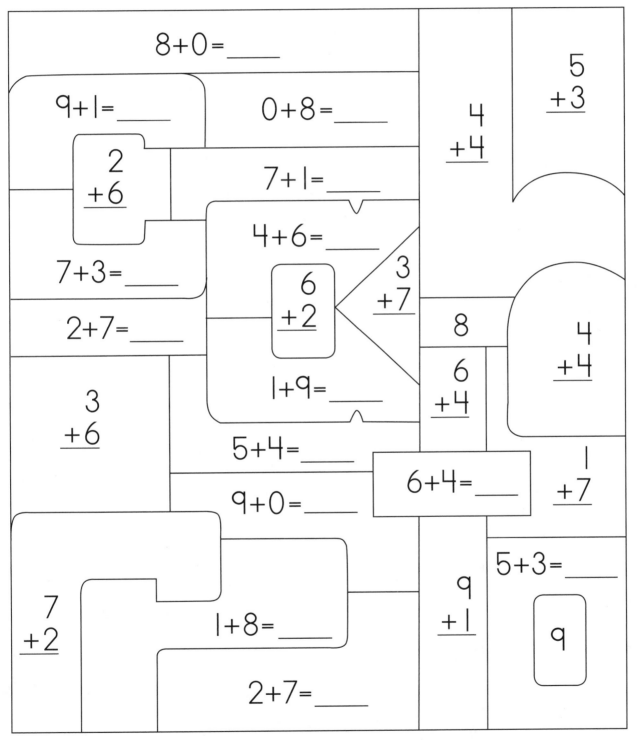

$8+0=$ _____

$9+1=$ _____

$0+8=$ _____

$\begin{array}{r} 4 \\ +4 \\ \hline \end{array}$

$\begin{array}{r} 5 \\ +3 \\ \hline \end{array}$

$\begin{array}{r} 2 \\ +6 \\ \hline \end{array}$

$7+1=$ _____

$4+6=$ _____

$\begin{array}{r} 3 \\ +7 \\ \hline \end{array}$

$7+3=$ _____

$\begin{array}{r} 6 \\ +2 \\ \hline \end{array}$

$2+7=$ _____

8

$\begin{array}{r} 6 \\ +4 \\ \hline \end{array}$

$\begin{array}{r} 4 \\ +4 \\ \hline \end{array}$

$1+9=$ _____

$\begin{array}{r} 3 \\ +6 \\ \hline \end{array}$

$5+4=$ _____

$6+4=$ _____

$\begin{array}{r} 1 \\ +7 \\ \hline \end{array}$

$9+0=$ _____

$5+3=$ _____

$\begin{array}{r} 7 \\ +2 \\ \hline \end{array}$

$1+8=$ _____

$\begin{array}{r} 9 \\ +1 \\ \hline \end{array}$

9

$2+7=$ _____

Know the addition facts (sums to 10) and the corresponding subtraction facts

©2003 by Evan-Moor Corp. • Basic Math Skills, Grade 2 • EMC 3015

Fly Away Home

Find the answers. Then make a path for Mother bird back to her nest.
If the answer is **1**, **2**, or **3**, color the box **brown**.

$\begin{array}{r} 10 \\ -\ 9 \\ \hline \end{array}$	$\begin{array}{r} 9 \\ -6 \\ \hline \end{array}$	$\begin{array}{r} 5 \\ -3 \\ \hline \end{array}$	$\begin{array}{r} 4 \\ -1 \\ \hline \end{array}$	$\begin{array}{r} 3 \\ +2 \\ \hline \end{array}$
$\begin{array}{r} 1 \\ +3 \\ \hline \end{array}$	$\begin{array}{r} 5 \\ -5 \\ \hline \end{array}$	$\begin{array}{r} 7 \\ -2 \\ \hline \end{array}$	$\begin{array}{r} 4 \\ +2 \\ \hline \end{array}$	$\begin{array}{r} 10 \\ -\ 8 \\ \hline \end{array}$	$\begin{array}{r} 2 \\ +2 \\ \hline \end{array}$
$\begin{array}{r} 7 \\ -5 \\ \hline \end{array}$	$\begin{array}{r} 5 \\ -4 \\ \hline \end{array}$	$\begin{array}{r} 2 \\ +0 \\ \hline \end{array}$	$\begin{array}{r} 6 \\ -4 \\ \hline \end{array}$	$\begin{array}{r} 8 \\ -7 \\ \hline \end{array}$	$\begin{array}{r} 3 \\ +4 \\ \hline \end{array}$
$\begin{array}{r} 7 \\ -4 \\ \hline \end{array}$	$\begin{array}{r} 3 \\ +3 \\ \hline \end{array}$	$\begin{array}{r} 3 \\ +5 \\ \hline \end{array}$	$\begin{array}{r} 10 \\ -\ 6 \\ \hline \end{array}$	$\begin{array}{r} 5 \\ +4 \\ \hline \end{array}$	$\begin{array}{r} 9 \\ -\ 9 \\ \hline \end{array}$
$\begin{array}{r} 10 \\ -\ 7 \\ \hline \end{array}$	$\begin{array}{r} 1 \\ +5 \\ \hline \end{array}$	$\begin{array}{r} 9 \\ -7 \\ \hline \end{array}$	$\begin{array}{r} 7 \\ -6 \\ \hline \end{array}$	$\begin{array}{r} 10 \\ -\ 7 \\ \hline \end{array}$	$\begin{array}{r} 1 \\ +1 \\ \hline \end{array}$
$\begin{array}{r} 8 \\ -6 \\ \hline \end{array}$	$\begin{array}{r} 7 \\ -4 \\ \hline \end{array}$	$\begin{array}{r} 4 \\ -3 \\ \hline \end{array}$	$\begin{array}{r} 6 \\ +3 \\ \hline \end{array}$	$\begin{array}{r} 4 \\ +6 \\ \hline \end{array}$	$\begin{array}{r} 9 \\ -6 \\ \hline \end{array}$
$\begin{array}{r} 4 \\ +4 \\ \hline \end{array}$	$\begin{array}{r} 0 \\ +5 \\ \hline \end{array}$	$\begin{array}{r} 8 \\ -8 \\ \hline \end{array}$	$\begin{array}{r} 2 \\ +7 \\ \hline \end{array}$	$\begin{array}{r} 3 \\ +4 \\ \hline \end{array}$	

Know the addition facts (sums to 10) and the corresponding subtraction facts

EMC 3015 • Basic Math Skills, Grade 2 • ©2003 by Evan-Moor Corp.

Feed the Elephants

Name _____

Find the answers and then draw a line to the correct elephant.

9 – 1 = ____

10 – 0 = ____

3 + 4 = ____

10 – 1 = ____

2 + 8 = ____

10 – 4 = ____

5 + 3 = ____

9 – 3 = ____

6 + 3 = ____

9 – 2 = ____

6 + 4 = ____

10 – 2 = ____

4 + 5 = ____

3 + 3 = ____

9 – 0 = ____

3 + 7 = ____

8 + 0 = ____

2 + 5 = ____

10 – 3 = ____

4 + 2 = ____

Know the addition facts (sums to 10) and the corresponding subtraction facts

Number & Operations

How Many Do You Remember?

Name _____

Add or subtract.

1.

$\begin{array}{r} 9 \\ -6 \\ \hline \end{array}$
$\begin{array}{r} 4 \\ -3 \\ \hline \end{array}$
$\begin{array}{r} 2 \\ +6 \\ \hline \end{array}$
$\begin{array}{r} 7 \\ -4 \\ \hline \end{array}$
$\begin{array}{r} 5 \\ -1 \\ \hline \end{array}$
$\begin{array}{r} 10 \\ -7 \\ \hline \end{array}$
$\begin{array}{r} 6 \\ -2 \\ \hline \end{array}$
$\begin{array}{r} 3 \\ +7 \\ \hline \end{array}$

2.

$\begin{array}{r} 9 \\ -3 \\ \hline \end{array}$
$\begin{array}{r} 5 \\ +5 \\ \hline \end{array}$
$\begin{array}{r} 8 \\ -6 \\ \hline \end{array}$
$\begin{array}{r} 6 \\ +4 \\ \hline \end{array}$
$\begin{array}{r} 10 \\ -5 \\ \hline \end{array}$
$\begin{array}{r} 6 \\ -6 \\ \hline \end{array}$
$\begin{array}{r} 3 \\ +6 \\ \hline \end{array}$
$\begin{array}{r} 3 \\ +4 \\ \hline \end{array}$

3.

$\begin{array}{r} 8 \\ -4 \\ \hline \end{array}$
$\begin{array}{r} 4 \\ +1 \\ \hline \end{array}$
$\begin{array}{r} 6 \\ +3 \\ \hline \end{array}$
$\begin{array}{r} 3 \\ +7 \\ \hline \end{array}$
$\begin{array}{r} 10 \\ -3 \\ \hline \end{array}$
$\begin{array}{r} 4 \\ +2 \\ \hline \end{array}$
$\begin{array}{r} 5 \\ +4 \\ \hline \end{array}$
$\begin{array}{r} 6 \\ -3 \\ \hline \end{array}$

4.

$\begin{array}{r} 4 \\ +1 \\ \hline \end{array}$
$\begin{array}{r} 5 \\ -4 \\ \hline \end{array}$
$\begin{array}{r} 4 \\ +2 \\ \hline \end{array}$
$\begin{array}{r} 6 \\ -4 \\ \hline \end{array}$
$\begin{array}{r} 6 \\ +2 \\ \hline \end{array}$
$\begin{array}{r} 7 \\ -1 \\ \hline \end{array}$
$\begin{array}{r} 2 \\ +4 \\ \hline \end{array}$
$\begin{array}{r} 6 \\ -2 \\ \hline \end{array}$

5.

$\begin{array}{r} 1 \\ +6 \\ \hline \end{array}$
$\begin{array}{r} 10 \\ -4 \\ \hline \end{array}$
$\begin{array}{r} 7 \\ +2 \\ \hline \end{array}$
$\begin{array}{r} 9 \\ -7 \\ \hline \end{array}$
$\begin{array}{r} 10 \\ -2 \\ \hline \end{array}$
$\begin{array}{r} 8 \\ -6 \\ \hline \end{array}$
$\begin{array}{r} 2 \\ +7 \\ \hline \end{array}$
$\begin{array}{r} 5 \\ +5 \\ \hline \end{array}$

Know the addition facts (sums to 10) and the corresponding subtraction facts

EMC 3015 • Basic Math Skills, Grade 2 • ©2003 by Evan-Moor Corp.

Grandpa's Garden

Name _____

1. Grandpa picked 4 pumpkins this morning. He picked 5 pumpkins this afternoon. How many pumpkins did he pick today?

_____ pumpkins

Which did you do?   add   subtract

2. Grandpa picked 7 baskets of beans. Grandma cooked 3 baskets. How many baskets of beans were not cooked?

_____ baskets of beans

Which did you do?   add   subtract

3. Grandma put 5 carrots in the stew and 3 carrots in the salad. How many carrots did she use?

_____ carrots

Which did you do?   add   subtract

4. We helped Grandpa pick cabbage. I picked four heads of cabbage. My sister picked three heads of cabbage. How many heads of cabbage did we pick?

_____ heads of cabbage

Which did you do?   add   subtract

5. Grandpa picked 10 ears of corn. He gave 6 ears of corn to the neighbors. He gave the rest of the corn to Grandma. How many ears of corn did he give Grandma?

_____ ears of corn

Which did you do?   add   subtract

6. There were four potatoes and two heads of cabbage in a basket. How many vegetables were in the basket?

_____ vegetables

Which did you do?   add   subtract

7. Write a word problem about this picture. Then write a number sentence about it.

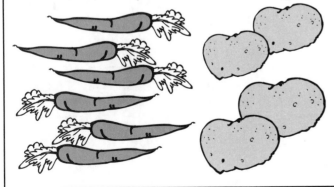

_____

_____

_____ ◯ _____ = _____

Which did you do?   add   subtract

Know the addition facts (sums to 10) and the corresponding subtraction facts

Number & Operations

Name _____

Fill in the circle next to the correct answer.

1. 7 + 3 = _____
   Ⓐ 1
   Ⓑ 10
   Ⓒ 8
   Ⓓ 4

2. 5 + 2 = _____
   Ⓐ 10
   Ⓑ 9
   Ⓒ 7
   Ⓓ 3

3. 10 – 8 = _____
   Ⓐ 3
   Ⓑ 5
   Ⓒ 1
   Ⓓ 2

4. 7 – 5 = _____
   Ⓐ 10
   Ⓑ 5
   Ⓒ 0
   Ⓓ 2

5. Find another name for 10.
   Ⓐ 8 + 1
   Ⓑ 4 + 4
   Ⓒ 1 + 3
   Ⓓ 3 + 7

6. Which problem has the same answer as 10 – 6?
   Ⓐ 0 + 6
   Ⓑ 10 – 8
   Ⓒ 6 – 2
   Ⓓ 3 + 5

7. Find the number sentence that is NOT correct.
   Ⓐ 10 – 5 = 5
   Ⓑ 9 – 4 = 5
   Ⓒ 7 – 3 = 9
   Ⓓ 10 + 0 = 10

8. Aretha made 5 apple pies. She made 4 pumpkin pies. How many pies did she make in all?
   Ⓐ 10
   Ⓑ 8
   Ⓒ 1
   Ⓓ 9

9. Ted and Ernie were playing basketball. Ted made 7 baskets. Ernie made 10 baskets. How many more baskets did Ernie make than Ted?
   Ⓐ 8
   Ⓑ 3
   Ⓒ 4
   Ⓓ 10

10. Find the number sentence for this picture.
   Ⓐ 5 – 3 = 2
   Ⓑ 5 + 3 = 8
   Ⓒ 8 – 3 = 5
   Ⓓ 8 – 3 = 10

Know the addition facts (sums to 10) and the corresponding subtraction facts

The Thirsty Giraffe

Name _____

Show the thirsty giraffe the trail to the watering hole.
Find the answers. Color all the boxes that equal **9** brown.

4 +8	11 − 7	10 +5	15 − 6 9	
8 +7	9 − 0	5 +4	14 − 5	12 − 2
15 − 9	12 − 3	4 +7	5 +9	13 − 5
15 − 7	11 − 2	13 − 4	10 + 3	7 + 5
15 − 8	4 +9	6 +3	13 − 6	9 +6
12 − 8	9 +2	15 − 6	8 +3	14 − 8
12 − 6	3 +8	13 − 4	14 − 6	8 +7

Know the addition facts (sums to 15) and the corresponding subtraction facts

Number & Operations

Elephant Riddle

Name _____

Use the code to solve the riddle. Write the matching letter below each answer.

Why did the elephant sit on a marshmallow?

Code

2–i	3–f	4–d	5–u	6–w
7–c	8–a	9–s	10–n	11–e
12–l	13–o	14–t	15–h	

15 − 6	9 + 4

___ ___

11 − 9	9 + 5

___ ___

12 − 6	8 + 5	14 − 9	9 + 3	11 − 7	8 + 2	5 + 9

___ ___ ___ ___ ___ ___ ___ ,

9 − 6	12 − 4	8 + 4	6 + 6

___ ___ ___ ___

10 − 8	13 − 3	6 + 8	7 + 6

7 + 7	9 + 6	5 + 6

6 + 9	4 + 9	8 + 6

___ ___ ___

15 − 8	7 + 8	6 + 7	13 − 6	5 + 8	7 + 5	14 − 6	9 + 5	4 + 7

___ ___ ___ ___ ___ ___ ___ ___ ___

Know the addition facts (sums to 15) and the corresponding subtraction facts

EMC 3015 • Basic Math Skills, Grade 2 • ©2003 by Evan-Moor Corp.

Downhill Racer

Name _____

Make a trail down the hill by marking an **X**
on problems with **15** as an answer.

1. $3 \atop +9$ $14 \atop -5$ $15 \atop -6$ $8 \atop +3$ $11 \atop -2$ ~~$9 \atop +6$~~
                                                                          15

2. $4 \atop +8$ $12 \atop -9$ $6 \atop +5$ $7 \atop +8$ $10 \atop +5$ $13 \atop -9$ $4 \atop +7$ $9 \atop +3$

3. $15 \atop -7$ $13 \atop -8$ $12 \atop -8$ $8 \atop +7$ $6 \atop +6$ $14 \atop -7$ $12 \atop -4$ $4 \atop +9$

4. $15 \atop -8$ $13 \atop -5$ $6 \atop +9$ $7 \atop +8$ $3 \atop +8$ $12 \atop -7$ $13 \atop -6$ $6 \atop +8$

5. $15 \atop -9$ $5 \atop +9$ $9 \atop +6$ $13 \atop -7$ $9 \atop +3$ $11 \atop -8$ $14 \atop -6$ $12 \atop -3$

6.  $10 \atop +5$ $9 \atop +5$ $8 \atop +6$ $12 \atop -5$ $14 \atop -9$ $12 \atop -6$

Know the addition facts (sums to 15) and the corresponding subtraction facts

Number & Operations

Which Answers Are the Same?

Name _____

Circle the two problems in each row that have the same answer.

1. $\begin{array}{r}12\\-8\end{array}$ $\begin{array}{r}8\\+5\end{array}$ $\begin{array}{r}13\\-3\end{array}$ $\begin{array}{r}8\\+4\end{array}$ $\begin{array}{r}14\\-5\end{array}$ $\begin{array}{r}4\\+9\end{array}$ $\begin{array}{r}14\\-8\end{array}$ $\begin{array}{r}13\\-8\end{array}$

2. $\begin{array}{r}6\\+8\end{array}$ $\begin{array}{r}5\\+6\end{array}$ $\begin{array}{r}8\\+7\end{array}$ $\begin{array}{r}14\\-6\end{array}$ $\begin{array}{r}7\\+3\end{array}$ $\begin{array}{r}5\\+9\end{array}$ $\begin{array}{r}15\\-8\end{array}$ $\begin{array}{r}11\\-8\end{array}$

3. $\begin{array}{r}9\\+6\end{array}$ $\begin{array}{r}15\\-9\end{array}$ $\begin{array}{r}13\\-6\end{array}$ $\begin{array}{r}12\\-3\end{array}$ $\begin{array}{r}9\\+4\end{array}$ $\begin{array}{r}14\\-7\end{array}$ $\begin{array}{r}8\\+6\end{array}$ $\begin{array}{r}11\\-7\end{array}$

4. $\begin{array}{r}13\\-7\end{array}$ $\begin{array}{r}14\\-9\end{array}$ $\begin{array}{r}4\\+9\end{array}$ $\begin{array}{r}7\\+4\end{array}$ $\begin{array}{r}15\\-7\end{array}$ $\begin{array}{r}11\\+4\end{array}$ $\begin{array}{r}5\\+8\end{array}$ $\begin{array}{r}13\\-9\end{array}$

Know the addition facts (sums to 15) and the corresponding subtraction facts

EMC 3015 • Basic Math Skills, Grade 2 • ©2003 by Evan-Moor Corp.

Collections

Name _____

Write the number sentence.

---

1. Carmen collects rocks. She has 15 small rocks and 6 big rocks. How many more small rocks than big rocks does Carmen have?

_____ ◯ _____ = _____

_____ more small rocks

2. Jamal wants to collect baseball cards. His brother gave him 4 cards. His father bought him 9 cards. How many baseball cards does Jamal have?

_____ ◯ _____ = _____

_____ baseball cards

---

3. Sally has 15 stickers. Maggie has 9 stickers. How many more stickers does Sally have than Maggie?

_____ ◯ _____ = _____

_____ more stickers

4. Ali collects stamps. He has 4 stamps from the U.S.A. He has 6 stamps from Canada. How many stamps does he have in all?

_____ ◯ _____ = _____

_____ stamps

---

5. There are 7 girls and 8 boys in Miss Bell's room who collect stickers. How many children collect stickers?

_____ ◯ _____ = _____

_____ children

6. Jorge and Carlos are twins. They both collect model cars. Jorge has 3 more cars than Carlos. If Jorge has 11 cars, how many does Carlos have?

_____ ◯ _____ = _____

_____ model cars

---

7. Write a word problem about this picture. Then write a number sentence about it.

_____

_____

_____ ◯ _____ = _____

Know the addition facts (sums to 15) and the corresponding subtraction facts

Number & Operations

Math Test

Fill in the circle next to the correct answer.

1. $9 + 5 =$ _____
- Ⓐ 15
- Ⓑ 14
- Ⓒ 13
- Ⓓ 11

2. $4 + 8 =$ _____
- Ⓐ 10
- Ⓑ 13
- Ⓒ 11
- Ⓓ 12

3. $15 - 8 =$ _____
- Ⓐ 3
- Ⓑ 5
- Ⓒ 7
- Ⓓ 9

4. $13 - 4 =$ _____
- Ⓐ 9
- Ⓑ 5
- Ⓒ 7
- Ⓓ 8

5. Find another name for 14.
- Ⓐ $8 + 4$
- Ⓑ $4 + 7$
- Ⓒ $9 + 5$
- Ⓓ $3 + 7$

6. Which problem has the same answer as $7 + 6$?
- Ⓐ $6 + 7$
- Ⓑ $15 - 4$
- Ⓒ $8 + 3$
- Ⓓ $14 - 2$

7. Find the number sentence that is NOT correct.
- Ⓐ $14 - 5 = 9$
- Ⓑ $11 - 3 = 8$
- Ⓒ $12 - 4 = 9$
- Ⓓ $13 - 3 = 10$

8. Carlos caught 4 fish in the morning. He caught 7 fish in the afternoon. How many fish did he catch?
- Ⓐ 8
- Ⓑ 9
- Ⓒ 10
- Ⓓ 11

9. Mattie had 15 cents. She spent 9 cents. How much money did she have left?
- Ⓐ 8 cents
- Ⓑ 3 cents
- Ⓒ 10 cents
- Ⓓ 6 cents

10. Find the number sentence for this picture.
- Ⓐ $7 - 6 = 1$
- Ⓑ $7 + 6 = 13$
- Ⓒ $12 - 7 = 5$
- Ⓓ $13 + 6 = 7$

Know the addition facts (sums to 15) and the corresponding subtraction facts

Mr. Lee's Bakery

Name _____

Mr. Lee has the best bakery in town. At the end of the day, he has to count the baked goods below to see what is left. Can you help him?

1.

_____ doughnuts

2.

_____ pies

3.

_____ cupcakes

4.

_____ gingerbread boys

5.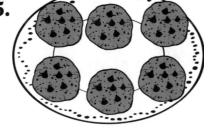

_____ chocolate cookies

6.

_____ sugar cookies

Mr. Lee started the day with the amounts below. How many of each did he sell?

7. 16 doughnuts $\begin{array}{r} 16 \\ -\ 8 \\ \hline 8 \end{array}$ __8__ sold	**8.** 12 sugar cookies _____ sold
9. 5 pies _____ sold	**10.** 7 gingerbread boys _____ sold
11. 13 cupcakes _____ sold	**12.** 14 chocolate cookies _____ sold

Know the addition facts (sums to 20) and the corresponding subtraction facts

Number & Operations

Up, Up, and Away

Find the answers. Start at **0** to connect the dots. Color the picture.

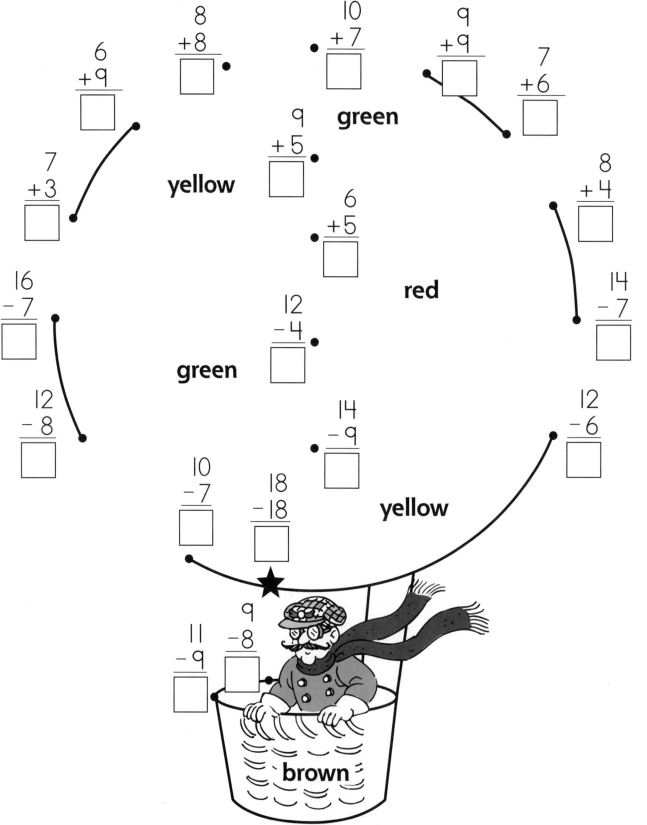

$$\begin{array}{r} 6 \\ +9 \\ \hline \end{array}$$

$$\begin{array}{r} 8 \\ +8 \\ \hline \end{array}$$

$$\begin{array}{r} 10 \\ +7 \\ \hline \end{array}$$

$$\begin{array}{r} 9 \\ +9 \\ \hline \end{array}$$

$$\begin{array}{r} 7 \\ +6 \\ \hline \end{array}$$

green

$$\begin{array}{r} 7 \\ +3 \\ \hline \end{array}$$

$$\begin{array}{r} 9 \\ +5 \\ \hline \end{array}$$

yellow

$$\begin{array}{r} 6 \\ +5 \\ \hline \end{array}$$

$$\begin{array}{r} 8 \\ +4 \\ \hline \end{array}$$

red

$$\begin{array}{r} 16 \\ -7 \\ \hline \end{array}$$

$$\begin{array}{r} 12 \\ -4 \\ \hline \end{array}$$

$$\begin{array}{r} 14 \\ -7 \\ \hline \end{array}$$

green

$$\begin{array}{r} 12 \\ -8 \\ \hline \end{array}$$

$$\begin{array}{r} 14 \\ -9 \\ \hline \end{array}$$

$$\begin{array}{r} 12 \\ -6 \\ \hline \end{array}$$

yellow

$$\begin{array}{r} 10 \\ -7 \\ \hline \end{array}$$

$$\begin{array}{r} 18 \\ -18 \\ \hline \end{array}$$

$$\begin{array}{r} 11 \\ -9 \\ \hline \end{array}$$

$$\begin{array}{r} 9 \\ -8 \\ \hline \end{array}$$

brown

Know the addition facts (sums to 20) and the corresponding subtraction facts

Number & Operations

Max's Math Challenge

Name _____

Help Max answer these problems.

1.
$$9 + 9$$ $$8 + 6$$ $$16 - 9$$ $$13 - 7$$ $$7 + 6$$ $$14 - 7$$ $$12 - 8$$ $$18 - 8$$

2.
$$8 + 5$$ $$18 - 9$$ $$15 - 7$$ $$7 + 7$$ $$16 - 8$$ $$6 + 6$$ $$11 - 5$$ $$6 + 5$$

3.
$$8 + 8$$ $$13 - 4$$ $$15 - 6$$ $$6 + 8$$ $$16 - 7$$ $$17 - 8$$ $$9 + 7$$ $$3 + 9$$

4.
$$17 - 9$$ $$5 + 7$$ $$15 - 9$$ $$7 + 8$$ $$8 + 5$$ $$16 - 9$$ $$12 - 6$$ $$4 + 8$$

5.
$$14 - 8$$ $$8 + 9$$ $$17 - 7$$ $$9 + 4$$ $$8 + 3$$ $$8 + 8$$ $$7 + 6$$ $$5 + 9$$

Know the addition facts (sums to 20) and the corresponding subtraction facts

Number & Operations

In & Out Robots

Name _____

Add the number at the top of each robot.

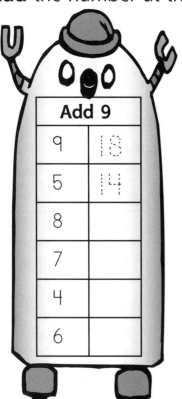

Add 9	
9	18
5	14
8	
7	
4	
6	

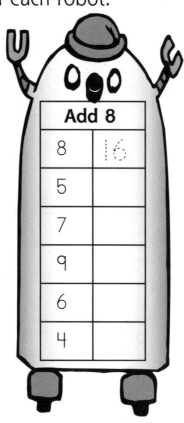

Add 8	
8	16
5	
7	
9	
6	
4	

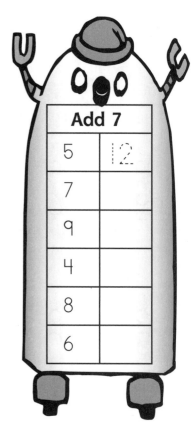

Add 7	
5	12
7	
9	
4	
8	
6	

Subtract the number at the top of each robot.

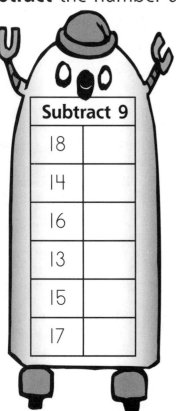

Subtract 9	
18	
14	
16	
13	
15	
17	

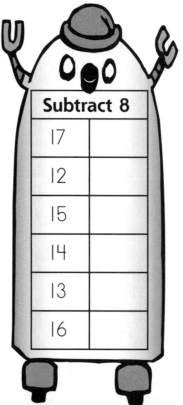

Subtract 8	
17	
12	
15	
14	
13	
16	

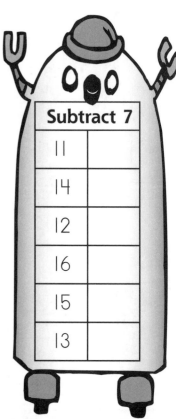

Subtract 7	
11	
14	
12	
16	
15	
13	

Know the addition facts (sums to 20) and the corresponding subtraction facts

Number & Operations

EMC 3015 • Basic Math Skills, Grade 2 • ©2003 by Evan-Moor Corp.

A Visit by the S.P.C.A.

Name _____

Find the answers. Circle **add** or **subtract**.

1. Mrs. Sakata came to school with animals from the S.P.C.A. She had 4 kittens and 1 puppy in a box. How many animals were in the box?

_____ animals

What did you do?   add   subtract

2. We fed bits of carrot to the bunnies. One ate 7 carrot bits. One ate 6 carrot bits. How many carrot bits did the bunnies eat in all?

_____ carrot bits

What did you do?   add   subtract

3. There are 19 children in our class. There are 9 girls in all. How many boys are in our class?

_____ boys

What did you do?   add   subtract

4. One kitten eats 3 cans of food a week. How many cans of food will the kitten need for two weeks?

_____ cans of food

What did you do?   add   subtract

5. A total of 9 boys and girls would not touch the snake. But 15 children did touch the snake. How many more children did touch the snake?

_____ more children

What did you do?   add   subtract

6. Mrs. Sakata asked the class, "How many of you have pets?" There were 14 children who had pets and 6 who had no pets. How many more children had pets than had no pets?

_____ more had pets

What did you do?   add   subtract

7. Write a word problem about this picture. Then write a number sentence about it.

_____

_____

_____

_____ ◯ _____ = _____

What did you do?   add   subtract

Know the addition facts (sums to 20) and the corresponding subtraction facts

Name _____

Math Test

Fill in the circle next to the correct answer.

1. 8 + 9 = _____
- Ⓐ 16
- Ⓑ 13
- Ⓒ 15
- Ⓓ 17

2. 16 − 7 = _____
- Ⓐ 10
- Ⓑ 5
- Ⓒ 9
- Ⓓ 8

3. Which problem equals 20?
- Ⓐ 18 − 18
- Ⓑ 10 + 10
- Ⓒ 10 − 10
- Ⓓ 9 + 9

4. Which number sentence is NOT correct?
- Ⓐ 17 − 8 = 9
- Ⓑ 14 − 8 = 6
- Ⓒ 15 − 8 = 6
- Ⓓ 16 − 8 = 8

5. Which problem has the same answer as 9 + 7?
- Ⓐ 17 − 7
- Ⓑ 15 − 4
- Ⓒ 8 + 8
- Ⓓ 18 − 9

6. Find the missing sign.

    12 ◯ 6 = 6
- Ⓐ +
- Ⓑ −
- Ⓒ =

7. Which two problems have the same answer?
- Ⓐ 9 + 2 and 5 + 6
- Ⓑ 5 + 7 and 2 + 9
- Ⓒ 5 + 4 and 3 + 7
- Ⓓ 7 + 3 and 7 − 3

8. Dan picked 20 apples. Walter picked 10 apples. How many more apples did Dan pick than Walter?
- Ⓐ 18
- Ⓑ 7
- Ⓒ 10
- Ⓓ 11

9. Peggy saw 8 blue birds and 6 crows. How many birds did Peggy see?
- Ⓐ 12
- Ⓑ 13
- Ⓒ 15
- Ⓓ 14

10. What is the number sentence for this picture?
- Ⓐ 9 + 8 = 1
- Ⓑ 17 + 9 = 8
- Ⓒ 9 − 1 = 8
- Ⓓ 17 − 8 = 9

Know the addition facts (sums to 20) and the corresponding subtraction facts

What Is It?

Name _____

What can you wear that everyone will like?

A–24	E–22	I–12	M–53	S–86
B–35	G–99	L–16	R–45	T–17

Use the code to solve the riddle. Write the matching letter below each answer.

$$\begin{array}{r} 87 \\ -63 \\ \hline \end{array}$$

⌐24¬

A

$$\begin{array}{r} 31 \\ +68 \\ \hline \end{array}$$
☐

_____

$$\begin{array}{r} 14 \\ +31 \\ \hline \end{array}$$
☐

_____

$$\begin{array}{r} 59 \\ -37 \\ \hline \end{array}$$
☐

_____

$$\begin{array}{r} 78 \\ -54 \\ \hline \end{array}$$
☐

_____

$$\begin{array}{r} 78 \\ -61 \\ \hline \end{array}$$
☐

_____

$$\begin{array}{r} 69 \\ -34 \\ \hline \end{array}$$
☐

_____

$$\begin{array}{r} 74 \\ -62 \\ \hline \end{array}$$
☐

_____

$$\begin{array}{r} 54 \\ +45 \\ \hline \end{array}$$
☐

_____

$$\begin{array}{r} 42 \\ +44 \\ \hline \end{array}$$
☐

_____

$$\begin{array}{r} 99 \\ -46 \\ \hline \end{array}$$
☐

_____

$$\begin{array}{r} 48 \\ -36 \\ \hline \end{array}$$
☐

_____

$$\begin{array}{r} 99 \\ -83 \\ \hline \end{array}$$
☐

_____

$$\begin{array}{r} 37 \\ -15 \\ \hline \end{array}$$
☐

_____

Draw the answer here.

Solve addition and subtraction problems of two 2-digit numbers without regrouping

Peter's Favorite Food

Name _____

Color each square where the answer has **6** in the **tens** place. This will tell you the first letter of Peter's favorite food. Then circle the picture of his favorite food.

62 +36	79 −15 64	87 −23	36 +33	88 −24	47 +12
77 −52	95 −35	34 +14	87 −54	68 − 6	25 +62
99 −86	41 +25	54 +15	74 −12	99 −35	52 +31
96 −71	67 − 7	66 +33	48 +51	97 −63	80 +18
16 +62	82 −20	98 −24	99 − 4	43 +34	56 −25
60 +27	77 −11	83 −42	80 −40	57 +41	56 +23

Solve addition and subtraction problems of two 2-digit numbers without regrouping

66

EMC 3015 • Basic Math Skills, Grade 2 • ©2003 by Evan-Moor Corp.

Add or Subtract?

Fill in the missing signs.   **+**   **–**

1. 67 ◯ 46 = 21	73 ◯ 14 = 87	25 ◯ 33 = 58
2. 29 ◯ 16 = 13	78 ◯ 45 = 33	65 ◯ 31 = 96
3. 28 ◯ 24 = 4	68 ◯ 37 = 31	40 ◯ 38 = 78
4. 65 ◯ 22 = 87	86 ◯ 53 = 33	59 ◯ 47 = 12
5. 33 ◯ 66 = 99	75 ◯ 43 = 32	68 ◯ 54 = 14
6. 12 ◯ 65 = 77	87 ◯ 64 = 23	94 ◯ 53 = 41
7. 66 ◯ 41 = 25	32 ◯ 52 = 84	79 ◯ 46 = 33
8. 62 ◯ 11 = 73	35 ◯ 23 = 58	80 ◯ 17 = 97
9. 20 ◯ 50 = 70	50 ◯ 10 = 40	62 ◯ 17 = 79
10. 45 ◯ 53 = 98	85 ◯ 32 = 53	72 ◯ 24 = 96

Solve addition and subtraction problems of two 2-digit numbers without regrouping

Number & Operations

Add to Check Subtraction

Name _____

Subtract to find the answer.
Add to check your answer.

1.

$$\begin{array}{r} 69 \\ -23 \\ \hline \boxed{46} \end{array} \qquad \begin{array}{r} 46 \\ +23 \\ \hline \boxed{69} \end{array}$$

$$\begin{array}{r} 29 \\ -16 \\ \hline \Box \end{array} \qquad \begin{array}{r} \Box \\ +16 \\ \hline \Box \end{array}$$

$$\begin{array}{r} 37 \\ -24 \\ \hline \Box \end{array} \qquad \begin{array}{r} \Box \\ +24 \\ \hline \Box \end{array}$$

2.

$$\begin{array}{r} 68 \\ -45 \\ \hline \Box \end{array} \qquad \begin{array}{r} \Box \\ +45 \\ \hline \Box \end{array}$$

$$\begin{array}{r} 75 \\ -34 \\ \hline \Box \end{array} \qquad \begin{array}{r} \Box \\ +34 \\ \hline \Box \end{array}$$

$$\begin{array}{r} 55 \\ -35 \\ \hline \Box \end{array} \qquad \begin{array}{r} \Box \\ +35 \\ \hline \Box \end{array}$$

3.

$$\begin{array}{r} 87 \\ -46 \\ \hline \Box \end{array} \qquad \begin{array}{r} \Box \\ +46 \\ \hline \Box \end{array}$$

$$\begin{array}{r} 43 \\ -20 \\ \hline \Box \end{array} \qquad \begin{array}{r} \Box \\ +20 \\ \hline \Box \end{array}$$

$$\begin{array}{r} 29 \\ -26 \\ \hline \Box \end{array} \qquad \begin{array}{r} \Box \\ +26 \\ \hline \Box \end{array}$$

4.

$$\begin{array}{r} 94 \\ -53 \\ \hline \Box \end{array} \qquad \begin{array}{r} \Box \\ +53 \\ \hline \Box \end{array}$$

$$\begin{array}{r} 45 \\ -30 \\ \hline \Box \end{array} \qquad \begin{array}{r} \Box \\ +30 \\ \hline \Box \end{array}$$

$$\begin{array}{r} 68 \\ -37 \\ \hline \Box \end{array} \qquad \begin{array}{r} \Box \\ +37 \\ \hline \Box \end{array}$$

5.

$$\begin{array}{r} 79 \\ -35 \\ \hline \Box \end{array} \qquad \begin{array}{r} \Box \\ +35 \\ \hline \Box \end{array}$$

$$\begin{array}{r} 66 \\ -32 \\ \hline \Box \end{array} \qquad \begin{array}{r} \Box \\ +32 \\ \hline \Box \end{array}$$

$$\begin{array}{r} 78 \\ -43 \\ \hline \Box \end{array} \qquad \begin{array}{r} \Box \\ +43 \\ \hline \Box \end{array}$$

Solve addition and subtraction problems of two 2-digit numbers without regrouping

Number & Operations

EMC 3015 • Basic Math Skills, Grade 2 • ©2003 by Evan-Moor Corp.

Marbles

Name _____

Add or subtract to find the answer.
Show how you found the answer.

---

1. Fred has 26 marbles. How many marbles will he have if his friend gives him 12 more?

$$26 + 12 = 38$$

_38_ marbles

2. Marsha has 36 marbles. Janice has 48 marbles. How many more marbles does Janice have than Marsha?

_____ more marbles

---

3. Marcus, Clyde, and Jerome collect marbles. Each boy has 23 marbles. How many marbles do they have in all?

_____ marbles

4. If Edgar has 35 small marbles and 24 large marbles, how many does he have in all?

_____ marbles

---

5. Edgar found a bag of marbles. There were 38 small marbles. There were 24 large marbles. How many more marbles were small?

_____ more small marbles

6. David has 38 marbles. His brother Kai has 12 marbles. His sister Meg has 15 marbles. Meg gave her marbles to Kai. Does Kai have more or less than David?

He has _____ marbles than David.

---

7. Write a word problem about this picture. Write a number sentence about it.

_____

_____

_____

____ ◯ ____ = ____

Solve addition and subtraction problems of two 2-digit numbers without regrouping

Math Test

Fill in the circle next to the correct answer.

1. 52 + 32 = _____
- Ⓐ 80
- Ⓑ 74
- Ⓒ 84
- Ⓓ 20

2. 79 – 46 = _____
- Ⓐ 33
- Ⓑ 35
- Ⓒ 24
- Ⓓ 23

3. Which problem equals 44?
- Ⓐ 35 + 23
- Ⓑ 22 + 22
- Ⓒ 62 – 22
- Ⓓ 88 – 54

4. Which number sentence is NOT correct?
- Ⓐ 94 – 64 = 30
- Ⓑ 80 + 17 = 97
- Ⓒ 85 – 21 = 64
- Ⓓ 16 + 22 = 83

5. Which problem has the same answer as 30 + 50?
- Ⓐ 50 – 32
- Ⓑ 80 – 40
- Ⓒ 20 + 60
- Ⓓ 70 – 10

6. Find the missing sign.

85 ◯ 32 = 53
- Ⓐ +
- Ⓑ –
- Ⓒ =

7. Find the missing sign.

24 ◯ 14 = 38
- Ⓐ +
- Ⓑ –
- Ⓒ =

8. There were 75 oranges on the tree. Hank picked 24 oranges. How many oranges were left on the tree?
- Ⓐ 91
- Ⓑ 59
- Ⓒ 99
- Ⓓ 51

9. There were 46 boys and 33 girls on the school bus. How many children rode the bus?
- Ⓐ 13
- Ⓑ 79
- Ⓒ 73
- Ⓓ 19

10. Find the number sentence for this picture.
- Ⓐ 43 – 12 = 31
- Ⓑ 53 + 12 = 21
- Ⓒ 53 – 12 = 65
- Ⓓ 53 + 12 = 65

Solve addition and subtraction problems of two 2-digit numbers without regrouping

EMC 3015 • Basic Math Skills, Grade 2 • ©2003 by Evan-Moor Corp.

Riddle Time

Name _____

When is an old car like a baby?

412-a	378-h	897-l	779-r
129-e	303-i	339-n	999-s
	768-t	533-w	

Use the code to solve the riddle. Write the matching letter below each answer.

433 +100	226 +152	659 −530	126 +213

828 −525	645 +123

699 −321	646 −234	594 +405

879 −467

274 +505	202 +210	999 −231	263 +505	684 +213	739 −610

Solve addition and subtraction problems of two 3-digit numbers without regrouping

Number & Operations

Race Through the Maze

Name _____

Add or subtract.

613 +360	182 +415	659 −324	323 +473	873 −571

645 −213	520 +138	888 −123	222 +164	678 −432

192 +807	937 −315	235 +460	456 +330	854 −123

EXIT

568 −163	475 +223	320 +525	657 −223	888 −536

Solve addition and subtraction problems of two 3-digit numbers without regrouping

Number & Operations   EMC 3015 • Basic Math Skills, Grade 2 • ©2003 by Evan-Moor Corp.

It Marks the Spot!

Name _____

The pirate made a map to show where he hid his treasure. Color the boxes that have an answer **3** in the **ones** place to show what marks the spot where the treasure is buried.

483 −233	404 +300	995 −870	556 +401	887 −343	545 −204
999 −405	275 −252	555 +341	236 +752	456 −123	274 +505
315 +260	777 −543	507 −104	567 −234	304 +464	567 +122
888 −123	164 +222	678 −345	192 +801	997 −303	235 +663
214 +183	789 −456	355 +341	446 −132	330 +123	534 +140
456 +123	854 −330	475 +223	568 −163	657 −223	629 −525

What marks the spot? _____

Solve addition and subtraction problems of two 3-digit numbers without regrouping

Can You Answer My Problems?

Add or subtract to help
Panda answer his problems.

689 −465	655 −324	406 +372	599 −267	252 +346
405 +550	721 +156	488 −408	958 −427	777 −453
105 +382	263 +336	369 −352	687 −445	153 +443
692 −290	200 +199	735 −123	500 +326	947 −627

Solve addition and subtraction problems of two 3-digit numbers without regrouping

Fish Market

Fill in the sales slips to see how much each shopper spent.

Prices

trout	$1.23	tuna	$4.30
squid	$1.42	crab	$3.10
shrimp	$3.14	lobster	$5.00

1.

Sales Slip

tuna $ 4.30

crab $ 3.10

total $ 7.40

2.

Sales Slip

trout $_____

squid $_____

total $_____

3.

Sales Slip

lobster $_____

shrimp $_____

total $_____

4.

Sales Slip

tuna $_____

trout $_____

total $_____

5.

Sales Slip

lobster $_____

tuna $_____

total $_____

6. What would you buy?
What would it cost?

Sales Slip

_____ $_____

_____ $_____

total $_____

Solve addition and subtraction problems of two 3-digit numbers without regrouping

Name _____

Fill in the circle next to the correct answer.

1. 524 + 235 = _____
- Ⓐ 957
- Ⓑ 314
- Ⓒ 759
- Ⓓ 700

2. 479 – 226 = _____
- Ⓐ 245
- Ⓑ 546
- Ⓒ 693
- Ⓓ 253

3. Which problem equals 555?
- Ⓐ 353 + 223
- Ⓑ 122 + 242
- Ⓒ 233 + 322
- Ⓓ 188 – 154

4. Which number sentence is NOT correct?
- Ⓐ 300 + 200 = 500
- Ⓑ 700 – 200 = 900
- Ⓒ 300 + 300 = 600
- Ⓓ 600 – 200 = 400

5. Find the missing sign.

286 ◯ 135 = 151
- Ⓐ +
- Ⓑ –
- Ⓒ =

6. Find the missing sign.

815 ◯ 132 = 947
- Ⓐ +
- Ⓑ –
- Ⓒ =

7. Amy spent $1.25. Then she spent $2.10. How much did she spend in all?
- Ⓐ $3.50
- Ⓑ $2.35
- Ⓒ $3.35
- Ⓓ $3.15

8. There were 157 crows on a wall. Then 100 crows flew away. How many crows were left on the wall?
- Ⓐ 107
- Ⓑ 100
- Ⓒ 57
- Ⓓ 5

9. There were 245 girls and 224 boys on a trip. How many children went on the trip?
- Ⓐ 121
- Ⓑ 469
- Ⓒ 269
- Ⓓ 421

10. Find the number sentence for this picture.
- Ⓐ 125 – 14 = 111
- Ⓑ 125 + 14 = 111
- Ⓒ 125 – 14 = 139
- Ⓓ 125 + 14 = 193

Solve addition and subtraction problems of two 3-digit numbers without regrouping

Playtime for Kitty

Name _____

Add or subtract. Draw a line through the addition problems from Kitty to her ball of yarn.

1. $\begin{array}{r} 40 \\ -\ 6 \\ \hline \end{array}$ $\qquad$ $\begin{array}{r} 72 \\ +\ 9 \\ \hline \end{array}$ $\qquad$ $\begin{array}{r} 51 \\ -\ 5 \\ \hline \end{array}$ $\qquad$ $\begin{array}{r} 32 \\ -\ 4 \\ \hline \end{array}$

2. $\begin{array}{r} 82 \\ -\ 5 \\ \hline \end{array}$ $\qquad$ $\begin{array}{r} 48 \\ +\ 5 \\ \hline \end{array}$ $\qquad$ $\begin{array}{r} 65 \\ -\ 9 \\ \hline \end{array}$ $\qquad$ $\begin{array}{r} 33 \\ -\ 7 \\ \hline \end{array}$

3. $\begin{array}{r} 20 \\ -\ 3 \\ \hline \end{array}$ $\qquad$ $\begin{array}{r} 90 \\ -\ 1 \\ \hline \end{array}$ $\qquad$ $\begin{array}{r} 37 \\ +\ 4 \\ \hline \end{array}$ $\qquad$ $\begin{array}{r} 74 \\ -\ 8 \\ \hline \end{array}$

4. $\begin{array}{r} 50 \\ -\ 2 \\ \hline \end{array}$ $\qquad$ $\begin{array}{r} 22 \\ -\ 4 \\ \hline \end{array}$ $\qquad$ $\begin{array}{r} 76 \\ +\ 7 \\ \hline \end{array}$ $\qquad$ $\begin{array}{r} 63 \\ -\ 9 \\ \hline \end{array}$

5. $\begin{array}{r} 46 \\ -\ 8 \\ \hline \end{array}$ $\qquad$ $\begin{array}{r} 55 \\ +\ 9 \\ \hline \end{array}$ $\qquad$ $\begin{array}{r} 89 \\ +\ 3 \\ \hline \end{array}$ $\qquad$ $\begin{array}{r} 62 \\ +\ 8 \\ \hline \end{array}$

Solve addition and subtraction problems of two 2-digit numbers with regrouping

Number & Operations

Help the Hippo

Name _____

What did the hippo say when she sat on the box of cookies?

Use the code to solve the riddle.
Write the matching letter below each answer.

17 – k
19 – i
22 – e
27 – w
42 – m
47 – r
48 – c
49 – s
50 – u
59 – h
61 – a
67 – y
70 – t
73 – l
81 – o
91 – b

46 +24	73 – 14	25 +36	55 + 15	80 –31
70				

37 +33	72 – 13	50 –28

___ ___ ___ ___ ___ , ___ ___ ___

63 –36	49 + 12	91 –24

28 +42	81 –22	61 –39

___ ___ ___ ___ ___ ___

70 –22	48 +33	52 +29	55 –38	31 –12	90 –68

___ ___ ___ ___ ___ ___

61 – 13	81 – 34	35 + 15	25 + 17	42 +49	36 +37	40 – 18	73 –24

___ ___ ___ ___ ___ ___ ___ ___

Solve addition and subtraction problems of two 2-digit numbers with regrouping

78

Number & Operations

EMC 3015 • Basic Math Skills, Grade 2 • ©2003 by Evan-Moor Corp.

Regroup to Find the Answer

Name _____

Regroup to add.

16 +16	1 16 +16 2	1 16 +16 32
Add the **ones**.	Write the ones. Move the tens to the tens place.	Add the **tens**.

Solve the problems.

72 + 9	56 + 7	24 + 6	39 + 9	67 +29	19 +19	48 +37	18 + 3

Regroup to subtract.

2 10 3̶0̶ −12	2 10 3̶0̶ −12 8	2 10 3̶0̶ −12 18
Regroup a ten to make more ones. Move the ones to the ones place.	Subtract the **ones**.	Subtract the **tens**.

Solve the problems.

30 −16	70 −25	41 −29	53 −48	95 −38	66 −17	55 −28	74 −36

Solve addition and subtraction problems of two 2-digit numbers with regrouping

©2003 by Evan-Moor Corp. • Basic Math Skills, Grade 2 • EMC 3015

Number & Operations

Check Your Answers

Answer the subtraction problems.
Then add the numbers to see if you are correct.

1.

$\begin{array}{r} 5\;10 \\ \cancel{60} \\ -49 \\ \hline \square\square \end{array}$ $\begin{array}{r} \square\square \\ +49 \\ \hline 60 \end{array}$

$\begin{array}{r} 74 \\ -37 \\ \hline \square \end{array}$ $\begin{array}{r} \square \\ +37 \\ \hline \square \end{array}$

$\begin{array}{r} 52 \\ -29 \\ \hline \square \end{array}$ $\begin{array}{r} \square \\ +29 \\ \hline \square \end{array}$

2.

$\begin{array}{r} 35 \\ -18 \\ \hline \square \end{array}$ $\begin{array}{r} \square \\ +18 \\ \hline \square \end{array}$

$\begin{array}{r} 43 \\ -16 \\ \hline \square \end{array}$ $\begin{array}{r} \square \\ +16 \\ \hline \square \end{array}$

$\begin{array}{r} 91 \\ -58 \\ \hline \square \end{array}$ $\begin{array}{r} \square \\ +58 \\ \hline \square \end{array}$

3.

$\begin{array}{r} 76 \\ -47 \\ \hline \square \end{array}$ $\begin{array}{r} \square \\ +47 \\ \hline \square \end{array}$

$\begin{array}{r} 58 \\ -39 \\ \hline \square \end{array}$ $\begin{array}{r} \square \\ +39 \\ \hline \square \end{array}$

$\begin{array}{r} 80 \\ -42 \\ \hline \square \end{array}$ $\begin{array}{r} \square \\ +42 \\ \hline \square \end{array}$

4.

$\begin{array}{r} 64 \\ -29 \\ \hline \square \end{array}$ $\begin{array}{r} \square \\ +29 \\ \hline \square \end{array}$

$\begin{array}{r} 53 \\ -27 \\ \hline \square \end{array}$ $\begin{array}{r} \square \\ +27 \\ \hline \square \end{array}$

$\begin{array}{r} 46 \\ -18 \\ \hline \square \end{array}$ $\begin{array}{r} \square \\ +18 \\ \hline \square \end{array}$

5.

$\begin{array}{r} 75 \\ -39 \\ \hline \square \end{array}$ $\begin{array}{r} \square \\ +39 \\ \hline \square \end{array}$

$\begin{array}{r} 62 \\ -36 \\ \hline \square \end{array}$ $\begin{array}{r} \square \\ +36 \\ \hline \square \end{array}$

$\begin{array}{r} 73 \\ -48 \\ \hline \square \end{array}$ $\begin{array}{r} \square \\ +48 \\ \hline \square \end{array}$

Solve addition and subtraction problems of two 2-digit numbers with regrouping

EMC 3015 • Basic Math Skills, Grade 2 • ©2003 by Evan-Moor Corp.

Jake's Vacation

Name _____

Jake and his family went on a trip. The map shows where they traveled.
Use the map to help you answer the questions.

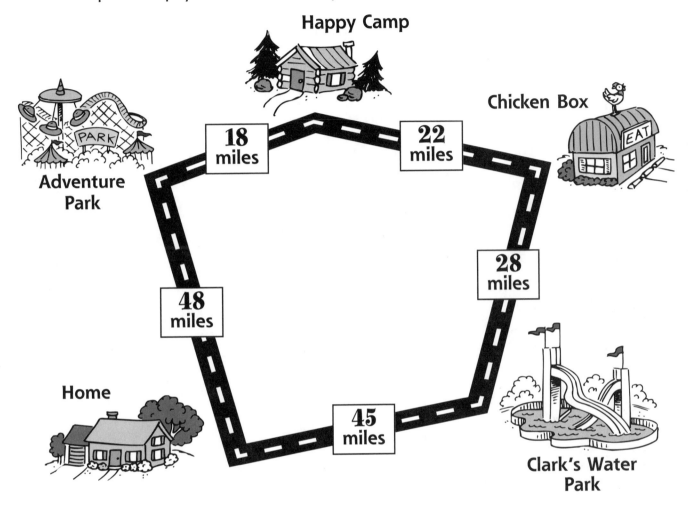

Happy Camp

Chicken Box

18 miles

22 miles

Adventure Park

28 miles

48 miles

Home

45 miles

Clark's Water Park

1. Yesterday we drove from home to Clark's Water Park and
   stopped for a while. Then we drove to the Chicken Box for lunch.
   After lunch we drove to Happy Camp to spend the night.

   How many miles did we drive yesterday? _____ miles

2. Today we drove from Happy Camp to Adventure Park.
   We stayed all day. Then we drove home.

   How many miles did we drive today? _____ miles

3. How many fewer miles did we travel today than yesterday? _____ miles

4. Plan a trip for your family. Where would you go the first day?

   How many miles would you travel? _____ miles

Solve addition and subtraction problems of two 2-digit numbers with regrouping

Math Test

Fill in the circle next to the correct answer.

1. 52 + 29 = _____
- Ⓐ 80
- Ⓑ 74
- Ⓒ 81
- Ⓓ 20

2. 60 − 24 = _____
- Ⓐ 33
- Ⓑ 36
- Ⓒ 24
- Ⓓ 23

3. Which problem equals 37?
- Ⓐ 19 + 18
- Ⓑ 22 + 22
- Ⓒ 62 − 22
- Ⓓ 88 − 54

4. Which number sentence is NOT correct?
- Ⓐ 90 − 64 = 26
- Ⓑ 73 + 17 = 90
- Ⓒ 81 − 25 = 64
- Ⓓ 46 + 24 = 70

5. Which problem has the same answer as 30 + 50?
- Ⓐ 50 − 32
- Ⓑ 80 − 31
- Ⓒ 35 + 45
- Ⓓ 70 + 18

6. Find the missing sign.

82 ◯ 35 = 47
- Ⓐ +
- Ⓑ −
- Ⓒ =

7. Find the missing sign.

26 ◯ 26 = 52
- Ⓐ +
- Ⓑ −
- Ⓒ =

8. There were 70 children on the bus. There were 29 girls. How many boys were on the bus?
- Ⓐ 91
- Ⓑ 59
- Ⓒ 99
- Ⓓ 41

9. Emma has 11 stuffed bears. She has 9 stuffed rabbits. How many stuffed animals does she have?
- Ⓐ 18
- Ⓑ 29
- Ⓒ 20
- Ⓓ 12

10. Find the number sentence for this picture.
- Ⓐ 39¢ + 52¢ = 81¢
- Ⓑ 52¢ − 39¢ = 27¢
- Ⓒ 52¢ − 39¢ = 23¢
- Ⓓ 39¢ + 52¢ = 91¢

Solve addition and subtraction problems of two 2-digit numbers with regrouping

EMC 3015 • Basic Math Skills, Grade 2 • ©2003 by Evan-Moor Corp.

Riddle Fun

Name _____

What is the opposite of a cool cat?

Use the code to solve the riddle.
Write the matching letter below each answer.

218 +316

867 +114	429 +158	753 −227

349 +129	692 −105	468 −239

___ ___   ___ ___ ___   ___ ___ ___

Draw your answer here.

Solve addition and subtraction problems of two 3-digit numbers with regrouping

Number & Operations

What Is in the Box?

Name _____

Find the answers.

1.
$$\begin{array}{r} 220 \\ -119 \\ \hline 101 \end{array}$$
$$\begin{array}{r} 753 \\ -628 \\ \hline \end{array}$$
$$\begin{array}{r} 184 \\ +109 \\ \hline \end{array}$$
$$\begin{array}{r} 630 \\ -315 \\ \hline \end{array}$$

2.
$$\begin{array}{r} 229 \\ +129 \\ \hline \end{array}$$
$$\begin{array}{r} 303 \\ +109 \\ \hline \end{array}$$
$$\begin{array}{r} 983 \\ -528 \\ \hline \end{array}$$
$$\begin{array}{r} 148 \\ +328 \\ \hline \end{array}$$

3.
$$\begin{array}{r} 860 \\ -327 \\ \hline \end{array}$$
$$\begin{array}{r} 734 \\ -228 \\ \hline \end{array}$$
$$\begin{array}{r} 219 \\ +432 \\ \hline \end{array}$$
$$\begin{array}{r} 327 \\ +327 \\ \hline \end{array}$$

4.
$$\begin{array}{r} 940 \\ -236 \\ \hline \end{array}$$
$$\begin{array}{r} 415 \\ +428 \\ \hline \end{array}$$
$$\begin{array}{r} 971 \\ -109 \\ \hline \end{array}$$
$$\begin{array}{r} 349 \\ +639 \\ \hline \end{array}$$

Start at **101**. Connect the dots in the order of the answers above.

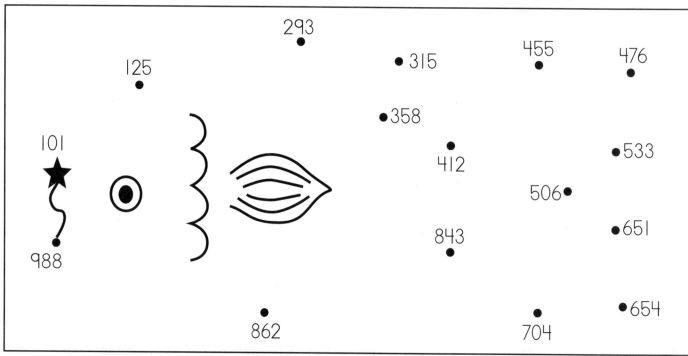

Solve addition and subtraction problems of two 3-digit numbers with regrouping

Number & Operations

EMC 3015 • Basic Math Skills, Grade 2 • ©2003 by Evan-Moor Corp.

Feed the Hungry Mouse

Name _____

I can only eat the cheese with correct answers.

Check the answers.
Color the cheese the mouse can eat.

1.

$$\begin{array}{r} 425 \\ +317 \\ \hline 742 \end{array}$$

$$\begin{array}{r} 138 \\ +522 \\ \hline 663 \end{array}$$

$$\begin{array}{r} 630 \\ -428 \\ \hline 212 \end{array}$$

$$\begin{array}{r} 325 \\ +549 \\ \hline 847 \end{array}$$

2.

$$\begin{array}{r} 582 \\ -167 \\ \hline 415 \end{array}$$

$$\begin{array}{r} 148 \\ +349 \\ \hline 497 \end{array}$$

$$\begin{array}{r} 239 \\ +149 \\ \hline 278 \end{array}$$

$$\begin{array}{r} 249 \\ -136 \\ \hline 483 \end{array}$$

3.

$$\begin{array}{r} 629 \\ +235 \\ \hline 964 \end{array}$$

$$\begin{array}{r} 720 \\ -609 \\ \hline 111 \end{array}$$

$$\begin{array}{r} 514 \\ +240 \\ \hline 354 \end{array}$$

$$\begin{array}{r} 541 \\ +331 \\ \hline 972 \end{array}$$

4.

$$\begin{array}{r} 964 \\ -318 \\ \hline 646 \end{array}$$

$$\begin{array}{r} 892 \\ -484 \\ \hline 408 \end{array}$$

$$\begin{array}{r} 394 \\ +402 \\ \hline 796 \end{array}$$

$$\begin{array}{r} 393 \\ -258 \\ \hline 135 \end{array}$$

Solve addition and subtraction problems of two 3-digit numbers with regrouping

Make a Match

Draw lines to match problems with the same answers.

1. $343 + 419$	**9.** $992 - 22$
2. $206 + 117$	**10.** $787 - 39$
3. $268 + 503$	**11.** $880 - 118$
4. $803 + 167$	**12.** $683 - 418$
5. $609 + 139$	**13.** $980 - 209$
6. $534 + 137$	**14.** $732 - 409$
7. $119 + 328$	**15.** $990 - 319$
8. $127 + 138$	**16.** $555 - 108$

addition

subtraction

Solve addition and subtraction problems of two 3-digit numbers with regrouping

Let's Go Shopping!

Name _____

Alex got a dog for his birthday. He is shopping for things for his dog. How much could he spend?

1. How much are a dish and a leash? $1.37 +2.55 ―――― $3.92 $ ___3.92___	**2.** How much are a sweater and a ball? $ _____ . _____
3. How much are a dog bone and a ball? $ _____ . _____	**4.** How much more does a leash cost than a dish? $ _____ . _____
5. How much more does a ball cost than a dog bone? $ _____ . _____	**6.** How much more does a sweater cost than a dish? $ _____ . _____
7. What two things would you buy for your dog? _____ _____	

Solve addition and subtraction problems of two 3-digit numbers with regrouping

Number & Operations

Name _____

Fill in the circle next to the correct answer.

1. 252 + 129 = _____
- Ⓐ 377
- Ⓑ 381
- Ⓒ 137
- Ⓓ 373

2. 560 − 224 = _____
- Ⓐ 344
- Ⓑ 784
- Ⓒ 332
- Ⓓ 336

3. 201 + 229 = _____
- Ⓐ 18
- Ⓑ 410
- Ⓒ 430
- Ⓓ 429

4. Which number sentence is NOT correct?
- Ⓐ 302 + 129 = 431
- Ⓑ 128 + 224 = 352
- Ⓒ 145 + 325 = 470
- Ⓓ 306 + 216 = 533

5. Which problem has the same answer as 282 − 106?
- Ⓐ 295 − 116
- Ⓑ 294 − 118
- Ⓒ 203 + 298
- Ⓓ 159 + 216

6. Find the missing sign.

354 ◯ 126 = 228
- Ⓐ +
- Ⓑ −
- Ⓒ =

7. Find the missing sign.

426 ◯ 318 = 744
- Ⓐ +
- Ⓑ −
- Ⓒ =

8. Tod had 252 ants in his ant farm. But then 126 ants got away. How many ants were left?
- Ⓐ 378
- Ⓑ 126
- Ⓒ 178
- Ⓓ 226

9. Mom made cookies for the bake sale. She made 125 sugar cookies. She made 218 peanut butter cookies. How many cookies did she make for the sale?
- Ⓐ 143
- Ⓑ 313
- Ⓒ 113
- Ⓓ 343

10. Find the number sentence for this picture.

- Ⓐ 209 − 108 = 107
- Ⓑ 209 − 108 = 201
- Ⓒ 209 + 108 = 317
- Ⓓ 209 + 108 = 307

Solve addition and subtraction problems of two 3-digit numbers with regrouping

EMC 3015 • Basic Math Skills, Grade 2 • ©2003 by Evan-Moor Corp.

Squirrel's Nest

Color the boxes to help Squirrel get to his nest.

parts are equal – **brown**

parts are NOT equal – **green**

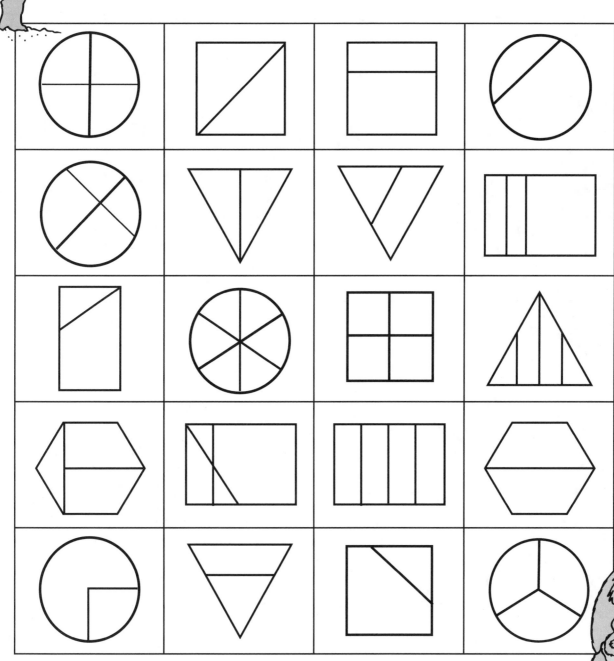

Recognize, name, and compare fractions as part of a whole

Apple Pies

Name _____

Grandma has baked apple pies for dinner. Color and cut out the pieces.
Paste them to the pie pans to make two whole pies.

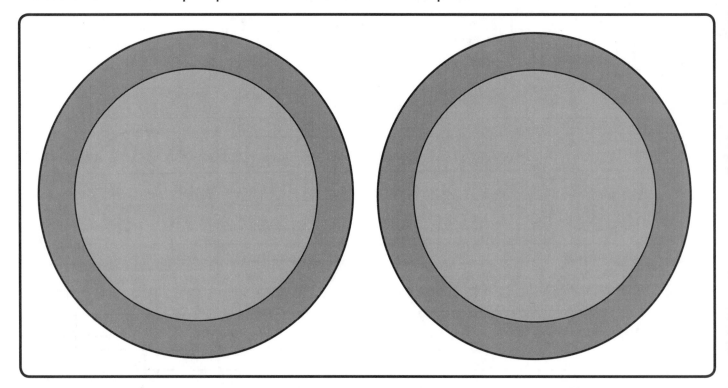

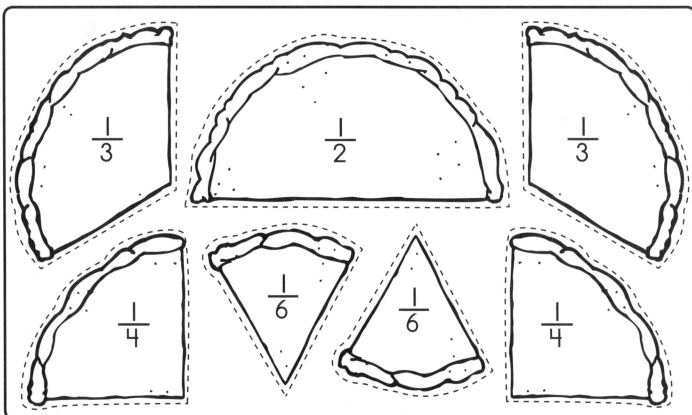

Recognize, name, and compare fractions as part of a whole

Find the Fractions

Name _____

Color the shapes that show the correct parts.

halves	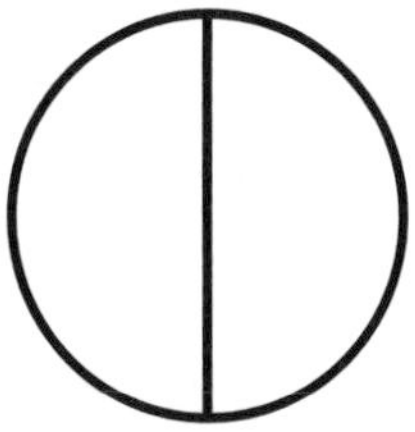	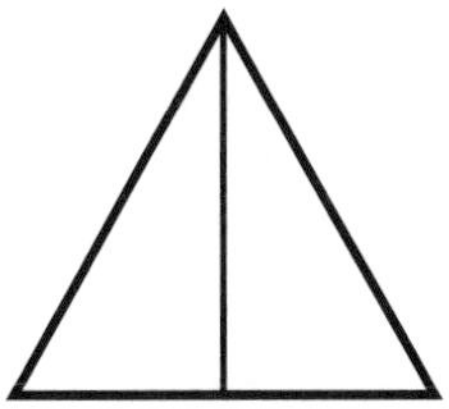	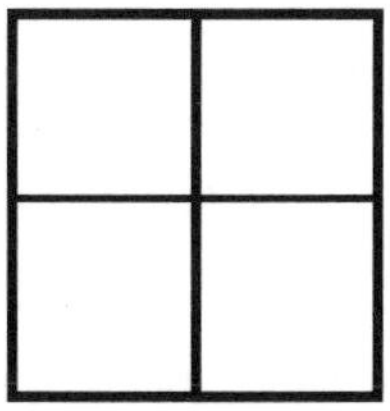	
thirds			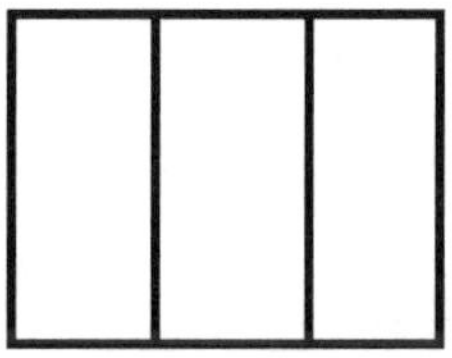	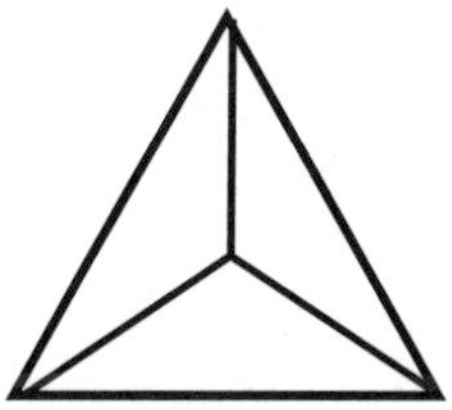
sixths	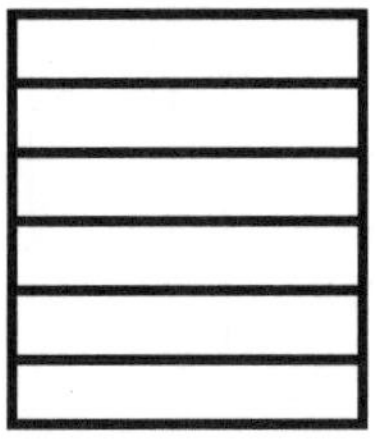	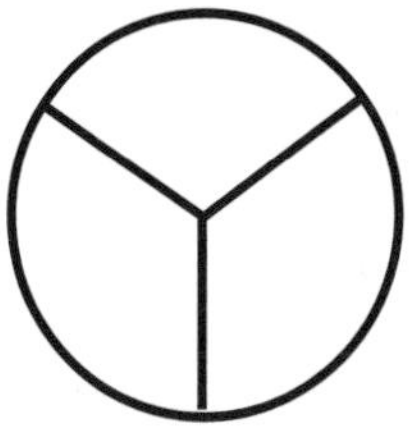		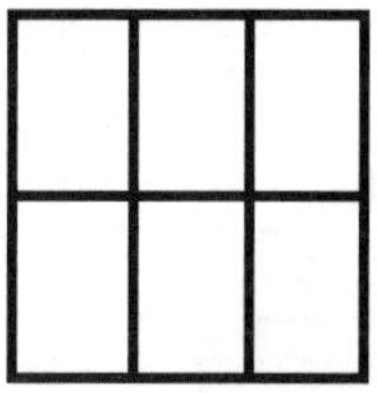
fourths		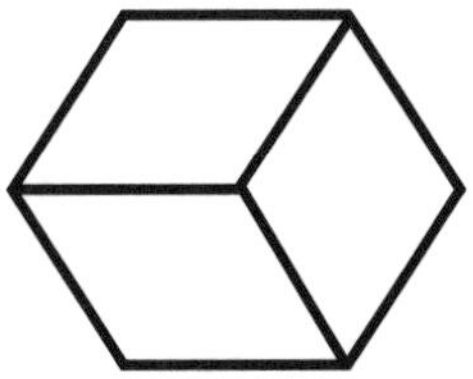		
tenths	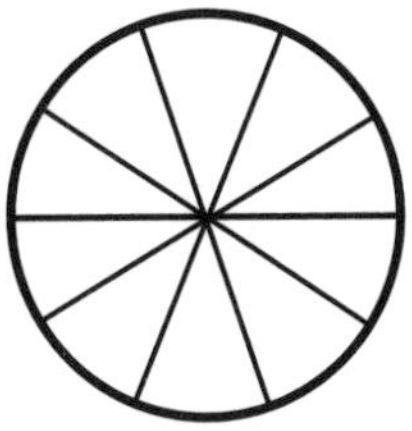	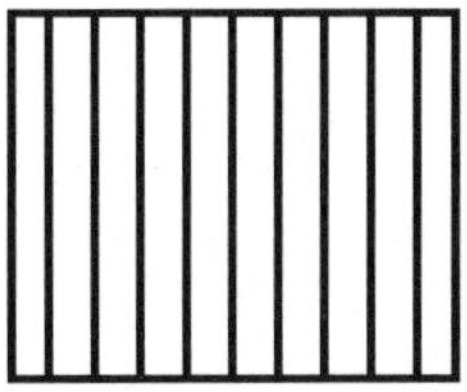	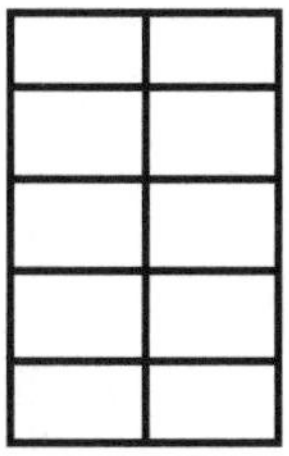	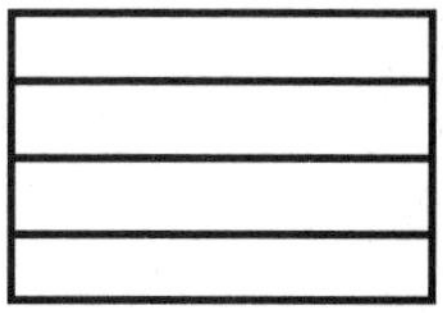
fifths			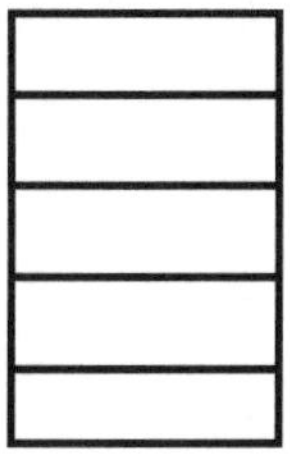	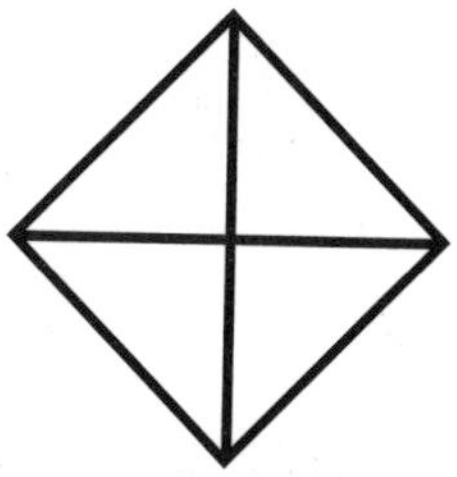

Recognize, name, and compare fractions as part of a whole

Fraction Fun

Name _____

Color the shape. Write the fraction.

1. Color one-fourth.

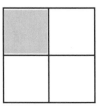

parts colored

equal parts

2. Color one-half.

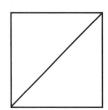 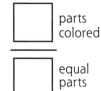

parts colored

equal parts

3. Color two-fourths.

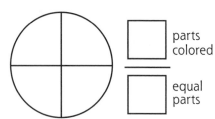

parts colored

equal parts

4. Color five-eighths.

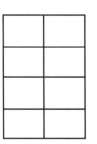 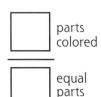

parts colored

equal parts

5. Color one-third.

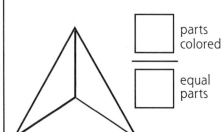

parts colored

equal parts

6. Color four-sixths.

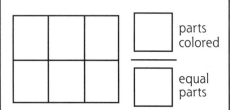

parts colored

equal parts

Color to show the fraction.

$\frac{1}{6}$

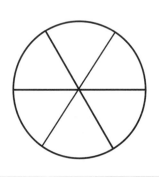

$\frac{3}{4}$

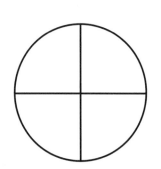

$\frac{4}{10}$

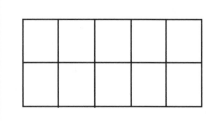

$\frac{2}{3}$

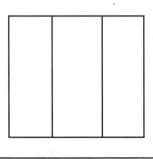

$\frac{1}{2}$

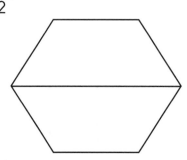

$\frac{3}{8}$

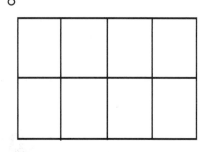

Recognize, name, and compare fractions as part of a whole

Baking Cookies

Name _____

Father is making butter nut cookies.
Color to show how much of each item he needs.

1. Father needs $1\frac{1}{2}$ cups of milk.

2. He needs $2\frac{3}{4}$ cups of flour.

3. He needs $1\frac{1}{3}$ sticks of butter.

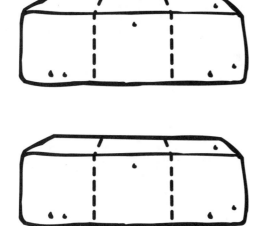

4. He needs $\frac{1}{2}$ cup of nuts.

Recognize, name, and compare fractions as part of a whole

Math Test

Fill in the circle next to the correct answer.

1. Which shape is divided into equal parts?

  Ⓐ   Ⓑ   Ⓒ   Ⓓ

2. Which shape is NOT divided into equal parts?

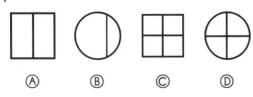

  Ⓐ   Ⓑ   Ⓒ   Ⓓ

3. How many equal parts are in this shape?

Ⓐ 5
Ⓑ 2
Ⓒ 8
Ⓓ 4

4. Which shape is divided in half?

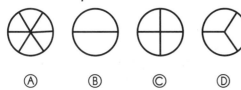

  Ⓐ   Ⓑ   Ⓒ   Ⓓ

5. Which shape is divided into fourths?

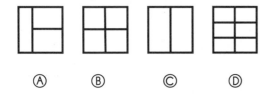

  Ⓐ   Ⓑ   Ⓒ   Ⓓ

6. Which shape shows $\frac{2}{3}$?

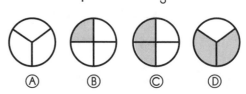

  Ⓐ   Ⓑ   Ⓒ   Ⓓ

7. Find the fraction.

Ⓐ $\frac{1}{3}$
Ⓑ $\frac{1}{8}$
Ⓒ $\frac{1}{5}$
Ⓓ $\frac{1}{4}$

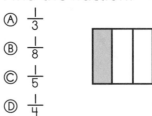

8. Find the fraction.

Ⓐ $\frac{1}{4}$
Ⓑ $\frac{1}{8}$
Ⓒ $\frac{1}{2}$
Ⓓ $\frac{1}{3}$

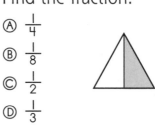

9. Find the fraction.

Ⓐ $\frac{3}{4}$
Ⓑ $\frac{3}{8}$
Ⓒ $\frac{3}{5}$
Ⓓ $\frac{3}{6}$

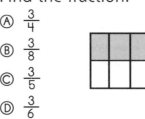

10. Find the fraction.

Ⓐ $\frac{3}{5}$
Ⓑ $\frac{2}{8}$
Ⓒ $\frac{2}{5}$
Ⓓ $\frac{2}{6}$

Recognize, name, and compare fractions as part of a whole

Berry Picking

Color and cut out the berries that Mary and Max picked.
Paste the same number of berries in each bowl.

1. Mary shared her berries with her friend Anna.

2. Max shared his berries with Carl and Tony.

Mary's Berries
Color the berries purple.

Max's Berries
Color the berries red.

Recognize, name, and compare fractions as part of a group

Number & Operations

Ladybugs, Ladybugs

Color the ladybugs.

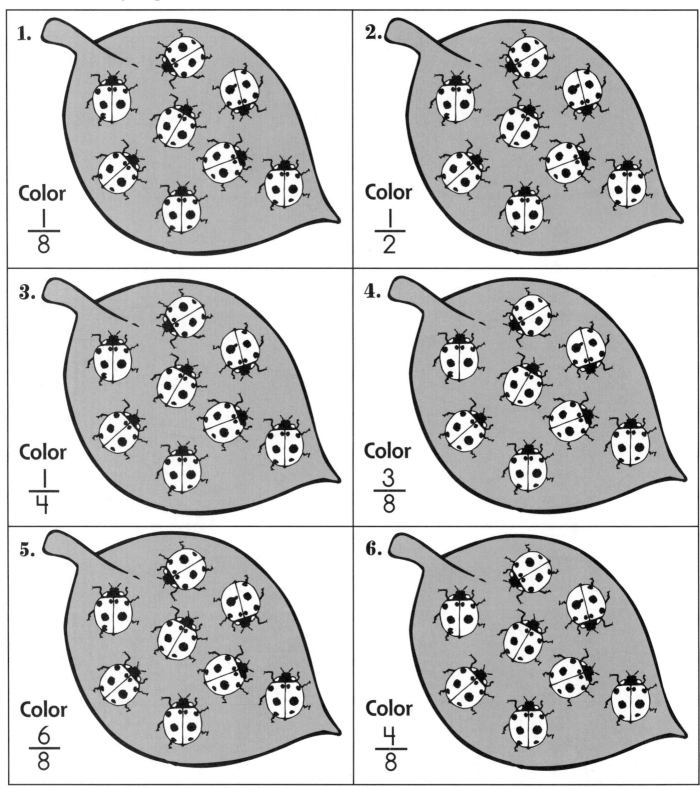

1. Color $\frac{1}{8}$

2. Color $\frac{1}{2}$

3. Color $\frac{1}{4}$

4. Color $\frac{3}{8}$

5. Color $\frac{6}{8}$

6. Color $\frac{4}{8}$

Circle the two leaves where you colored **half** of the ladybugs.

Recognize, name, and compare fractions as part of a group

Under the Sea

Circle the fractional part of each group of sea animals.

1. $\dfrac{1}{2}$

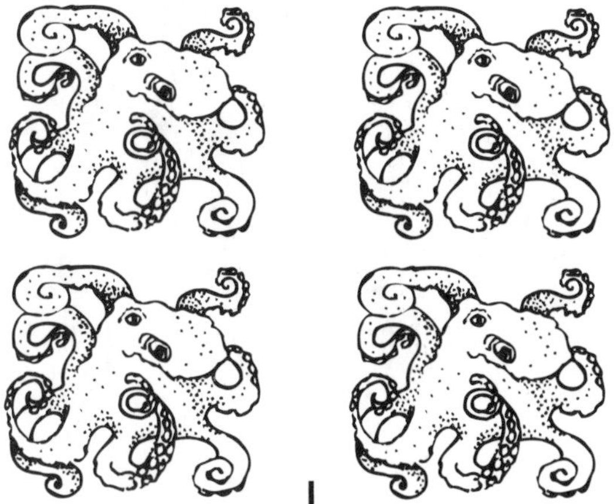

2. $\dfrac{1}{6}$

3. $\dfrac{1}{8}$

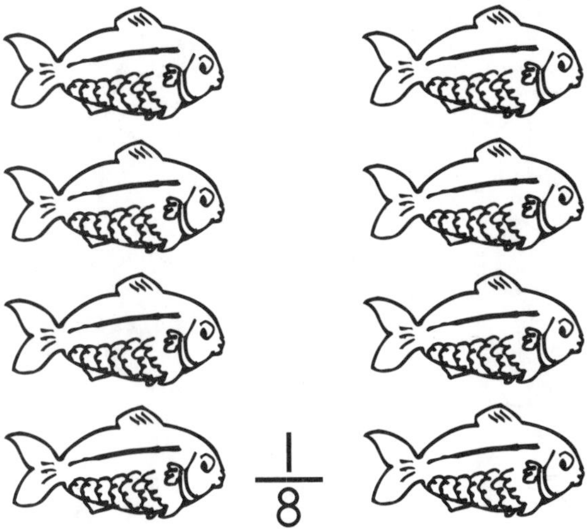

4. $\dfrac{3}{4}$

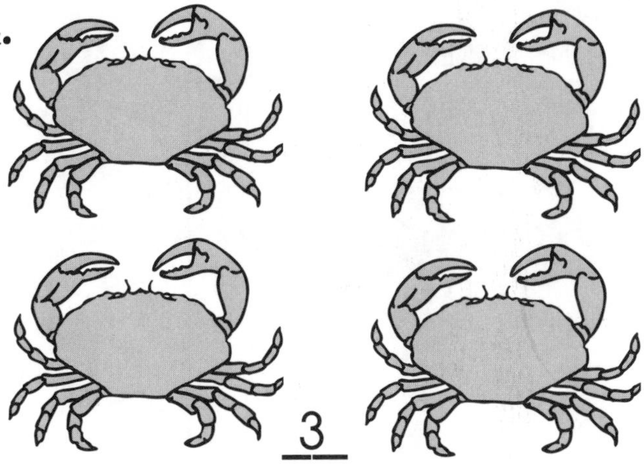

5. $\dfrac{4}{6}$

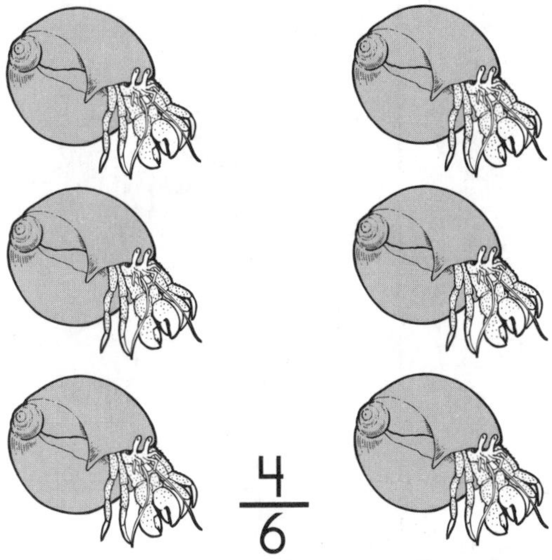

6. $\dfrac{5}{8}$

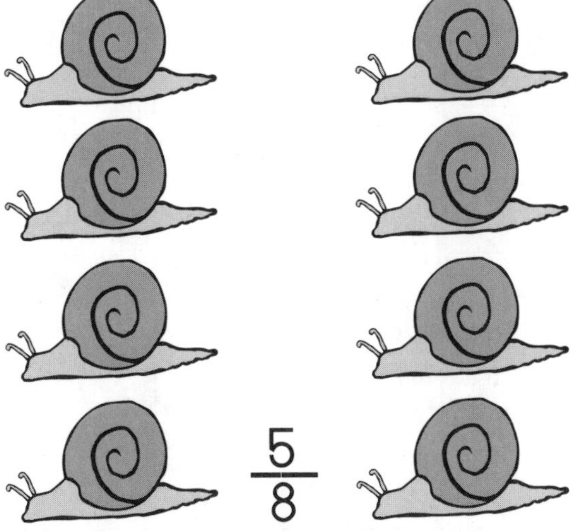

Recognize, name, and compare fractions as part of a group

Number & Operations

Nuts!

How much is circled?

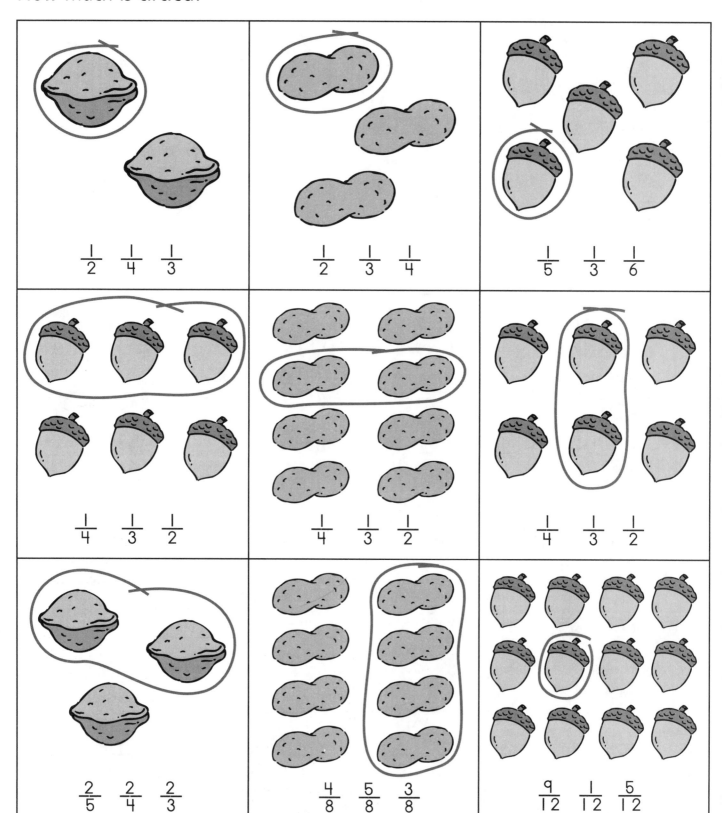

Row 1:
$\frac{1}{2}$ $\frac{1}{4}$ $\frac{1}{3}$ $\frac{1}{2}$ $\frac{1}{3}$ $\frac{1}{4}$ $\frac{1}{5}$ $\frac{1}{3}$ $\frac{1}{6}$

Row 2:
$\frac{1}{4}$ $\frac{1}{3}$ $\frac{1}{2}$ $\frac{1}{4}$ $\frac{1}{3}$ $\frac{1}{2}$ $\frac{1}{4}$ $\frac{1}{3}$ $\frac{1}{2}$

Row 3:
$\frac{2}{5}$ $\frac{2}{4}$ $\frac{2}{3}$ $\frac{4}{8}$ $\frac{5}{8}$ $\frac{3}{8}$ $\frac{9}{12}$ $\frac{1}{12}$ $\frac{5}{12}$

Recognize, name, and compare fractions as part of a group

   EMC 3015 • Basic Math Skills, Grade 2 • ©2003 by Evan-Moor Corp.

May I Have Some?

Name _____

Color the objects to show the answer.

1. Isaac gave $\frac{1}{2}$ of his cookies to me. How many cookies did he give me?

2. Susie lost $\frac{1}{3}$ of her balls in the park. How many did she have left?

3. Stan caught $\frac{2}{3}$ of the mice in the barn. How many did he catch?

Draw to show the answer.

4. Aunt Jill made 12 cookies. She put $\frac{1}{2}$ of the cookies in a bag for me. She put $\frac{1}{2}$ in a bag for my sister.

Draw the cookies.

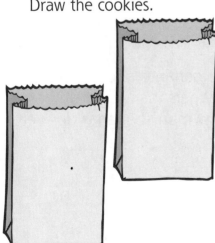

5. Uncle Ned picked three apples. He put $\frac{1}{3}$ of them in one basket. He put $\frac{2}{3}$ in the other basket.

Draw the apples.

6. Arnold bought 8 goldfish. He put $\frac{1}{2}$ of the goldfish in the big bowl. He put $\frac{1}{4}$ of the goldfish in one small bowl. He put $\frac{1}{4}$ of the goldfish in the other small bowl.

Draw the goldfish.

Recognize, name, and compare fractions as part of a group

Name _____

Fill in the circle next to the correct answer.

1. Which group is divided in half?

Ⓐ   Ⓑ   Ⓒ   Ⓓ

2. Which group is NOT divided in half?

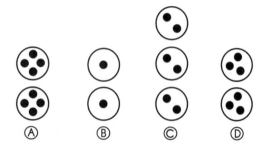

Ⓐ   Ⓑ   Ⓒ   Ⓓ

3. Find the set that is divided into thirds.

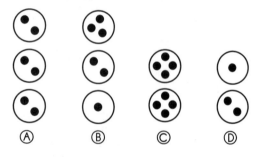

Ⓐ   Ⓑ   Ⓒ   Ⓓ

4. Find the number for $\frac{1}{3}$ of the stars.

Ⓐ 6
Ⓑ 2
Ⓒ 4
Ⓓ 3

5. Find the number for $\frac{1}{2}$ of the fish.

Ⓐ 6
Ⓑ 2
Ⓒ 8
Ⓓ 3

6. Find the number for $\frac{3}{4}$ of the hearts.

Ⓐ 4   Ⓑ 2   Ⓒ 3   Ⓓ 1

7. Find the fraction that names the black dots.

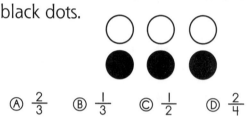

Ⓐ $\frac{2}{3}$ Ⓑ $\frac{1}{3}$ Ⓒ $\frac{1}{2}$ Ⓓ $\frac{2}{4}$

8. Find the fraction that names the white mice.

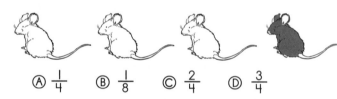

Ⓐ $\frac{1}{4}$ Ⓑ $\frac{1}{8}$ Ⓒ $\frac{2}{4}$ Ⓓ $\frac{3}{4}$

9. There are 6 pieces of cheese and 2 mice. Each mouse gets the same number of pieces. How many pieces of cheese does each mouse get?

Ⓐ 1
Ⓑ 2
Ⓒ 3
Ⓓ 4

10. There are 12 bananas and 3 monkeys. Each monkey gets the same number of bananas. How many bananas does each monkey get?

Ⓐ 2
Ⓑ 4
Ⓒ 6
Ⓓ 8

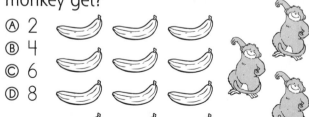

Recognize, name, and compare fractions as part of a group

Tic-Tac-Toe

Write an **X** on 75¢.
Write an **O** on 49¢.

X   **O**

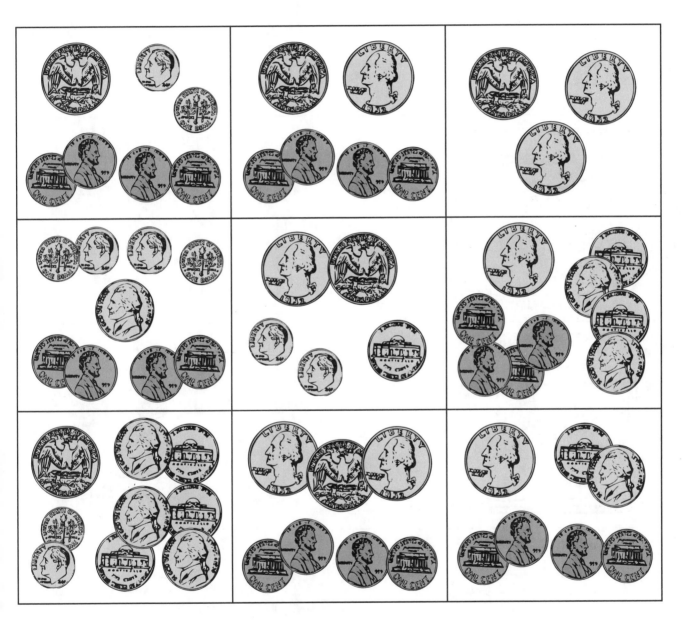

Who won the game?   **X**    **O**

Identify and know the value of coins (penny, nickel, dime, quarter) and show different combinations of coins that equal the same value

Number & Operations

In the Fishbowl

Name _____

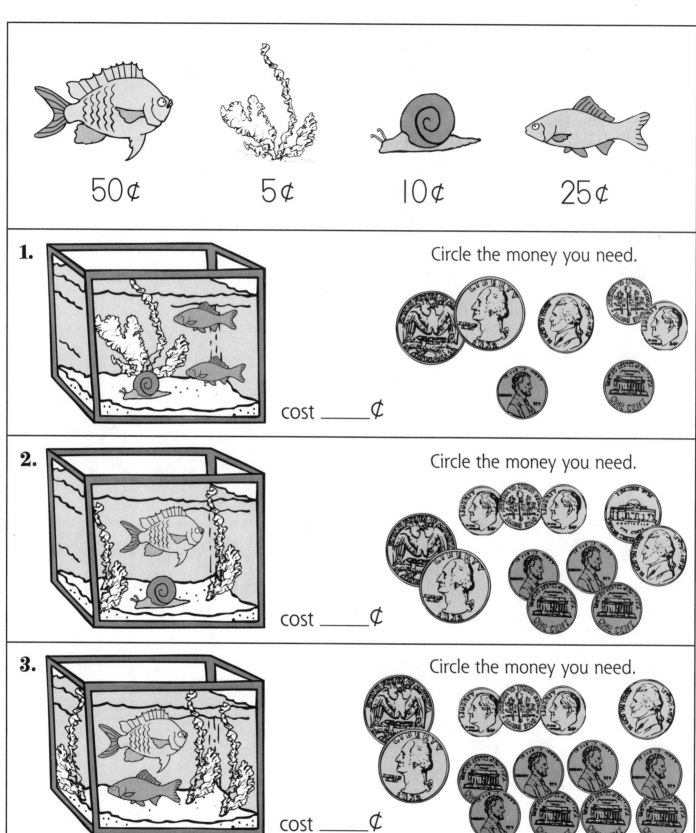

50¢   5¢   10¢   25¢

1. cost _____¢

Circle the money you need.

2. cost _____¢

Circle the money you need.

3. cost _____¢

Circle the money you need.

Identify and know the value of coins (penny, nickel, dime, quarter) and show different combinations of coins that equal the same value

How Much Money Do I Have?

Name _____

1. Tanya

10 20 21 22 23 | 23¢ |

2. Kareem

___ ___ ___ ___ ___ | ¢ |

3. Yolanda

___ ___ ___ ___ ___ | ¢ |

4. Kim

___ ___ ___ ___ ___ | ¢ |

5. Otis

___ ___ ___ ___ ___ | ¢ |

6. Hamid

___ ___ ___ ___ ___ | ¢ |

7. Who has the most money? _____

8. Who has the least amount of money? _____

Identify and know the value of coins (penny, nickel, dime, quarter) and show different combinations of coins that equal the same value

Number & Operations **103**

School Supplies

Name _____

It's time to buy school supplies. Count the money to see how much you give the clerk. Circle the coins you would get back in change.

Cost	Give Clerk	How Much Change?
1. 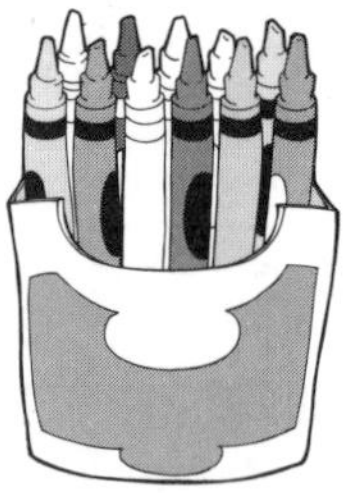 64¢		
2.  35¢		
3. 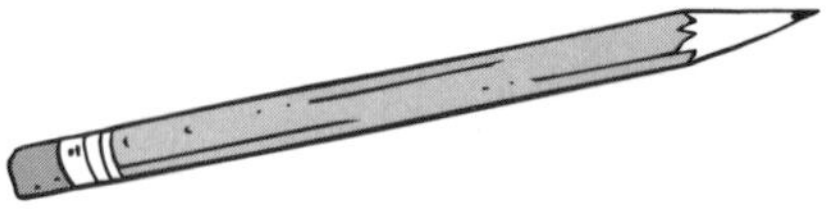 23¢		
4.  57¢		
5.  85¢		

Identify and know the value of coins (penny, nickel, dime, quarter) and show different combinations of coins that equal the same value

At the Candy Store

Answer the questions.
Use the symbols **< = >** to show why.

---

1. Jan is going to the store. She has

     .

She wants to buy some candy for 14¢.
Does she have enough money?

yes   Show why. __15¢ > 14¢__

---

2. Ryan has

    .

He wants to buy some suckers for 18¢.
Does he have enough money?

_____ Show why. _____

---

3. Angela has

 .

She wants to buy some gumballs for
16¢. Does she have enough money?

_____ Show why. _____

---

4. Jerome wants to buy gum for 20¢.
He has

  .

Does he have enough money?

_____ Show why. _____

---

5. John wants to buy jawbreakers for 12¢.
He has .

Does he have enough money?

_____ Show why. _____

---

6. Jasmine wants to buy five chocolate
drops for 25¢. She has .

Does she have enough money?

_____ Show why. _____

---

7. Write a word problem about this picture. Show the answer.

_____

_____

_____

_____ ◯ _____ = _____

Identify and know the value of coins (penny, nickel, dime, quarter) and show different combinations of coins that equal the same value

Number & Operations

Math Test

Fill in the circle next to the correct answer.

1. What is the name of this coin?

ⓐ nickel
ⓑ dime
ⓒ quarter
ⓓ penny

2. What is the name of this coin?

ⓐ nickel
ⓑ dime
ⓒ quarter
ⓓ penny

3. How do you count nickels?

ⓐ count by ones
ⓑ count by twos
ⓒ count by fives
ⓓ count by tens

4. Which coin is worth 25¢?

ⓐ   ⓑ   ⓒ   ⓓ

5. Which one shows the same amount?

ⓐ 50¢   ⓑ 31¢   ⓒ 36¢   ⓓ 26¢

6. An ice-cream cone costs 60¢. Mark gave the clerk 70¢. How much change did he get back?

ⓐ 1¢   ⓑ 10¢   ⓒ 5¢   ⓓ 25¢

7. Which coin shows the same amount?

ⓐ   ⓑ   ⓒ   ⓓ

8. Which coins are worth more than 40¢?

ⓐ   ⓑ   ⓒ   ⓓ

9. Which coins are worth less than 25¢?

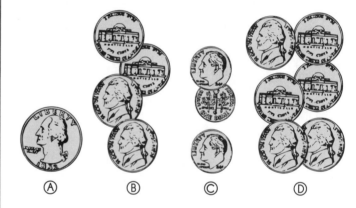

ⓐ   ⓑ   ⓒ   ⓓ

10. Which one costs the same?

ⓐ 26¢   ⓑ 18¢   ⓒ 35¢   ⓓ 25¢

Identify and know the value of coins (penny, nickel, dime, quarter) and show different combinations of coins that equal the same value

Making One Dollar

Name _____

There are 100 pennies or 100¢ in $1.00.
Count to find out how many other coins equal $1.00.

Count nickels.					
	$ .05	$ .10	$.	$.	$.
	$.	$.	$.	$.	$.
	$.	$.	$.	$.	$.
	$.	$.	$.	$.	$.

	$ .10	$.	$.	$.	$.
	$.	$.	$.	$.	$.

	$ .25	$.	$.

	$.	$.

How many in $1.00? _____   How many in $1.00? _____

How many in $1.00? _____   How many in $1.00? _____

Solve problems using combinations of coins and bills

©2003 by Evan-Moor Corp. • Basic Math Skills, Grade 2 • EMC 3015

What Will It Cost?

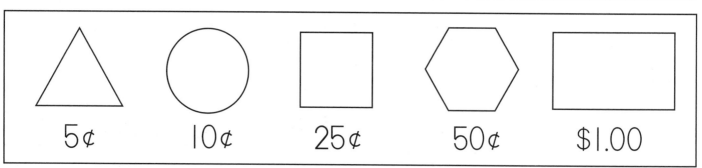

5¢   10¢   25¢   50¢ $1.00

How much will each object cost?

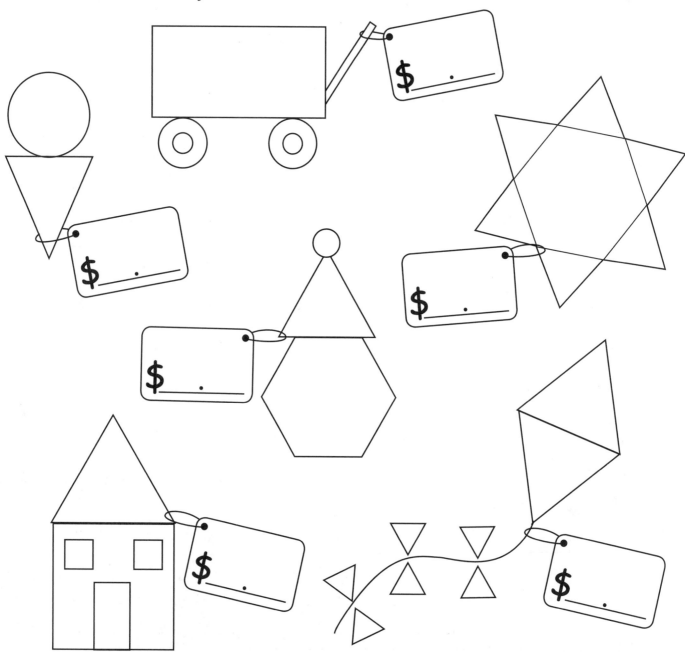

Solve problems using combinations of coins and bills

EMC 3015 • Basic Math Skills, Grade 2 • ©2003 by Evan-Moor Corp.

Counting Money

Name _____

Write the number of dollar bills and coins you need to make each amount of money.

$0.85						
$1.27						
$1.55						
$2.87						
$3.30						

Mark the coins to show two ways to make each sum of money.

$0.80		
$1.25		

Solve problems using combinations of coins and bills

A School of Fish

Cut out the tails and paste them on the correct fish.
Color the fish that is worth the most money.

$1.38

$1.75 $3.45 $2.80

Solve problems using combinations of coins and bills

Shopping at the Zoo

Name _____

Millie, George, Kim, Anthony, and Carlos went to the zoo on Saturday.
They each bought a small toy animal.
Count the money to see how much each toy cost.

1. Millie bought a toy monkey.
   How much did it cost?

$ 1.16

2. George bought a toy lion.
   How much did it cost?

$. _____

3. Kim bought a toy zebra.
   How much did it cost?

$. _____

4. Anthony bought a toy giraffe.
   How much did it cost?

$. _____

5. Carlos bought a toy elephant.
   How much did it cost?

   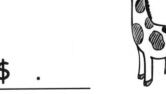 

$. _____

Solve problems using combinations of coins and bills

Number & Operations

Name _____

Fill in the circle next to the correct answer.

Math Test

1. What is the name of this coin?
   Ⓐ nickel
   Ⓑ dime
   Ⓒ quarter
   Ⓓ half-dollar

2. How many pennies make one dollar?
   Ⓐ I　　Ⓑ I0　　Ⓒ I00　　Ⓓ I,000

3. How do you count quarters?
   Ⓐ count by 5s
   Ⓑ count by 2s
   Ⓒ count by 25s
   Ⓓ count by 10s

4. Which coins show one dollar?

   Ⓐ　　Ⓑ　　Ⓒ　　Ⓓ

5. How much is this worth?
   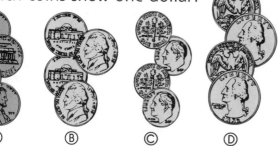
   Ⓐ $0.75　Ⓑ $0.30　Ⓒ $1.00　Ⓓ $1.50

6. Which coin shows the same amount?

   Ⓐ　　Ⓑ　　Ⓒ　　Ⓓ

7. Find the coins worth more than $1.00.
   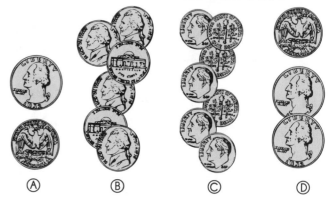
   Ⓐ　　Ⓑ　　Ⓒ　　Ⓓ

8. Find the coins worth less than 50¢.
   Ⓐ　　Ⓑ　　Ⓒ　　Ⓓ

9. A kite costs $1.30. Jon gave the clerk $1.50. How much change should he get back?
   Ⓐ 5¢　　Ⓑ 20¢　　Ⓒ 40¢　　Ⓓ 25¢

10. Which one costs the same?

    $6.75　　$3.75　　$3.99　　$3.82
    Ⓐ　　Ⓑ　　Ⓒ　　Ⓓ

Solve problems using combinations of coins and bills

EMC 3015 • Basic Math Skills, Grade 2 • ©2003 by Evan-Moor Corp.

Collect the Carrots for Bunny!

Name _____

Write in the missing numbers to help Bunny get to the carrots.

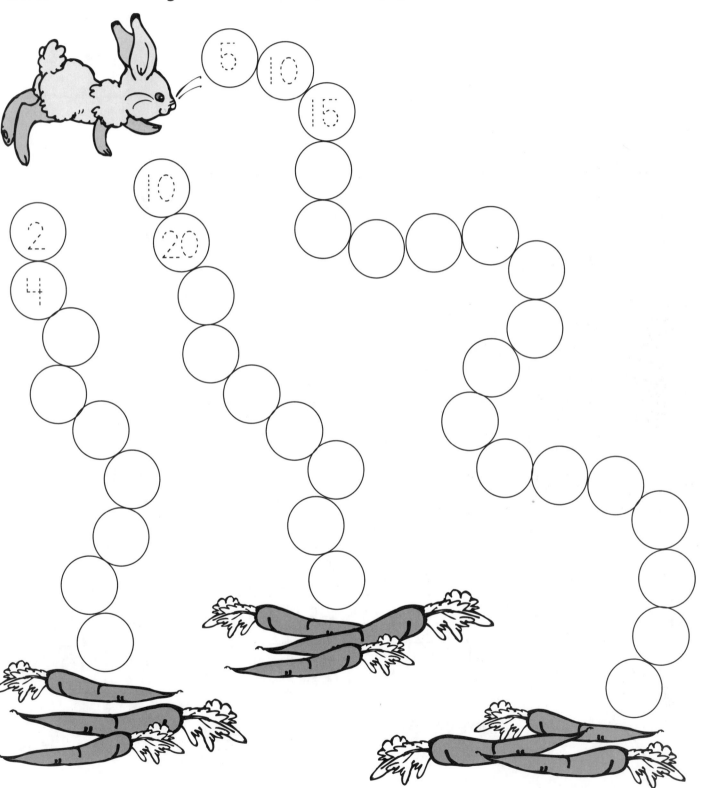

Count by tens, fives, and twos

Where Are We Going?

Name _____

Mark, Angela, and Tony went shopping.

Mark took the counting by **tens** path. Color the tens path **red**.

Angela took the counting by **fives** path. Color the fives path **blue**.

Tony took the counting by **twos** path. Color the twos path **green**.

Write each name beside the store where his or her path led.

Tony

Angela

Mark

Pet Store _____ (name)

Video Store _____ (name)

Shoe Store _____ (name)

Count by tens, fives, and twos

EMC 3015 • Basic Math Skills, Grade 2 • ©2003 by Evan-Moor Corp.

Skip Counting

Count by **tens** – outline the boxes in **red**

Count by **twos** – color the boxes **yellow**

Count by **fives** – make a **blue X** on the boxes

Some boxes will be marked more than one time.

1	2	3	4	X5	6	7	8	9	X10
11	12	13	14	15	16	17	18	19	20
21	22	23	24	25	26	27	28	29	30
31	32	33	34	35	36	37	38	39	40
41	42	43	44	45	46	47	48	49	50
51	52	53	54	55	56	57	58	59	60
61	62	63	64	65	66	67	68	69	70
71	72	73	74	75	76	77	78	79	80
81	82	83	84	85	86	87	88	89	90
91	92	93	94	95	96	97	98	99	100

Count by tens, fives, and twos

Number & Operations

How Many Legs?

Name _____

Count by twos, fives, or tens to find the answers.

---

1. Flock of Chickens

How many legs? _____ legs

How did you find the answer?

I counted by _____ because _____ .

---

2. Crowd of Caterpillars

How many legs? _____ legs

How did you find the answer?

I counted by _____ because _____ .

---

3. Bunch of Alien Bugs

How many legs? _____ legs

How did you find the answer?

I counted by _____ because _____ .

Count by tens, fives, and twos

Mrs. Washington's Vegetable Stand

Name _____

Mrs. Washington sells vegetables from her garden. She puts the vegetables in bags and boxes to sell. How many vegetables does she have to sell?

Draw pictures. Then count by twos, fives, or tens to answer the questions.

1. She packed 6 paper bags. She put 5 ears of corn in each bag.

How many ears of corn did she pack?

_____ ears of corn

2. She packed 4 baskets. She put 10 tomatoes in each basket.

How many tomatoes did she pack?

_____ tomatoes

3. She packed 8 sacks. She put 2 big squash in each sack.

How many squash did she pack?

_____ squash

4. Write a number story about this picture. Tell how to pack the potatoes in boxes.

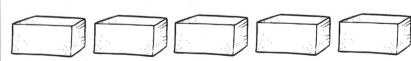

_____

_____

_____

_____

Count by tens, fives, and twos

Number & Operations

Name _____

Math Test

Fill in the circle next to the correct answer.

1. What number comes next?

25, 30, 35, 40, _____

- Ⓐ 30
- Ⓑ 41
- Ⓒ 50
- Ⓓ 45

2. What number comes next?

18, 20, 22, 24, _____

- Ⓐ 26
- Ⓑ 27
- Ⓒ 34
- Ⓓ 28

3. What number is missing?

_____, 80, 90, 100, 110

- Ⓐ 40
- Ⓑ 70
- Ⓒ 50
- Ⓓ 79

4. What number is missing?

85, 90, _____, 100, 105

- Ⓐ 95
- Ⓑ 80
- Ⓒ 91
- Ⓓ 99

5. Put these numbers in order.

24, 22, 26, 20

- Ⓐ 20, 24, 22, 26
- Ⓑ 20, 22, 26, 24
- Ⓒ 20, 22, 24, 26
- Ⓓ 20, 26, 22, 24

6. Which number does NOT belong?

35, 40, 45, 46, 50, 55

- Ⓐ 45
- Ⓑ 35
- Ⓒ 46
- Ⓓ 50

7. Which number does NOT belong?

70, 80, 85, 90, 100

- Ⓐ 90
- Ⓑ 80
- Ⓒ 100
- Ⓓ 85

8. Which number is NOT in order?

45, 50, 55, 70, 60, 65

- Ⓐ 60
- Ⓑ 65
- Ⓒ 70
- Ⓓ 55

9. One nickel is 5¢. How much money is 9 nickels?

- Ⓐ 45¢
- Ⓑ 40¢
- Ⓒ 65¢
- Ⓓ 90¢

10. Each bucket holds 10 cups of water. How many cups of water are in 10 buckets?

- Ⓐ 50
- Ⓑ 70
- Ⓒ 95
- Ⓓ 100

Count by tens, fives, and twos

In the Barnyard

How many are there?

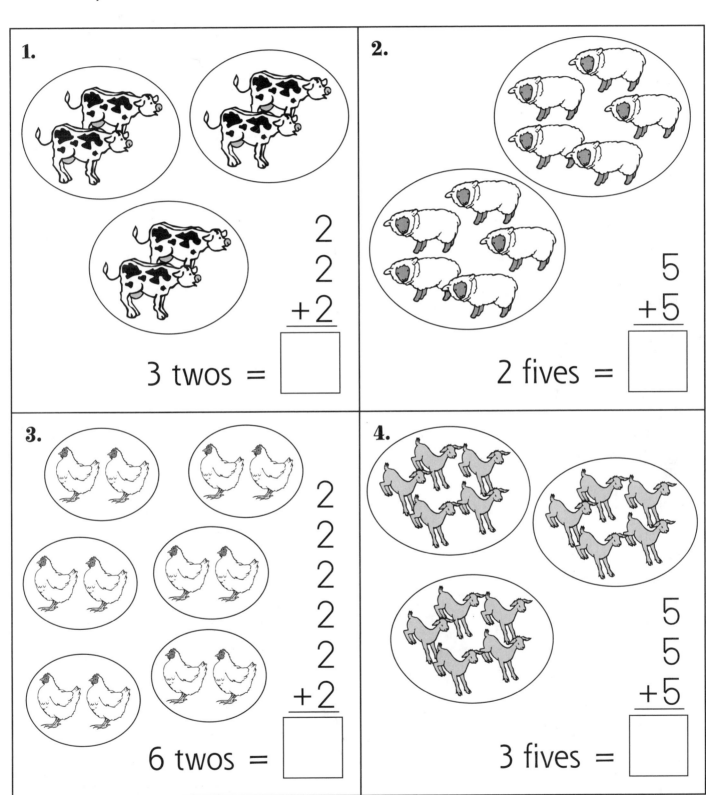

1.

$$\begin{array}{r} 2 \\ 2 \\ +2 \\ \hline \end{array}$$

3 twos = ☐

2.

$$\begin{array}{r} 5 \\ +5 \\ \hline \end{array}$$

2 fives = ☐

3.

$$\begin{array}{r} 2 \\ 2 \\ 2 \\ 2 \\ 2 \\ +2 \\ \hline \end{array}$$

6 twos = ☐

4.

$$\begin{array}{r} 5 \\ 5 \\ +5 \\ \hline \end{array}$$

3 fives = ☐

Use repeated addition, arrays, and counting by multiples to do multiplication

Number & Operations

It Came from Outer Space

Name _____

Look at the men from outer space. Answer the questions.

1. How many men from outer

space? _____

How many eyes on one man? _____

How many eyes in all? _____

2. How many men from outer

space? _____

How many feet on one man? _____

How many feet in all? _____

3. How many men from outer

space? _____

How many arms on one man? _____

How many arms in all? _____

4. How many men from outer

space? _____

How many ears on one man? _____

How many ears in all? _____

Use repeated addition, arrays, and counting by multiples to do multiplication

Number & Operations

EMC 3015 • Basic Math Skills, Grade 2 • ©2003 by Evan-Moor Corp.

Party Fun

Name _____

Circle the pictures. Answer the questions.

1. Circle 2 each time.

How many in all? _____

How many 2s? _____

_____ × 2 = _____

2. Circle 5 each time.

How many in all? _____

How many 5s? _____

_____ × 5 = _____

3. Circle 2 each time.

How many in all? _____

How many 2s? _____

_____ × 2 = _____

4. Circle 5 each time.

How many in all? _____

How many 5s? _____

_____ × 5 = _____

5. Circle 2 each time.

How many in all? _____

How many 2s? _____

_____ × 2 = _____

Use repeated addition, arrays, and counting by multiples to do multiplication

Number & Operations

Add, Then Multiply

Name _____

Read and follow the directions.

---

1. Draw 2 stars in each circle.

Add $\quad 2 + 2 =$ ___4___

Multiply $2 \times 2 =$ ___4___

---

2. Draw 2 hearts in each circle.

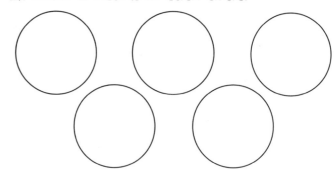

Add $\quad 2 + 2 + 2 + 2 + 2 =$ ___

Multiply $5 \times 2 =$ ___

---

3. Draw 5 squares in each circle.

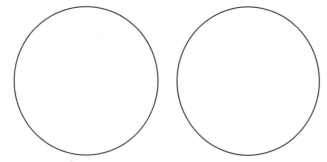

Add $\quad 5 + 5 =$ ___

Multiply $2 \times 5 =$ ___

---

4. Draw 5 balls in each circle.

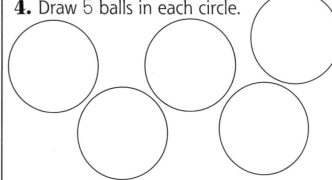

Add $\quad 5 + 5 + 5 + 5 + 5 =$ ___

Multiply $5 \times 5 =$ ___

---

5. Draw 2 buttons in each circle.

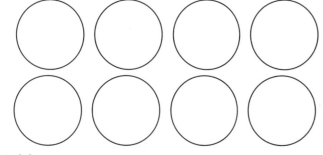

Add

$2 + 2 + 2 + 2 + 2 + 2 + 2 + 2 =$ ___

Multiply $8 \times 2 =$ ___

---

6. Draw 5 cookies in each circle.

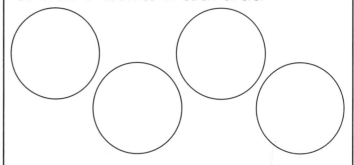

Add $\quad 5 + 5 + 5 + 5 =$ ___

Multiply $4 \times 5 =$ ___

Use repeated addition, arrays, and counting by multiples to do multiplication

EMC 3015 • Basic Math Skills, Grade 2 • ©2003 by Evan-Moor Corp.

A School Flower Garden

Name _____

---

1. John wants to plant daffodils. Daffodils are sold in bags of 5. He has 3 bags.

How many daffodils can he plant?

Add to find the answer.

_____ 5 + 5 + 5 = 15 _____ daffodils

Multiply to find the answer.

_____ 3 × 5 = 15 _____ daffodils

---

2. Elisa is planting bulbs. She bought 5 bags of tulip bulbs. There are 5 bulbs in each bag.

How many bulbs can she plant?

Add to find the answer.

_____ bulbs

Multiply to find the answer.

_____ bulbs

---

3. There are 3 bags of crocus bulbs on the shelf. Each bag holds 10 bulbs.

How many crocus bulbs are there?

Add to find the answer.

_____ bulbs

Multiply to find the answer.

_____ bulbs

---

4. Edna has 6 bags of paper whites. There are 2 bulbs in each bag. She will put one bulb in each hole.

How many holes must she dig for the paper whites?

Add to find the answer.

_____ holes

Multiply to find the answer.

_____ holes

---

5. Write a word problem about this picture. Then write a number sentence about it.

_____

_____

_____

_____ ◯ _____ = _____

Use repeated addition, arrays, and counting by multiples to do multiplication

Number & Operations

Math Test

Fill in the circle next to the correct answer.

1. Count by twos. Find the answer.

Ⓐ 5
Ⓑ 8
Ⓒ 9
Ⓓ 6

2. Count by fives. Find the answer.

Ⓐ 3
Ⓑ 5
Ⓒ 15
Ⓓ 20

3. Count by tens. Find the answer.

Ⓐ 30¢   Ⓑ 5¢   Ⓒ 50¢   Ⓓ 15¢

4. Which picture shows groups of two?

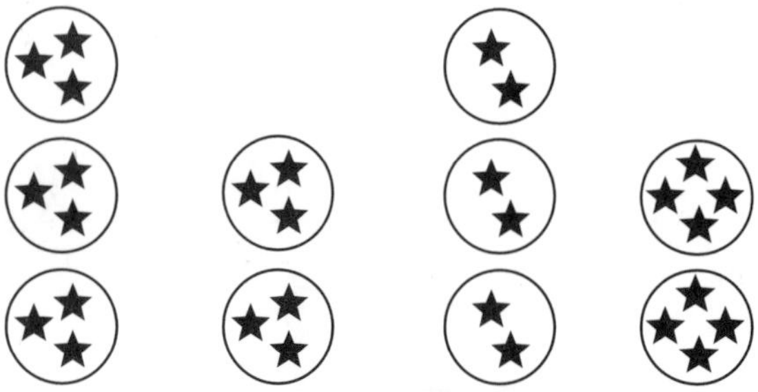

Ⓐ   Ⓑ   Ⓒ   Ⓓ

5. Which picture shows groups of five?

Ⓐ

Ⓑ

Ⓒ

Ⓓ

6. How many groups of five are there?

Ⓐ 2
Ⓑ 4
Ⓒ 5
Ⓓ 3

7. How many stars are there in all?

Ⓐ 10
Ⓑ 5
Ⓒ 50
Ⓓ 25

8. Find the addition problem that has the same answer as 3 x 2.

Ⓐ 3 + 2
Ⓑ 3 + 3 + 3
Ⓒ 2 + 2 + 2
Ⓓ 2 + 3

9. Find the addition problem that has the same answer as 5 x 10.

Ⓐ 5 + 5 + 5 + 5 + 5
Ⓑ 10 + 5
Ⓒ 5 + 10
Ⓓ 10 + 10 + 10 + 10 + 10

10. Mom made 3 boxes of cookies. She put 10 cookies in each box. Find the number sentence that shows this.

Ⓐ 10 + 10 + 10 = 30
Ⓑ 10 + 10 + 10 = 3
Ⓒ 3 + 3 + 3 = 9
Ⓓ 3 + 3 + 3 + 3 + 3 = 15

Use repeated addition, arrays, and counting by multiples to do multiplication

Kim's Toy Dinosaur

Name _____

Find the answers. Color Kim's dinosaur.

Key

4 and 40	–	yellow stripes
5 and 25	–	yellow
10 and 30	–	red dots
6 and 16	–	red
8 and 18	–	green
15 and 16	–	green dots
2 and 12	–	orange
20 and 50	–	orange stripes

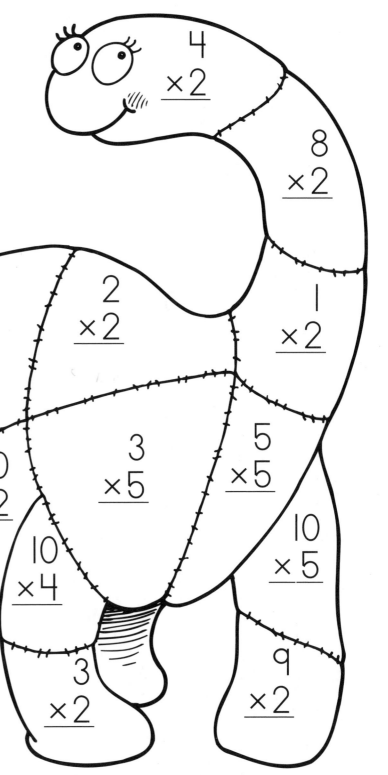

Find the Hidden Dinosaur

Name _____

Cut the puzzle pieces apart.
Paste the correct answer on top of the problem.

6 ×5	7 ×5	9 ×5	10 ×5	3 ×2	1 ×5
2 ×5	8 ×2	4 ×5	9 ×2	3 ×5	2 ×2
7 ×2	8 ×5	4 ×2	10 ×6	5 ×5	6 ×2

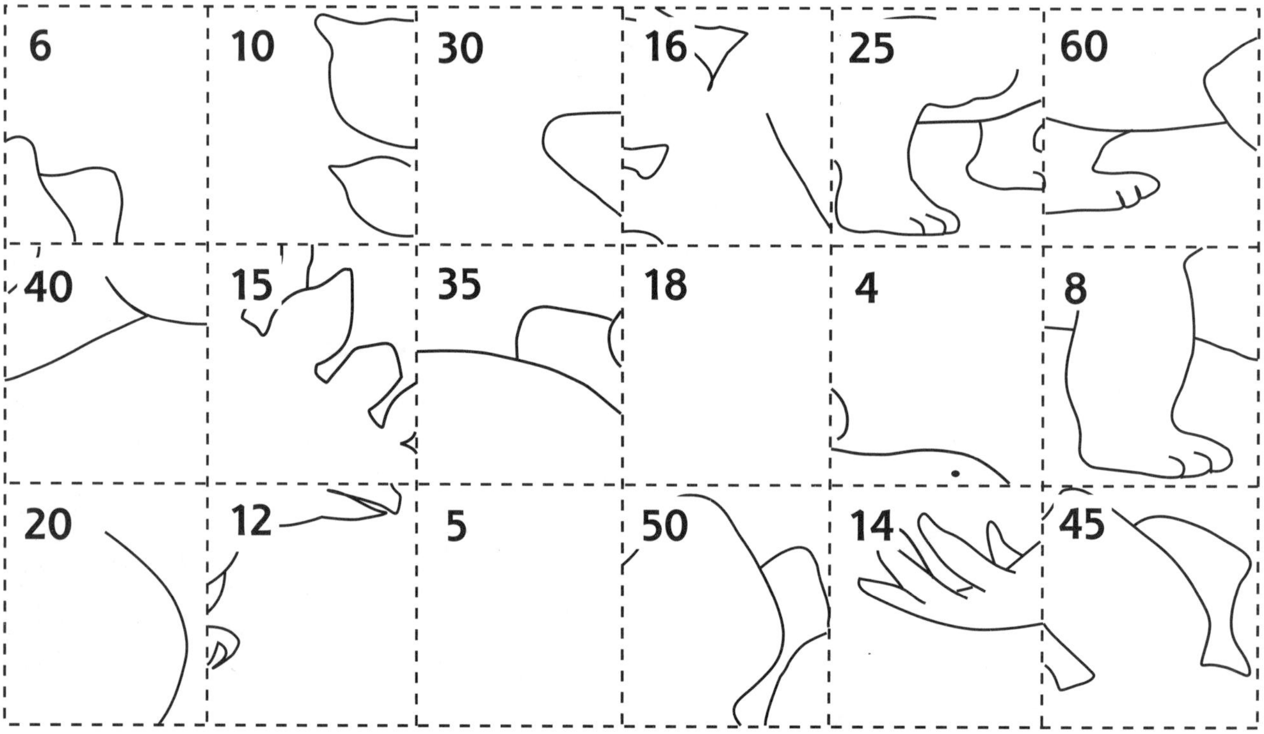

6	10	30	16	25	60
40	15	35	18	4	8
20	12	5	50	14	45

Solve multiplication problems of tens, fives, and twos

Twos, Fives, Tens

Count by 2s.

| 0 | 2 | __ | __ | __ | __ | __ | __ | __ | __ |

$$
\begin{array}{r} 3 \\ \times 2 \\ \hline \end{array} \qquad
\begin{array}{r} 2 \\ \times 2 \\ \hline \end{array} \qquad
\begin{array}{r} 8 \\ \times 2 \\ \hline \end{array} \qquad
\begin{array}{r} 0 \\ \times 2 \\ \hline \end{array} \qquad
\begin{array}{r} 5 \\ \times 2 \\ \hline \end{array}
$$

$$
\begin{array}{r} 4 \\ \times 2 \\ \hline \end{array} \qquad
\begin{array}{r} 1 \\ \times 2 \\ \hline \end{array} \qquad
\begin{array}{r} 6 \\ \times 2 \\ \hline \end{array} \qquad
\begin{array}{r} 7 \\ \times 2 \\ \hline \end{array} \qquad
\begin{array}{r} 9 \\ \times 2 \\ \hline \end{array}
$$

Count by 5s.

| 0 | 5 | __ | __ | __ | __ | __ | __ | __ | __ |

$$
\begin{array}{r} 5 \\ \times 5 \\ \hline \end{array} \qquad
\begin{array}{r} 2 \\ \times 5 \\ \hline \end{array} \qquad
\begin{array}{r} 9 \\ \times 5 \\ \hline \end{array} \qquad
\begin{array}{r} 3 \\ \times 5 \\ \hline \end{array} \qquad
\begin{array}{r} 7 \\ \times 5 \\ \hline \end{array}
$$

$$
\begin{array}{r} 0 \\ \times 5 \\ \hline \end{array} \qquad
\begin{array}{r} 4 \\ \times 5 \\ \hline \end{array} \qquad
\begin{array}{r} 8 \\ \times 5 \\ \hline \end{array} \qquad
\begin{array}{r} 1 \\ \times 5 \\ \hline \end{array} \qquad
\begin{array}{r} 6 \\ \times 5 \\ \hline \end{array}
$$

Count by 10s.

| 0 | 10 | __ | __ | __ | __ | __ | __ | __ | __ |

$$
\begin{array}{r} 3 \\ \times 10 \\ \hline \end{array} \qquad
\begin{array}{r} 1 \\ \times 10 \\ \hline \end{array} \qquad
\begin{array}{r} 5 \\ \times 10 \\ \hline \end{array} \qquad
\begin{array}{r} 0 \\ \times 10 \\ \hline \end{array} \qquad
\begin{array}{r} 8 \\ \times 10 \\ \hline \end{array}
$$

$$
\begin{array}{r} 4 \\ \times 10 \\ \hline \end{array} \qquad
\begin{array}{r} 2 \\ \times 10 \\ \hline \end{array} \qquad
\begin{array}{r} 9 \\ \times 10 \\ \hline \end{array} \qquad
\begin{array}{r} 7 \\ \times 10 \\ \hline \end{array} \qquad
\begin{array}{r} 6 \\ \times 10 \\ \hline \end{array}
$$

Solve multiplication problems of tens, fives, and twos

Number & Operations

Gone Fishing

Name _____

Write the answers on the fish tails.

$4 \times 10 =$

$8 \times 2 =$

$5 \times 2 =$

$2 \times 5 =$

$4 \times 5 =$

$2 \times 2 =$

$3 \times 2 =$

$9 \times 2 =$

$2 \times 10 =$

$5 \times 5 =$

$7 \times 2 =$

$9 \times 10 =$

$0 \times 2 =$

$0 \times 5 =$

$1 \times 5 =$

$3 \times 5 =$

$6 \times 5 =$

Solve multiplication problems of tens, fives, and twos

EMC 3015 • Basic Math Skills, Grade 2 • ©2003 by Evan-Moor Corp.

A Multiplication Table

Name _____

Alice is making a multiplication table. Help her complete the table by filling in the missing numbers.

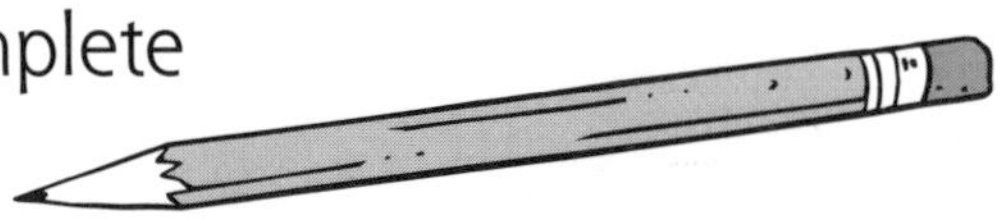

X	2	5	10
1	2		
2	4		
3			
4		20	
5			
6			60
7	14	35	
8			
9			90
10			

Solve multiplication problems of tens, fives, and twos

Name _____

Math Test

Fill in the circle next to the correct answer.

1. 5 x 2 = _____
- Ⓐ 12
- Ⓑ 3
- Ⓒ 7
- Ⓓ 10

2. 3 x 5 = _____
- Ⓐ 15
- Ⓑ 25
- Ⓒ 30
- Ⓓ 8

3. 6 x 10 = _____
- Ⓐ 16
- Ⓑ 4
- Ⓒ 60
- Ⓓ 61

4. 8 x 2 = _____
- Ⓐ 10
- Ⓑ 16
- Ⓒ 4
- Ⓓ 28

5. Which one shows this problem?
   4 x 5

- Ⓐ
- Ⓑ
- Ⓒ
- Ⓓ

6. What is the problem for this?

- Ⓐ 3 x 3
- Ⓑ 5 x 5
- Ⓒ 3 x 5
- Ⓓ 3 x 4

7. Which number sentence is NOT correct?
- Ⓐ 3 x 5 = 15
- Ⓑ 5 x 5 = 10
- Ⓒ 6 x 2 = 12
- Ⓓ 4 x 10 = 40

8. Find the missing sign.

   6 ◯ 5 = 30

- Ⓐ +
- Ⓑ −
- Ⓒ =
- Ⓓ x

9. There are 3 bags of peanuts. There are 10 peanuts in a bag. How many peanuts are there in all?
- Ⓐ 30
- Ⓑ 10
- Ⓒ 3
- Ⓓ 33

10. A dime is worth 10¢. How much are 7 dimes worth?
- Ⓐ 17¢
- Ⓑ 10¢
- Ⓒ 7¢
- Ⓓ 70¢

Solve multiplication problems of tens, fives, and twos

Number & Operations   EMC 3015 • Basic Math Skills, Grade 2 • ©2003 by Evan-Moor Corp.

Snack Time at the Zoo

Name _____

Morgan works in a zoo. She feeds the animals their afternoon snack. Help her divide the snacks for the animals. Circle the snacks to find the answer.

1. Divide the bananas into three equal groups.

How many bananas will she give each monkey?

_____ bananas

2. Divide the ears of corn into four equal groups.

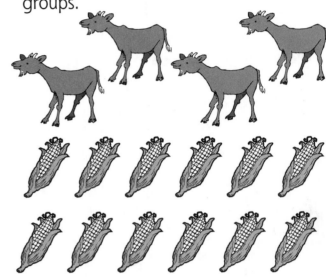

How many ears of corn will she give each goat?

_____ ears of corn

3. Divide the bundles of hay into two equal groups.

How many bundles of hay will she give each elephant?

_____ bundles of hay

4. Divide the fish into four equal parts.

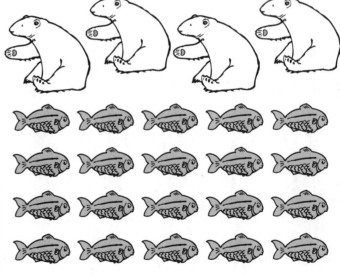

How many fish will she give each polar bear?

_____ fish

Use repeated subtraction, equal sharing, and forming equal groups to do division

Number & Operations

Cookie Count

Name _____

Circle cookies to find the answers.

1. Divide the cookies into 3 equal groups.  _____ in each group	**2.** Divide the cookies into 5 equal groups. 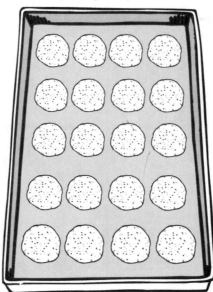 _____ in each group	**3.** Divide the cookies into 2 equal groups.  _____ in each group
4. Divide the cookies into 6 equal groups.  _____ in each group	**5.** Divide the cookies into 3 equal groups. 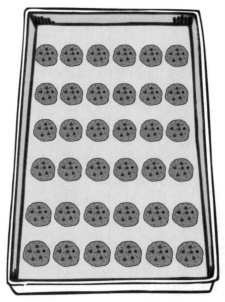 _____ in each group	**6.** Divide the cookies into 4 equal groups.  _____ in each group

Use repeated subtraction, equal sharing, and forming equal groups to do division

Number & Operations   EMC 3015 • Basic Math Skills, Grade 2 • ©2003 by Evan-Moor Corp.

Hearts and Stars

Name _____

Divide the hearts and stars into equal groups.

1. Divide the hearts into 2 equal groups.

_2_ groups

_____ in each group

2. Divide the stars into 4 equal groups.

_____ groups

_____ in each group

3. Divide the hearts into 3 equal groups.

_____ groups

_____ in each group

4. Divide the stars into 8 equal groups.

_____ groups

_____ in each group

5. Divide the hearts into 2 equal groups. How many are left over?

_____ groups

_____ in each group

_____ left over

6. Divide the stars into 3 equal groups. How many are left over?

_____ groups

_____ in each group

_____ left over

Use repeated subtraction, equal sharing, and forming equal groups to do division

Garden Rows

Divide the shapes into equal groups. Then subtract until you reach zero.

1. Divide 12 flowers into 4 equal groups.

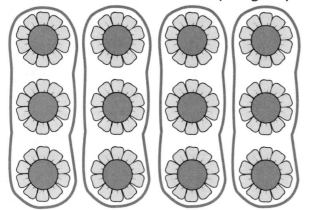

$12 - 4 = \underline{8}$

$\underline{8} - 4 = \underline{4}$

$\underline{4} - 4 = \underline{0}$

How many times did you subtract?

$\underline{3}$

$12 \div 4 = \underline{3}$

2. Divide 10 flowers into 5 equal groups.

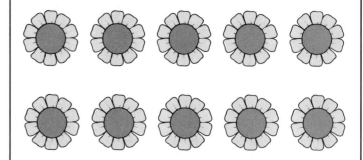

$10 - 5 = \underline{}$

$\underline{} - 5 = \underline{}$

How many times did you subtract?

$\underline{}$

$10 \div 5 = \underline{}$

3. Divide 15 flowers into 3 equal groups.

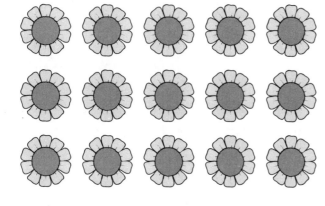

$15 - 3 = \underline{}$

$\underline{} - 3 = \underline{}$

$\underline{} - 3 = \underline{}$

$\underline{} - 3 = \underline{}$

$\underline{} - 3 = \underline{}$

How many times did you subtract?

$\underline{}$

$15 \div 3 = \underline{}$

4. Divide 20 flowers into 4 equal groups.

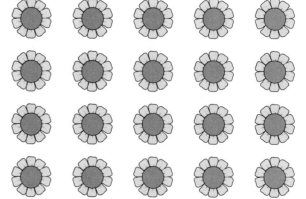

$20 - 4 = \underline{}$

$\underline{} - 4 = \underline{}$

$\underline{} - 4 = \underline{}$

$\underline{} - 4 = \underline{}$

$\underline{} - 4 = \underline{}$

How many times did you subtract?

$\underline{}$

$20 \div 4 = \underline{}$

Use repeated subtraction, equal sharing, and forming equal groups to do division

EMC 3015 • Basic Math Skills, Grade 2 • ©2003 by Evan-Moor Corp.

At the Pond

Name _____

Read the word problem. Draw pictures and write the answers.

1. Five boys went fishing in the pond.
Each boy caught the same number of fish.
Together they caught 25 fish.
How many fish did each boy catch?

Each boy caught __5__ fish.

$$25 \div 5 = 5$$

2. Miss Wilson caught 45 tadpoles
for science class. She put the same
number of tadpoles in each jar.
If she had 5 jars, how many
tadpoles were in each jar?

She put _____ tadpoles in each jar.

$$\underline{\quad} \div \underline{\quad} = \underline{\quad}$$

3. Two girls picked flowers growing by the
pond. Together they picked 20 flowers.
Each girl picked the same number of flowers.
How many flowers did each girl pick?

Each girl picked _____ flowers.

$$\underline{\quad} \div \underline{\quad} = \underline{\quad}$$

Use repeated subtraction, equal sharing, and forming equal groups to do division

Math Test

Name _____

Fill in the circle next to the correct answer.

1. How many equal groups of 2 can you divide 8 peanuts into?

- Ⓐ 2
- Ⓑ 3
- Ⓒ 4
- Ⓓ 5

2. How many equal groups of 3 can you divide 6 bananas into?

- Ⓐ 2
- Ⓑ 3
- Ⓒ 4
- Ⓓ 5

3. How many equal groups of 5 can you divide 10 acorns into?

- Ⓐ 2
- Ⓑ 3
- Ⓒ 4
- Ⓓ 5

4. Which group can be divided into 2 equal groups?

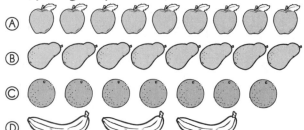

5. Which group can be divided into 2 equal groups?

- Ⓐ
- Ⓑ
- Ⓒ
- Ⓓ

6. Which group can NOT be divided into 2 equal groups?

7. How many times must you subtract to reach 0?

$$12 - 3 = 9, \quad 9 - 3 = 6,$$
$$6 - 3 = 3, \quad 3 - 3 = 0$$

- Ⓐ 2
- Ⓑ 3
- Ⓒ 4
- Ⓓ 5

8. $6 \div 2 =$ _____

- Ⓐ 2
- Ⓑ 3
- Ⓒ 4
- Ⓓ 5

9. $10 \div 5 =$ _____

- Ⓐ 2
- Ⓑ 3
- Ⓒ 4
- Ⓓ 5

10. Mark has 8 dog cookies. He has 4 dogs. Each dog gets the same number of cookies. How many cookies does each dog get?

- Ⓐ 2
- Ⓑ 3
- Ⓒ 4
- Ⓓ 5

Use repeated subtraction, equal sharing, and forming equal groups to do division

EMC 3015 • Basic Math Skills, Grade 2 • ©2003 by Evan-Moor Corp.

Algebra

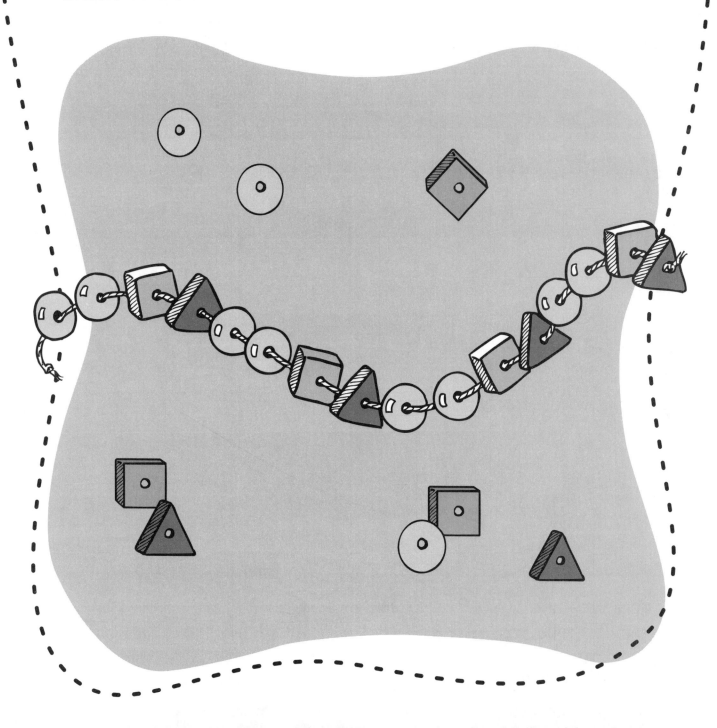

What Is It?

Circle numbers to complete the pattern.

1	2	③	4	5	⑥	7	8	⑨	10	11	⑫	13	14	⑮	16	17	18	19	20
21	22	23	24	25	26	27	28	29	30	31	32	33	34	35	36	37	38	39	40
41	42	43	44	45	46	47	48	49	50	51	52	53	54	55	56	57	58	59	60

Connect the numbers you circled in order to complete the dot-to-dot.

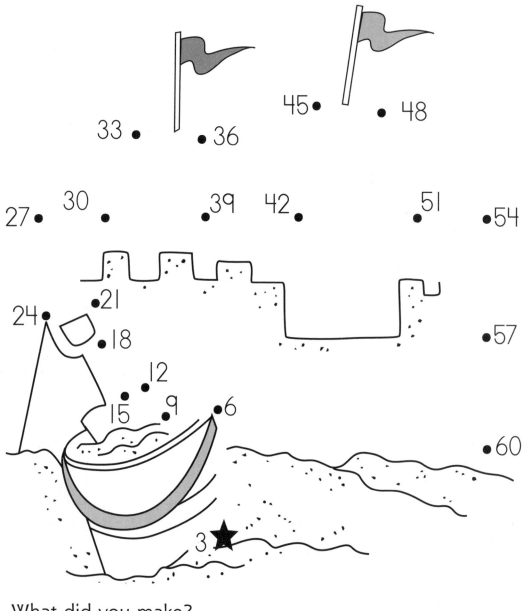

What did you make? _____

Recognize, describe, and extend patterns

EMC 3015 • Basic Math Skills, Grade 2 • ©2003 by Evan-Moor Corp.

Race to the Top

Think about the number pattern. Write the missing numbers.

12	17	27
24	5	9
26	3	6
28	1	3

Recognize, describe, and extend patterns

Algebra

Color Grandma's Blanket

Color the number patterns.

ones	– blue
twos	– red
threes	– yellow
fours	– orange
fives	– purple

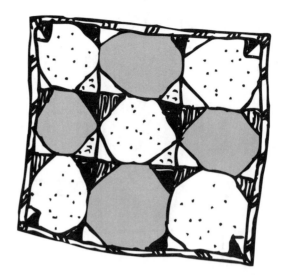

	1	2	3	4	5	6	7	8	9	10	11	12	13	14	15	16	17	18	19	20
ones	1	2	3	4	5	6	7	8	9	10	11	12	13	14	15	16	17	18	19	20
twos	1	2	3	4	5	6	7	8	9	10	11	12	13	14	15	16	17	18	19	20
threes	1	2	3	4	5	6	7	8	9	10	11	12	13	14	15	16	17	18	19	20
fours	1	2	3	4	5	6	7	8	9	10	11	12	13	14	15	16	17	18	19	20
fives	1	2	3	4	5	6	7	8	9	10	11	12	13	14	15	16	17	18	19	20
fours	1	2	3	4	5	6	7	8	9	10	11	12	13	14	15	16	17	18	19	20
threes	1	2	3	4	5	6	7	8	9	10	11	12	13	14	15	16	17	18	19	20
twos	1	2	3	4	5	6	7	8	9	10	11	12	13	14	15	16	17	18	19	20
ones	1	2	3	4	5	6	7	8	9	10	11	12	13	14	15	16	17	18	19	20

Recognize, describe, and extend patterns

EMC 3015 • Basic Math Skills, Grade 2 • ©2003 by Evan-Moor Corp.

Hippity, Hoppity Frogs

Name _____

Finish the number patterns by marking the jumps for each frog.

1. Write the number pattern here. _____

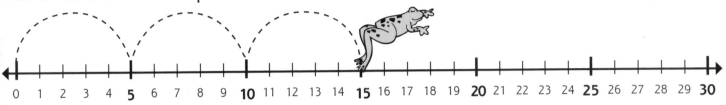

0 1 2 3 4 **5** 6 7 8 9 **10** 11 12 13 14 **15** 16 17 18 19 **20** 21 22 23 24 **25** 26 27 28 29 **30**

2. Write the number pattern here. _____

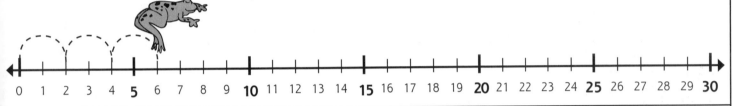

0 1 2 3 4 **5** 6 7 8 9 **10** 11 12 13 14 **15** 16 17 18 19 **20** 21 22 23 24 **25** 26 27 28 29 **30**

3. Write the number pattern here. _____

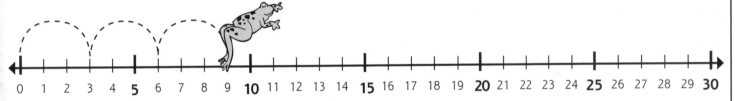

0 1 2 3 4 **5** 6 7 8 9 **10** 11 12 13 14 **15** 16 17 18 19 **20** 21 22 23 24 **25** 26 27 28 29 **30**

4. Write the number pattern here. _____

0 1 2 3 4 **5** 6 7 8 9 **10** 11 12 13 14 **15** 16 17 18 19 **20** 21 22 23 24 **25** 26 27 28 29 **30**

5. Make your own number pattern.

Write the number pattern here. _____

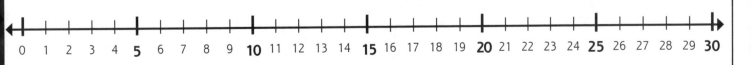

0 1 2 3 4 **5** 6 7 8 9 **10** 11 12 13 14 **15** 16 17 18 19 **20** 21 22 23 24 **25** 26 27 28 29 **30**

Recognize, describe, and extend patterns

©2003 by Evan-Moor Corp. • Basic Math Skills, Grade 2 • EMC 3015

Algebra

What's My Pattern?

Name _____

Finish the number patterns.

Then write the rule in the boxes.

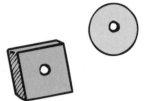

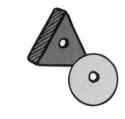

1. 1   3   5   _7_ ___ ___ ___ ___

[+2] [+2] [ ] [ ] [ ] [ ] [ ]

2. 15 13 11 ___ ___ ___ ___

[-2] [ ] [ ] [ ] [ ] [ ] [ ]

3. 1   6   5   10   9   ___ ___ ___ ___ ___

[ ] [ ] [ ] [ ] [ ] [ ] [ ] [ ] [ ] [ ]

Recognize, describe, and extend patterns

Algebra   EMC 3015 • Basic Math Skills, Grade 2 • ©2003 by Evan-Moor Corp.

Math Test

Fill in the circle next to the correct answer.

1. What number comes next?

   5, 10, 15, 20, _____
   - Ⓐ 21
   - Ⓑ 22
   - Ⓒ 25
   - Ⓓ 30

2. What number comes next?

   14, 12, 10, 8, _____
   - Ⓐ 7
   - Ⓑ 6
   - Ⓒ 5
   - Ⓓ 4

3. Find the missing number.

   _____, 6, 9, 12, 15
   - Ⓐ 2
   - Ⓑ 3
   - Ⓒ 4
   - Ⓓ 5

4. Find the missing number.

   _____, 15, 17, 19, 21
   - Ⓐ 11
   - Ⓑ 12
   - Ⓒ 13
   - Ⓓ 14

5. Which number is NOT part of the pattern?

   10, 15, 20, 22, 25, 30, 35
   - Ⓐ 20
   - Ⓑ 22
   - Ⓒ 25
   - Ⓓ 27

6. The rule is + 3. What is the next number?

   20, _____
   - Ⓐ 21
   - Ⓑ 22
   - Ⓒ 23
   - Ⓓ 24

7. The rule is – 6. What is the next number?

   12, _____
   - Ⓐ 6
   - Ⓑ 5
   - Ⓒ 4
   - Ⓓ 3

8. The rule is x 2. What is the next number?

   8, _____
   - Ⓐ 10
   - Ⓑ 12
   - Ⓒ 14
   - Ⓓ 16

9. What is the rule?

   3, 5, 7, 9, 11
   - Ⓐ add 2
   - Ⓑ add 3
   - Ⓒ subtract 2
   - Ⓓ subtract 3

10. What is the rule?

    15, 12, 9, 6
    - Ⓐ add 3
    - Ⓑ subtract 3
    - Ⓒ multiply by 3
    - Ⓓ subtract 6

Recognize, describe, and extend patterns

Algebra   **143**

Jill's Aquarium

Name _____

Jill has a big aquarium. She has room for more fish, snails, and plants. Write the answers. Then draw how many more she adds to her aquarium.

1. Jill has 1 big fish. She wants 4. How many more does she need? _____ more $1 +$ _____ $= 4$	**2.** Jill has 2 small fish. She wants 6. How many more does she need? _____ more $2 +$ _____ $= 6$
3. Jill has 1 snail. She wants 10. How many more does she need? _____ more $1 +$ _____ $= 10$	**4.** Jill has 3 water plants. She wants 7. How many more does she need? _____ more $3 +$ _____ $= 7$

Solve problems involving simple number patterns

Tasty Treats

Find the answers to help the animals reach their treats.

1. Timothy Turtle
Start at **1**.

$1 + 2 = \boxed{}$

$\boxed{} + 2 = \boxed{}$

$\boxed{} + 2 = \boxed{}$

$\boxed{} + 2 = \boxed{}$

2. Rita Robin
Start at **15**.

$15 - 3 = \boxed{}$

$\boxed{} - 3 = \boxed{}$

$\boxed{} - 3 = \boxed{}$

$\boxed{} - 3 = \boxed{}$

3. Peter Penguin
Start at **5**.

$5 + 5 = \boxed{}$

$\boxed{} + 5 = \boxed{}$

$\boxed{} + 5 = \boxed{}$

$\boxed{} + 5 = \boxed{}$

Solve problems involving simple number patterns

Mr. Martin's Math Machines

Name _____

Fill in the missing numbers.

+4

In	Out
4	8
2	6
	9
	5
9	

−2

In	Out
7	5
5	3
	1
	7
2	

−5

In	Out
10	5
	2
8	
14	
	6

+3

In	Out
3	6
4	
	9
	10
	12

Solve problems involving simple number patterns

Algebra

EMC 3015 • Basic Math Skills, Grade 2 • ©2003 by Evan-Moor Corp.

Who Will Win the Race?

Name _____

Fill in the missing numbers to see who wins the race.
The winner ends with the highest number.

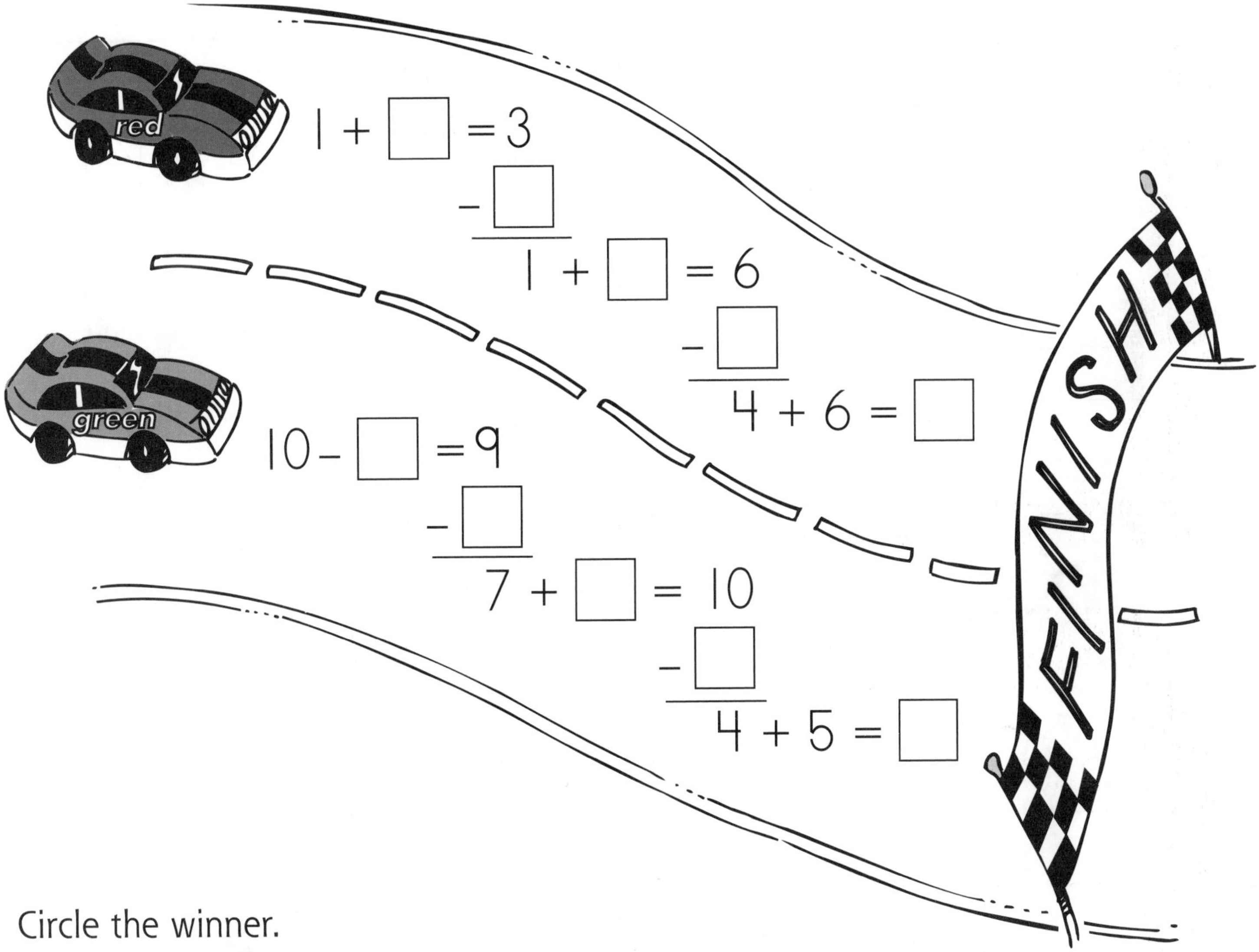

$1 + \boxed{} = 3$

$-\boxed{}$

$\overline{1 + \boxed{} = 6}$

$-\boxed{}$

$\overline{4 + 6 = \boxed{}}$

$10 - \boxed{} = 9$

$-\boxed{}$

$\overline{7 + \boxed{} = 10}$

$-\boxed{}$

$\overline{4 + 5 = \boxed{}}$

Circle the winner.

red   green

Mrs. Garcia's Chickens

Name _____

Complete the number sentence to answer each question.

---

1. Mrs. Garcia has 7 hens.
She wants 12.
How many more does she need?

_____ more

$7 + \underline{5} = 12$

2. The hens laid 9 eggs.
Mrs. Garcia wants 15 eggs.
How many more does she need?

_____ more

$9 + \underline{} = 15$

---

3. Mrs. Garcia has 8 eggs.
She started with 12.
How many did she sell?

_____ eggs

$12 - \underline{} = 4$

4. One hen sat on 9 eggs.
Only 3 of the eggs hatched.
How many more need to hatch?

_____ more

$3 + \underline{} = 9$

---

5. Write a word problem about this picture. Then write a number sentence about it.

_____

_____

_____

$\underline{} \bigcirc \underline{} = \underline{}$

Solve problems involving simple number patterns

Algebra

EMC 3015 • Basic Math Skills, Grade 2 • ©2003 by Evan-Moor Corp.

Name _____

Math Test

Fill in the circle next to the correct answer.

1. Find the missing number.

$$3 + \underline{\quad} = 12$$

- Ⓐ 7
- Ⓑ 8
- Ⓒ 9
- Ⓓ 10

2. Find the missing number.

$$\underline{\quad} + 7 = 13$$

- Ⓐ 5
- Ⓑ 6
- Ⓒ 7
- Ⓓ 8

3. Find the missing number.

$$8 - \underline{\quad} = 5$$

- Ⓐ 1
- Ⓑ 2
- Ⓒ 3
- Ⓓ 4

4. Find the missing number.

$$14 - \underline{\quad} = 7$$

- Ⓐ 6
- Ⓑ 7
- Ⓒ 8
- Ⓓ 9

5. Find the missing number.

$$2 + \underline{\quad} = 4$$

- Ⓐ 1
- Ⓑ 2
- Ⓒ 3
- Ⓓ 4

6. Which number sentence is missing **9**?

- Ⓐ $4 + \underline{\quad} = 13$
- Ⓑ $3 + \underline{\quad} = 11$
- Ⓒ $6 + \underline{\quad} = 12$
- Ⓓ $9 + \underline{\quad} = 15$

7. Which number sentence is missing **3**?

- Ⓐ $6 - \underline{\quad} = 5$
- Ⓑ $7 - \underline{\quad} = 2$
- Ⓒ $8 - \underline{\quad} = 0$
- Ⓓ $9 - \underline{\quad} = 6$

8. Jim has 4 goldfish. He wants 12. How many more does he need?

$$4 + \underline{\quad} = 12$$

- Ⓐ 6
- Ⓑ 7
- Ⓒ 8
- Ⓓ 9

9. Morgan has 3 toy cars. He wants 12. How many more does he need?

$$3 + \underline{\quad} = 12$$

- Ⓐ 6
- Ⓑ 7
- Ⓒ 8
- Ⓓ 9

10. The clown has 6 balloons. He started with 12 balloons. How many did he sell?

$$12 - \underline{\quad} = 6$$

- Ⓐ 4
- Ⓑ 6
- Ⓒ 8
- Ⓓ 9

Solve problems involving simple number patterns

At the Pond

Cut out the number sentences. Look at each picture.
Find the four number sentences that could tell about it.
Paste the number sentences under the correct pictures.

Relate problem situations to number sentences involving addition and subtraction

Counting Counters

You will need 12 small objects to use as counters.
Follow the directions.
Write the number sentence for each problem.

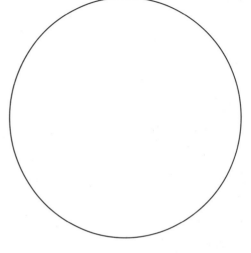

---

1. Put 12 counters in the square.
Move 2 counters to the circle.
How many counters are left in
the square?

12 – _____ = _____

2. Put 12 counters in the square.
Move 8 counters to the circle.
How many counters are left in
the square?

12 – _____ = _____

3. Put 12 counters in the square.
Move 6 counters to the circle.
How many counters are left in
the square?

12 – _____ = _____

4. Put 12 counters in the square.
Move 3 counters to the circle.
How many counters are left in
the square?

_____ – _____ = _____

5. Put 12 counters in the square.
Move 5 counters to the circle.
How many counters are left in
the square?

_____ – _____ = _____

6. Put 12 counters in the square.
Move 7 counters to the circle.
How many counters are left in
the square?

_____ – _____ = _____

Relate problem situations to number sentences involving addition and subtraction

Algebra

What Is the Missing Number?

Name _____

Look at how much you have. Look at how much you need.
Write and draw the missing amount.

1.

9¢ + ____ ¢ = 12¢

2.

9¢ + ____ ¢ = 16¢

3.

8¢ + ____ ¢ = 17¢

4.

6¢ + ____ ¢ = 15¢

5.

10¢ + ____ ¢ = 20¢

6.

40¢ + ____ ¢ = 60¢

7.

30¢ + ____ ¢ = 60¢

8.

70¢ + ____ ¢ = 90¢

Relate problem situations to number sentences involving addition and subtraction

Algebra   EMC 3015 • Basic Math Skills, Grade 2 • ©2003 by Evan-Moor Corp.

Birds and Bugs

Name _____

1. Write an addition problem about birds. Draw a picture about it. Write the number sentence.

| I saw 4 blue birds in a tree. 3 red birds came. How many birds did I see? |  | 4 + 3 = 7 |

2. Write a subtraction problem about birds. Draw a picture about it. Write the number sentence.

| | | |

3. Write a subtraction problem about bugs. Draw a picture about it. Write the number sentence.

| | | |

4. Write a subtraction problem about bugs. Draw a picture about it. Write the number sentence.

| | | |

Relate problem situations to number sentences involving addition and subtraction

Story Problems

Name _____

Write a word problem about this number sentence.

$$9 + 7 = 16$$

_____

_____

Draw a picture to show the problem.

_____

Write a word problem about this number sentence.

$$15 - 8 = 7$$

_____

_____

Draw a picture to show the problem.

Relate problem situations to number sentences involving addition and subtraction

EMC 3015 • Basic Math Skills, Grade 2 • ©2003 by Evan-Moor Corp.

Math Test

Fill in the circle next to the correct answer.

1. Find the number sentence that tells about this picture.

Ⓐ 3 − 2 = 1
Ⓑ 3 + 2 = 5
Ⓒ 5 + 3 = 8
Ⓓ 5 − 2 = 3

2. Find the number sentence that tells about this picture.

Ⓐ 6 − 2 = 4
Ⓑ 2 + 6 = 8
Ⓒ 8 − 2 = 6
Ⓓ 8 − 6 = 2

3. Find the number sentence that tells about this picture.

Ⓐ 7 − 4 = 3
Ⓑ 7 + 4 = 11
Ⓒ 7 + 3 = 10
Ⓓ 4 − 3 = 1

4. Find the missing number.
9¢ + _____ = 16¢

Ⓐ 6¢
Ⓑ 7¢
Ⓒ 8¢
Ⓓ 9¢

5. Find the missing number.
16¢ − _____ = 8¢

Ⓐ 6¢
Ⓑ 7¢
Ⓒ 8¢
Ⓓ 9¢

6. Find the missing number.
30¢ + _____ = 50¢

Ⓐ 10¢
Ⓑ 20¢
Ⓒ 30¢
Ⓓ 40¢

7. Bob had a bag of 15 jelly beans. After he ate some of them, 9 were left in the bag. How many jelly beans did he eat?

Ⓐ 5
Ⓑ 6
Ⓒ 7
Ⓓ 8

8. Three birds sat in a tree. Two more birds came. How many birds were in the tree? Find the number sentence for this problem.

Ⓐ 5 − 3 = 2
Ⓑ 3 − 2 = 1
Ⓒ 3 + 2 = 5
Ⓓ 5 − 2 = 3

9. Jake had 11 marbles. He gave 9 marbles to his sister. How many marbles did he have left?

Ⓐ 2
Ⓑ 8
Ⓒ 18
Ⓓ 20

10. There are 46 children in second grade. There are 23 girls. How many are boys?

Ⓐ 13
Ⓑ 69
Ⓒ 29
Ⓓ 23

Relate problem situations to number sentences involving addition and subtraction

Algebra

It's a Rule

The order of numbers may change, but the answer stays the same.

$4+2=6$
$2+4=6$

$2 \times 3 = 6$
$3 \times 2 = 6$

Add

1. $2 + 4 = \underline{6}$ so $4 + 2 = \underline{6}$

2. $8 + 4 = \underline{}$ so $4 + 8 = \underline{}$

3. $6 + 8 = \underline{}$ so $8 + 6 = \underline{}$

4. $8 + 7 = \underline{}$ so $7 + 8 = \underline{}$

5. $6 + 7 = \underline{}$ so $7 + 6 = \underline{}$

6. $7 + 5 = \underline{}$ so $5 + 7 = \underline{}$

7. $12 + 10 = \underline{}$ so $10 + 12 = \underline{}$

Add

8. $8 + 5 = \underline{}$ so $5 + 8 = \underline{}$

9. $4 + 9 = \underline{}$ so $9 + 4 = \underline{}$

10. $3 + 4 = \underline{}$ so $4 + 3 = \underline{}$

11. $9 + 8 = \underline{}$ so $8 + 9 = \underline{}$

12. $3 + 9 = \underline{}$ so $9 + 3 = \underline{}$

13. $4 + 6 = \underline{}$ so $6 + 4 = \underline{}$

14. $60 + 40 = \underline{}$ so $40 + 60 = \underline{}$

Multiply

15. $2 \times 5 = \underline{10}$ so $5 \times 2 = \underline{10}$

16. $5 \times 6 = \underline{}$ so $6 \times 5 = \underline{}$

17. $2 \times 3 = \underline{}$ so $3 \times 2 = \underline{}$

Multiply

18. $4 \times 2 = \underline{}$ so $2 \times 4 = \underline{}$

19. $10 \times 4 = \underline{}$ so $4 \times 10 = \underline{}$

20. $10 \times 5 = \underline{}$ so $5 \times 10 = \underline{}$

Use the commutative and associative rules to simplify mental calculations and to check results

Arnold's Homework

Name _____

This is Arnold's homework.
Help him find the answers.

Do the numbers in parentheses first.

Answer the addition problems.

1. $(1 + 2) + 5 =$ _____
  ___3___ $+ 5 =$ ___8___

$1 + (2 + 5) =$ _____
$1 +$ ___7___ $=$ ___8___

2. $(6 + 5) + 2 =$ _____
  _____ $+ 2 =$ _____

$6 + (5 + 2) =$ _____
$6 +$ _____ $=$ _____

3. $(6 + 5) + 4 =$ _____
  _____ $+ 4 =$ _____

$6 + (5 + 4) =$ _____
$6 +$ _____ $=$ _____

4. $(7 + 3) + 5 =$ _____
  _____ $+ 5 =$ _____

$7 + (3 + 5) =$ _____
$7 +$ _____ $=$ _____

5. $(2 + 2) + 8 =$ _____
  _____ $+ 8 =$ _____

$2 + (2 + 8) =$ _____
$2 +$ _____ $=$ _____

6. $(9 + 5) + 5 =$ _____
  _____ $+ 5 =$ _____

$9 + (5 + 5) =$ _____
$9 +$ _____ $=$ _____

7. $(4 + 8) + 0 =$ _____
  _____ $+ 0 =$ _____

$4 + (8 + 0) =$ _____
$4 +$ _____ $=$ _____

Answer the multiplication problems.

8. $(2 \times 2) \times 5 =$ _____
  _____ $\times 5 =$ _____

$2 \times (2 \times 5) =$ _____
$2 \times$ _____ $=$ _____

Use the commutative and associative rules to simplify mental calculations and to check results

Use What You Know

Name _____

Try to find the answer in your head without using a pencil and paper.
Then write the answer and tell how you found it.

> The problem is 3+7+4. I know 3 and 7 are 10. 10 and 4 are 14. The answer is 14!

1. $2 + 8 + 6 =$ ____

   This is what I did: _____

2. $2 + 5 + 5 =$ ____

   This is what I did: _____

3. $6 + 4 + 7 =$ ____

   This is what I did: _____

4. $1 + 9 + 3 =$ ____

   This is what I did: _____

5. $5 + 3 + 5 =$ ____

   This is what I did: _____

6. $8 + 7 + 3 =$ ____

   This is what I did: _____

Use the commutative and associative rules to simplify mental calculations and to check results

EMC 3015 • Basic Math Skills, Grade 2 • ©2003 by Evan-Moor Corp.

Make a Match

Add. Then make a match.

Name _____

$$\begin{array}{r} 2 \\ +5 \\ \hline \boxed{7} \end{array}$$

$$\begin{array}{r} 8 \\ +4 \\ \hline \boxed{} \end{array}$$

$$\begin{array}{r} 9 \\ +3 \\ \hline \boxed{} \end{array}$$

$$\begin{array}{r} 5 \\ +2 \\ \hline \boxed{7} \end{array}$$

$$\begin{array}{r} 6 \\ +2 \\ \hline \boxed{} \end{array}$$

$$\begin{array}{r} 6 \\ +3 \\ \hline \boxed{} \end{array}$$

$$\begin{array}{r} 9 \\ +1 \\ \hline \boxed{} \end{array}$$

$$\begin{array}{r} 3 \\ +9 \\ \hline \boxed{} \end{array}$$

$$\begin{array}{r} 4 \\ +8 \\ \hline \boxed{} \end{array}$$

$$\begin{array}{r} 2 \\ +6 \\ \hline \boxed{} \end{array}$$

$$\begin{array}{r} 3 \\ +6 \\ \hline \boxed{} \end{array}$$

$$\begin{array}{r} 1 \\ +9 \\ \hline \boxed{} \end{array}$$

Use the commutative and associative rules to simplify mental calculations and to check results

Algebra

What's It Worth?

Add the coins in the parentheses first.

1.

$\underline{6}$ ¢ + $\underline{10}$ ¢ = $\underline{16}$ ¢

$\underline{1}$ ¢ + $\underline{15}$ ¢ = $\underline{16}$ ¢

2.

___ + ___ = ___

___ + ___ = ___

3.

___ + ___ = ___

___ + ___ = ___

---

4. (5¢ + 5¢) + 10¢ =

___ + ___ = ___

5¢ + (5¢ + 10¢) =

___ + ___ = ___

5. (25¢ + 1¢) + 1¢ =

___ + ___ = ___

25¢ + (1¢ + 1¢) =

___ + ___ = ___

6. 5¢ + (10¢ + 25¢) =

___ + ___ = ___

(5¢ + 10¢) + 25¢ =

___ + ___ = ___

7. 25¢ + (5¢ + 25¢) =

___ + ___ = ___

(25¢ + 5¢) + 25¢ =

___ + ___ = ___

Use the commutative and associative rules to simplify mental calculations and to check results

Algebra

EMC 3015 • Basic Math Skills, Grade 2 • ©2003 by Evan-Moor Corp.

Name _____

Math Test

Fill in the circle next to the correct answer.

1. If $7 + 5 = 12$, what is $5 + 7$?

Ⓐ 2
Ⓑ 75
Ⓒ 12
Ⓓ 21

2. If $14 + 16 = 30$, what is $16 + 14$?

Ⓐ 22
Ⓑ 30
Ⓒ 16
Ⓓ 28

3. If $2 \times 8 = 16$, what is 8×2?

Ⓐ 10
Ⓑ 14
Ⓒ 16
Ⓓ 18

4. What should be added first?

$4 + (2 + 8) =$ _____

Ⓐ $4 + 2$
Ⓑ $2 + 8$
Ⓒ $4 + 8$
Ⓓ $4 + 10$

5. What should be added first?

$6 + (3 + 4) =$ _____

Ⓐ $6 + 3$
Ⓑ $6 + 4$
Ⓒ $3 + 4$
Ⓓ $9 + 4$

6. What should be multiplied first?

$(2 \times 3) \times 5 =$ _____

Ⓐ 2×3
Ⓑ 3×5
Ⓒ 2×5
Ⓓ 5×2

7. Find the answer.

$4 + (8 + 2) =$ _____

Ⓐ 10
Ⓑ 12
Ⓒ 14
Ⓓ 16

8. Find the answer.

$(10 + 10) + 20 =$ _____

Ⓐ 20
Ⓑ 50
Ⓒ 80
Ⓓ 40

9. Find the answer.

$(2 \times 2) \times 5 =$ _____

Ⓐ 9
Ⓑ 4
Ⓒ 10
Ⓓ 20

10. What number is missing?

$2 + (5 + 4) = (2 + 5) +$ _____

Ⓐ 7
Ⓑ 5
Ⓒ 4
Ⓓ 9

Use the commutative and associative rules to simplify mental calculations and to check results

Algebra

Geometry

EMC 3015 • Basic Math Skills, Grade 2 • ©2003 by Evan-Moor Corp.

It's a Puzzle

Name _____

Find the matching puzzle piece. Color it.

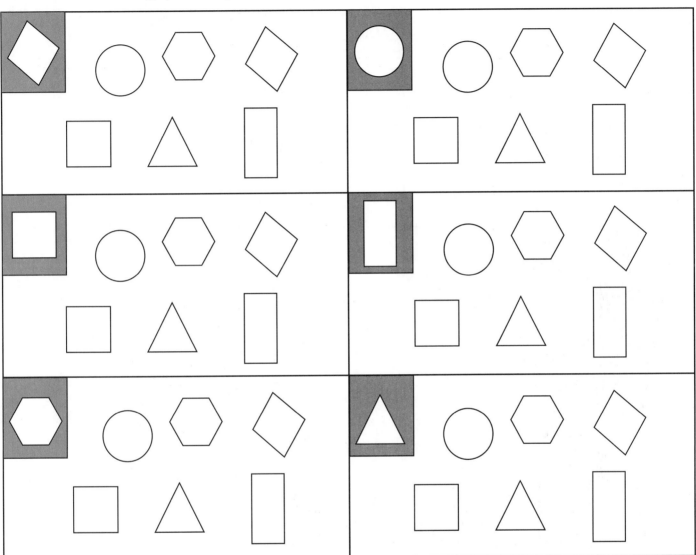

Draw each shape.

square	circle	triangle
rectangle	hexagon	diamond

Identify, describe, and compare plane objects according to the number of sides and corners

Rhyming Riddle

Name _____

It runs all night and runs all day,
but it never, ever runs away.
What is it?

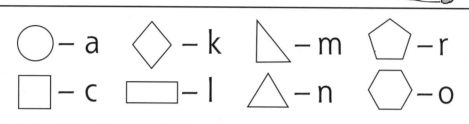

○ – a   ◇ – k   △ – m   ⬠ – r

▢ – c   ▭ – l   △ – n   ⬡ – o

Use the code to solve the riddle.
Write the matching letter under each shape.

a ___   ___ ___ ___ ___ ___

___ ___ ___ ___ ___

Circle the answer here.

Identify, describe, and compare plane objects according to the number of sides and corners

EMC 3015 • Basic Math Skills, Grade 2 • ©2003 by Evan-Moor Corp.

Name the Shape

Name _____

Mark the sides with a red crayon. Make an **X** on each corner.

square	rectangle
triangle	hexagon
circle	pentagon

1.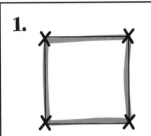

_____ name

_____ sides

_____ corners

2.

_____ name

_____ sides

_____ corners

3.

_____ name

_____ sides

_____ corners

4.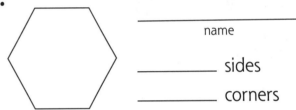

_____ name

_____ sides

_____ corners

5.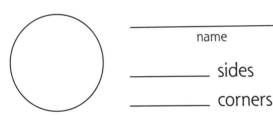

_____ name

_____ sides

_____ corners

6.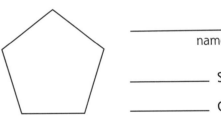

_____ name

_____ sides

_____ corners

7.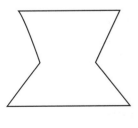

_____ sides

_____ corners

8.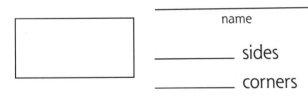

_____ sides

_____ corners

9.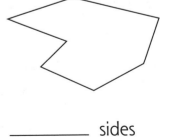

_____ sides

_____ corners

Identify, describe, and compare plane objects according to the number of sides and corners

Make the Shape

Draw a shape that has these sides and corners.

1. 3 sides

3 corners

2. 4 equal sides

4 corners

3. 4 sides – 2 long, 2 short

4 corners

4. 6 sides

6 corners

5. How are these shapes alike?

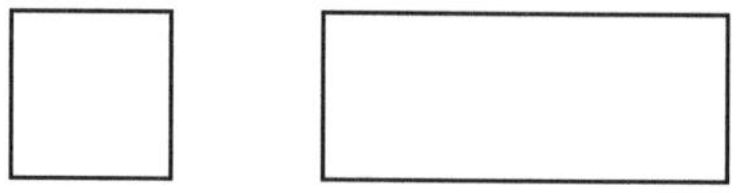

☐ ☐

_____

_____

How are they different?

_____

_____

Identify, describe, and compare plane objects according to the number of sides and corners

EMC 3015 • Basic Math Skills, Grade 2 • ©2003 by Evan-Moor Corp.

Shape Pictures

Name ____________________

Draw a large black square. Draw a large yellow circle inside the square.
Draw a red triangle inside the circle.

Draw a picture with these shapes.
Describe your picture.

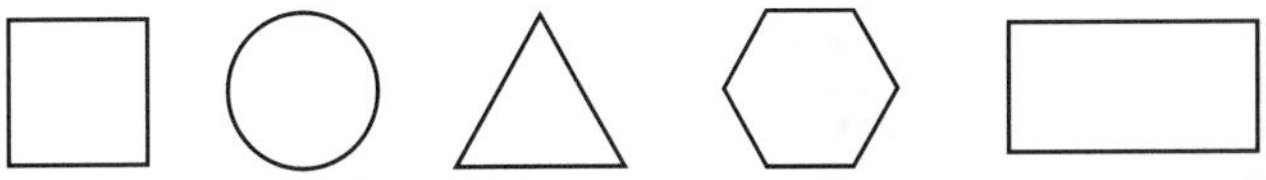

____

____

____

Identify, describe, and compare plane objects according to the number of sides and corners

Name _____

Fill in the circle next to the correct answer.

1. Find the rectangle.

   Ⓐ   Ⓑ   Ⓒ   Ⓓ

2. Find the circle.

   Ⓐ   Ⓑ   Ⓒ   Ⓓ

3. Find the square.

   Ⓐ   Ⓑ   Ⓒ   Ⓓ

4. Find the name of this shape.

  Ⓐ circle
  Ⓑ square
  Ⓒ rectangle
  Ⓓ triangle

5. Find the name of this shape.

  Ⓐ circle
  Ⓑ hexagon
  Ⓒ rectangle
  Ⓓ square

6. Find the name of this shape.

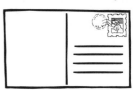

  Ⓐ circle
  Ⓑ square
  Ⓒ rectangle
  Ⓓ triangle

7. Which shape has no corners?

  Ⓐ circle
  Ⓑ hexagon
  Ⓒ rectangle
  Ⓓ triangle

8. Which sign is shaped like a hexagon?

   Ⓐ   Ⓑ   Ⓒ   Ⓓ

9. Which shape has 5 corners and 5 sides?

  Ⓐ pentagon
  Ⓑ square
  Ⓒ hexagon
  Ⓓ rectangle

10. Find the shape that is NOT a triangle.

   Ⓐ   Ⓑ   Ⓒ   Ⓓ

Identify, describe, and compare plane objects according to the number of sides and corners

Jump, Jackrabbits, Jump!

Name _____

These jackrabbits jump on different shapes to get to their holes. Color the shapes.

1. This jackrabbit jumps on shapes with straight sides.

2. This jackrabbit jumps on shapes with curved sides.

3. This jackrabbit jumps on shapes that have corners.

4. This jackrabbit jumps on shapes that can roll.

5. This jackrabbit jumps on shapes that can be stacked on top of each other.

Classify familiar plane and solid objects according to the number and shape of faces, edges, and vertices

Geometry

Which Go Together?

Name _____

Match the shapes.

sphere

rectangular prism

pyramid

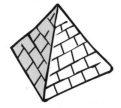

cone

cube

cylinder

Classify familiar plane and solid objects according to the number and shape of faces, edges, and vertices

EMC 3015 • Basic Math Skills, Grade 2 • ©2003 by Evan-Moor Corp.

Find the Shape

Look at the shape of each object. Write the name of the object in the correct box.

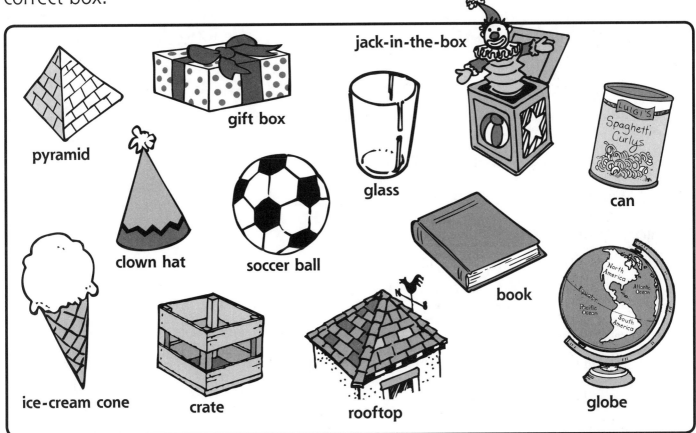

pyramid

gift box

jack-in-the-box

glass

can

clown hat

soccer ball

ice-cream cone

crate

book

rooftop

globe

⬤ sphere	⬛ cube	▭ rectangular prism
_____ _____	_____ _____	_____ _____
▽ cone	⬭ cylinder	△ pyramid
_____ _____	_____ _____	_____ _____

Classify familiar plane and solid objects according to the number and shape of faces, edges, and vertices

Looking for Shapes

Name _____

 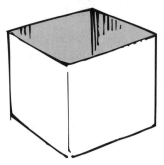  

1. Color the cone red.
How do you know which shape is the cone?

_____

2. Color the cube green.
How do you know which shape is the cube?

_____

3. Color the sphere orange.
How do you know which shape is the sphere?

_____

4. Color the cylinder purple.
How do you know which shape is the cylinder?

_____

5. Color the rectangular prism brown.
How do you know which shape is the rectangular prism?

_____

Outline this part of the solid shape.

      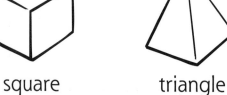   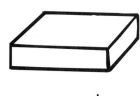

circle   square   triangle   rectangle

Classify familiar plane and solid objects according to the number and shape of faces, edges, and vertices

EMC 3015 • Basic Math Skills, Grade 2 • ©2003 by Evan-Moor Corp.

Shape Search

Look around the classroom. Find objects that are the shapes below.
Make an **X** by a shape you can find. Draw it in the box.

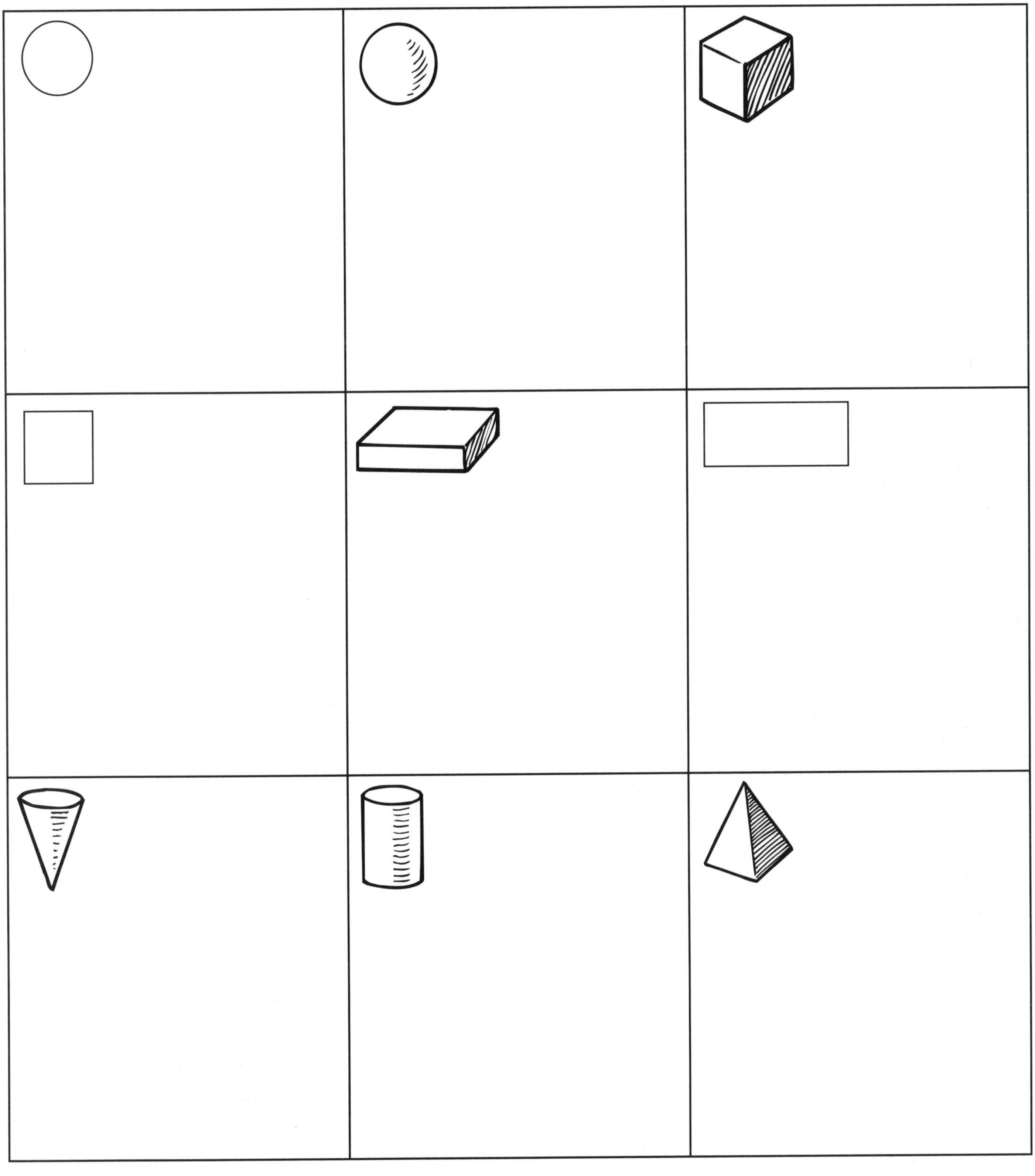

Classify familiar plane and solid objects according to the number and shape of faces, edges, and vertices

Name _____

Fill in the circle next to the correct answer.

1. Find the sphere.

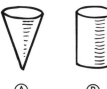

Ⓐ   Ⓑ   Ⓒ   Ⓓ

2. Find the cone.

Ⓐ   Ⓑ   Ⓒ   Ⓓ

3. Find the cylinder.

Ⓐ   Ⓑ   Ⓒ   Ⓓ

4. Find the pyramid.

Ⓐ   Ⓑ   Ⓒ   Ⓓ

5. Find the cube.

Ⓐ   Ⓑ   Ⓒ   Ⓓ

6. Which object has flat ends and can roll?

 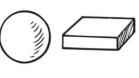

Ⓐ   Ⓑ   Ⓒ   Ⓓ

7. Which object has the same shape?

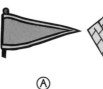

Ⓐ   Ⓑ   Ⓒ   Ⓓ

8. Which object has the same shape?

Ⓐ   Ⓑ   Ⓒ   Ⓓ

9. One side of a cube is a _____.
  Ⓐ rectangle
  Ⓑ triangle
  Ⓒ square
  Ⓓ circle

10. One end of a cylinder is a _____.
  Ⓐ rectangle
  Ⓑ triangle
  Ⓒ square
  Ⓓ circle

Classify familiar plane and solid objects according to the number and shape of faces, edges, and vertices

Symmetry–Both Sides the Same

Name _____

Fold the page along the middle line. Cut out the shapes.
Open the shapes. Are both sides the same?

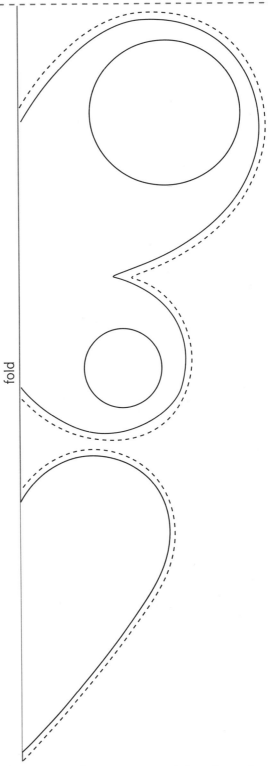

fold

Identify and construct congruent figures and draw lines of symmetry

The Other Half

Name _____

Draw the other side of each picture.

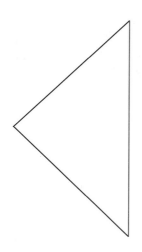

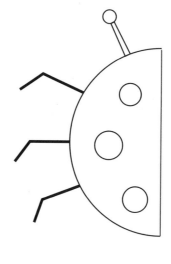

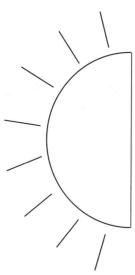

Identify and construct congruent figures and draw lines of symmetry

EMC 3015 • Basic Math Skills, Grade 2 • ©2003 by Evan-Moor Corp.

Playtime

Pete's dog will play with toys only when both sides are the same.

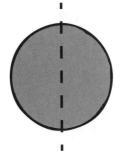

Pete's dog **won't** play with this toy.   His dog **will** play with this toy.

Look at each toy. Are both sides the same? Will Pete's dog play with the toy? Fill in the circle by the correct answer.

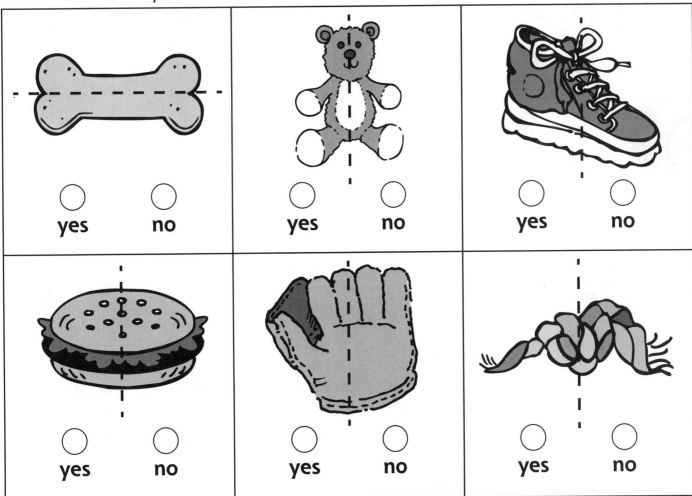

◯ yes ◯ no	◯ yes ◯ no	◯ yes ◯ no
◯ yes ◯ no	◯ yes ◯ no	◯ yes ◯ no

Identify and construct congruent figures and draw lines of symmetry

Divide the Shapes

Name _____

When an item is **symmetrical**, both sides are the same shape and size.

Draw a line of symmetry on each shape.

Think of four different ways to mark the cookies so the sides are the same.

  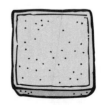 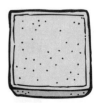

Identify and construct congruent figures and draw lines of symmetry

Same Size, Same Shape

Name _____

Color the figures that are both the same size and the same shape.

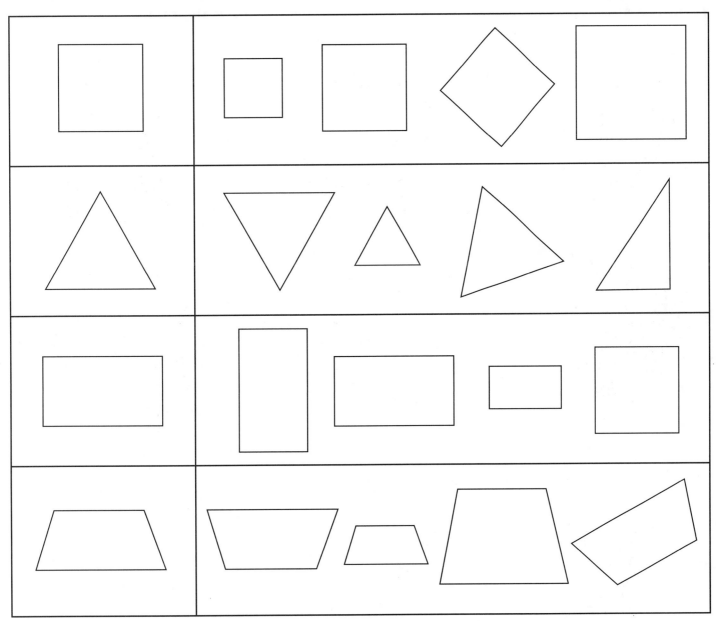

Draw a figure that has the same size and shape.

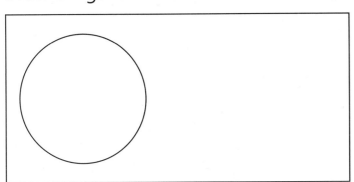

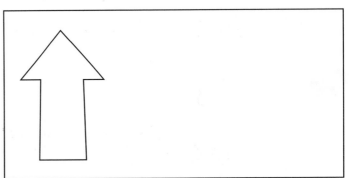

Identify and construct congruent figures and draw lines of symmetry

Math Test

Fill in the circle next to the correct answer.

1. Which shape shows a line of symmetry?

Ⓐ Ⓑ Ⓒ Ⓓ

2. Which shape is NOT the same on both sides?

Ⓐ Ⓑ Ⓒ Ⓓ

3. Find the objects that are the same size.

Ⓐ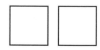

Ⓑ

Ⓒ

Ⓓ

4. Find the objects that are the same shape.

Ⓐ

Ⓑ

Ⓒ

Ⓓ

5. Which shape is the other side of this heart?

Ⓐ Ⓑ Ⓒ Ⓓ

6. Which shape is the other side of this butterfly?

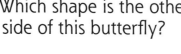

Ⓐ Ⓑ Ⓒ Ⓓ

7. Find the letter that is NOT symmetrical.

Ⓐ **H**

Ⓑ **A**

Ⓒ **T**

Ⓓ **R**

8. These shapes are congruent. Why?

Ⓐ same size, different shape
Ⓑ same size, same shape
Ⓒ different size, same shape
Ⓓ different size, different shape

9. Find the object that is the same size and shape.

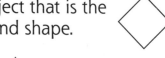

Ⓐ Ⓑ Ⓒ Ⓓ

10. How are these objects different?

Ⓐ different shape
Ⓑ different size
Ⓒ different color
Ⓓ they are the same

Identify and construct congruent figures and draw lines of symmetry

180

It's a Puzzle

Name _____

Cut out the triangles. Put the pieces together to make a hexagon.
Glue the pieces in place.

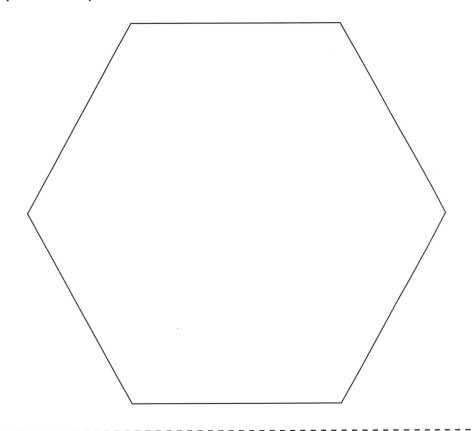

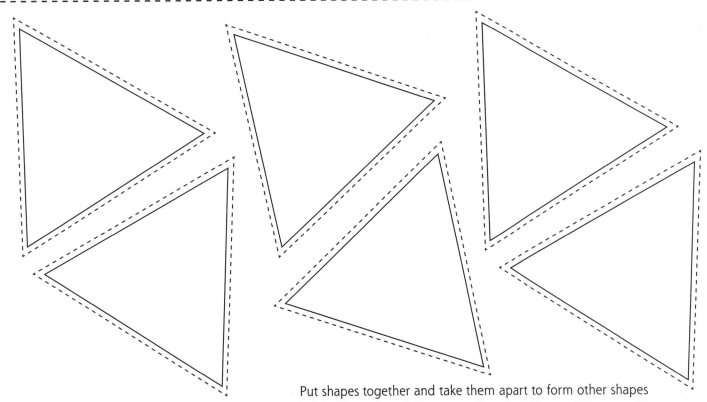

Put shapes together and take them apart to form other shapes

Sail Across the Sea

Name _____

Cut out the puzzle pieces.
Put the pieces together to make a sailboat. Glue the pieces in place.

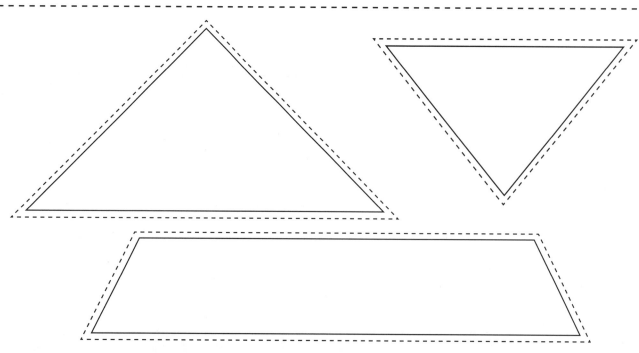

Put shapes together and take them apart to form other shapes

Geometry

EMC 3015 • Basic Math Skills, Grade 2 • ©2003 by Evan-Moor Corp.

Make a Shape

Name _____

Cut out the shapes.

Use 2 large triangles to make a square. Glue the pieces here.	Use 4 small triangles to make a square. Glue the pieces here.
Use 2 squares to make a rectangle. Glue the pieces here.	Use 2 trapezoids to make a hexagon. Glue the pieces here.

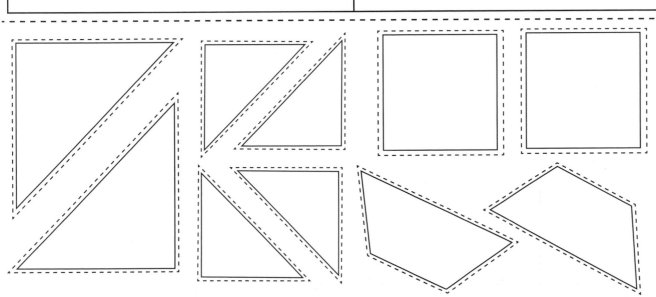

Put shapes together and take them apart to form other shapes

Find the Pieces

Name _____

Color the pieces you need to make each shape.

New Shapes

Cut out the shapes at the bottom of the page.
Follow the directions.
Then fill in the blanks.

1. Start with the square. Cut the square to make two triangles. Glue the triangles here.	**2.** Start with the rectangle. Cut the rectangle to make four squares. Glue the squares here.	**3.** Start with the hexagon. Cut the hexagon to make two trapezoids Glue the trapezoids here.
How did you make the triangles? _____ _____	How did you make the squares? _____ _____	How did you make the trapezoids? _____ _____

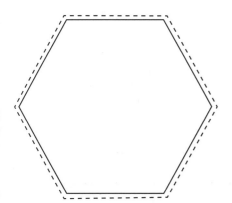

Put shapes together and take them apart to form other shapes

Name _____

Math Test

Fill in the circle next to the correct answer.

1. Find the shapes used to make this square.
- Ⓐ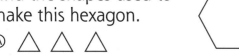
- Ⓑ
- Ⓒ
- Ⓓ

2. Find the shapes used to make this hexagon.
- Ⓐ
- Ⓑ
- Ⓒ
- Ⓓ

3. Find the shapes used to make this rectangle.
- Ⓐ
- Ⓑ
- Ⓒ
- Ⓓ

4. How many triangles were used to make this hexagon?
- Ⓐ 2
- Ⓑ 4
- Ⓒ 6
- Ⓓ 8

5. How many rectangles were used to make this sailboat?
- Ⓐ 0
- Ⓑ 1
- Ⓒ 2
- Ⓓ 3

6. How many trapezoids were used to make this hexagon?
- Ⓐ 0
- Ⓑ 1
- Ⓒ 2
- Ⓓ 3

7. What shapes will you get if you cut this square?
- Ⓐ 2 triangles
- Ⓑ 4 triangles
- Ⓒ 2 squares
- Ⓓ 2 rectangles

8. What shapes will you get if you cut this rectangle?
- Ⓐ 2 triangles
- Ⓑ 4 squares
- Ⓒ 2 squares
- Ⓓ 2 rectangles

9. Which shapes were used to make this house?
- Ⓐ circle, square, rectangle
- Ⓑ square, triangle, rectangle
- Ⓒ square, rectangle, hexagon
- Ⓓ circle, triangle, square

10. Which shapes were used to make this clown?
- Ⓐ circles, square, triangle
- Ⓑ triangle, rectangle, hexagon
- Ⓒ circles, triangle, hexagon
- Ⓓ square, circles, hexagon

Put shapes together and take them apart to form other shapes

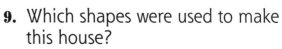

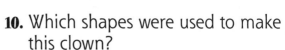

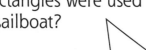
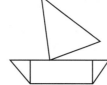

Pet Pens

Name _____

The children built fences to keep their pets in the yard.
Add the numbers to find how long each fence was.

10

8 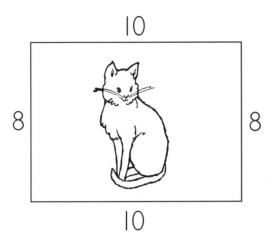 8

10

1. Ann built a _____-foot fence
for her cat.

13

12 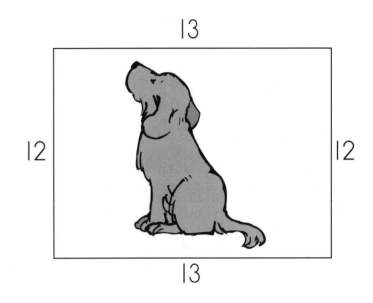 12

13

2. Tim built a _____-foot fence
for his dog.

8  8

4

3. Bob built a _____-foot fence
for his duck.

5

5   5

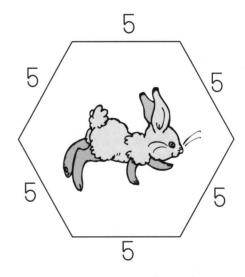

5   5

5

4. Sam built a _____-foot fence
for his rabbit.

5. Which animal has the pen with the longest fence? _____

Calculate the perimeter of a shape

Geometry

Presents for Kisha

Name _____

It is Kisha's birthday. One of her presents was a measuring tape. She used it to measure the distance around her presents.

The distance around something is called a "perimeter."

1. The perimeter is _____.

2. The perimeter is _____.

3. The perimeter is _____.

4. The perimeter is _____.

5. The perimeter is _____.

6. The perimeter is _____.

Calculate the perimeter of a shape

EMC 3015 • Basic Math Skills, Grade 2 • ©2003 by Evan-Moor Corp.

By the Sea

Name _____

What is the perimeter of each figure?
Circle the two figures that have the same perimeter.

1.

3

6   6

3

[ ]

2.

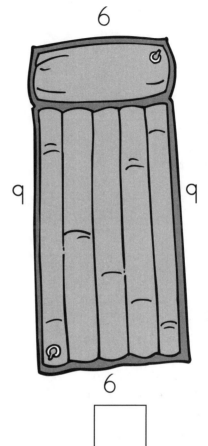

6

9   9

6

[ ]

3.

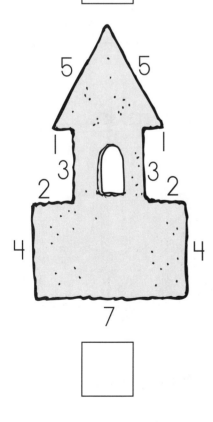

5   5

1   1

3   3

2   2

4   4

7

[ ]

4.

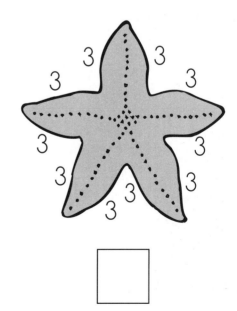

3   3

3   3

3   3

3   3

3 3

[ ]

Calculate the perimeter of a shape

Find the Perimeter

Name _____

Add the numbers to find the perimeter.

The distance around something is called the "perimeter."

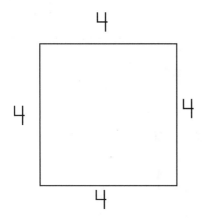

1. The perimeter is _____.

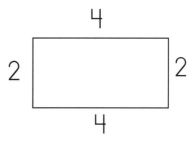

2. The perimeter is _____.

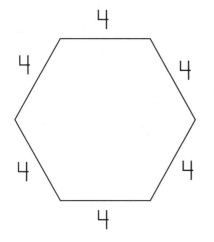

3. The perimeter is _____.

4. The perimeter is _____.

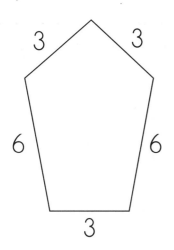

5. The perimeter is _____.

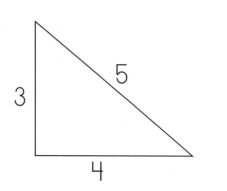

6. The perimeter is _____.

Calculate the perimeter of a shape

How Far Around?

Read the word problem.
Draw a picture to help you find the answer.

---

1. Anney drew a square.
Each side was 5 inches long.

What was the perimeter of her square?

___20___ inches

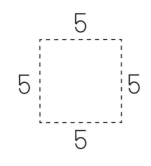

2. Ken drew a rectangle.
Two sides were 5 inches long.
Two sides were 7 inches long.

What was the perimeter of his rectangle?

_____ inches

---

3. Alfred built a raft.
Two sides were 4 feet long.
Two sides were 6 feet long.

What was the perimeter of his raft?

_____ feet

4. Miyeko drew a funny shape.
It had five sides. All five sides
were 10 centimeters long.

What was the perimeter of her shape?

_____ centimeters

---

5. Draw a shape with straight sides. Write a number on each side to tell how long it is.
Then answer the questions about your shape.

How many sides does it have? _____   What is the perimeter of your shape? _____

Calculate the perimeter of a shape

Geometry

Name _____

Fill in the circle next to the correct answer.

1. What does **perimeter** mean?

Ⓐ a shape with five sides
Ⓑ a kind of ruler
Ⓒ the distance around something
Ⓓ the sound a kitten makes

2. Find the perimeter.

Ⓐ 2
Ⓑ 4
Ⓒ 8
Ⓓ 12

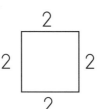

3. Find the perimeter.

Ⓐ 2
Ⓑ 4
Ⓒ 8
Ⓓ 12

4. Find the perimeter.

Ⓐ 3
Ⓑ 7
Ⓒ 9
Ⓓ 12

5. Find the perimeter.

Ⓐ 8
Ⓑ 24
Ⓒ 28
Ⓓ 16

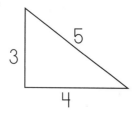

6. Find the perimeter.

Ⓐ 17
Ⓑ 18
Ⓒ 19
Ⓓ 20

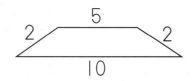

7. Find the number sentence that shows the perimeter.

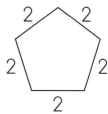

Ⓐ 4 x 2 = 8
Ⓑ 2 + 2 + 2 + 2 = 8
Ⓒ 5 x 2 = 10
Ⓓ 2 + 2 + 2 + 2 + 2 = 12

8. Alex drew a rectangle. Two sides were 5 inches long. Two sides were 7 inches long. What was the perimeter of his rectangle?

Ⓐ 12 inches
Ⓑ 17 inches
Ⓒ 24 inches
Ⓓ 35 inches

9. Bob built a raft. Two sides were 4 feet long. Two sides were 6 feet long. What was the perimeter of his raft?

Ⓐ 14 feet
Ⓑ 10 feet
Ⓒ 46 feet
Ⓓ 20 feet

10. Kent drew a funny shape. It had five sides. Three sides were 10 centimeters long. Two sides were 5 centimeters long. What was the perimeter of his shape?

Ⓐ 40 centimeters
Ⓑ 10 centimeters
Ⓒ 50 centimeters
Ⓓ 35 centimeters

Calculate the perimeter of a shape

EMC 3015 • Basic Math Skills, Grade 2 • ©2003 by Evan-Moor Corp.

Measurement

Dog Bone Measuring

Name _____

Use Rowdy's dog bones to measure.

Estimate and measure the length of objects using a variety of nonstandard units

EMC 3015 • Basic Math Skills, Grade 2 • ©2003 by Evan-Moor Corp.

Clowning Around

Name _____

Cut out the clown hats. Use the hats to measure the clowns.

3. _____ hats tall

1. __5__ hats tall

2. _____ hats tall

5. _____ hat tall

4. _____ hats tall

6. _____ hats tall

Estimate and measure the length of objects using a variety of nonstandard units

How Big Is the Fish?

Name _____

You will need 5 paper clips to measure the fish. Place the paper clips across a fish. Count how many you use. Then write the answer.

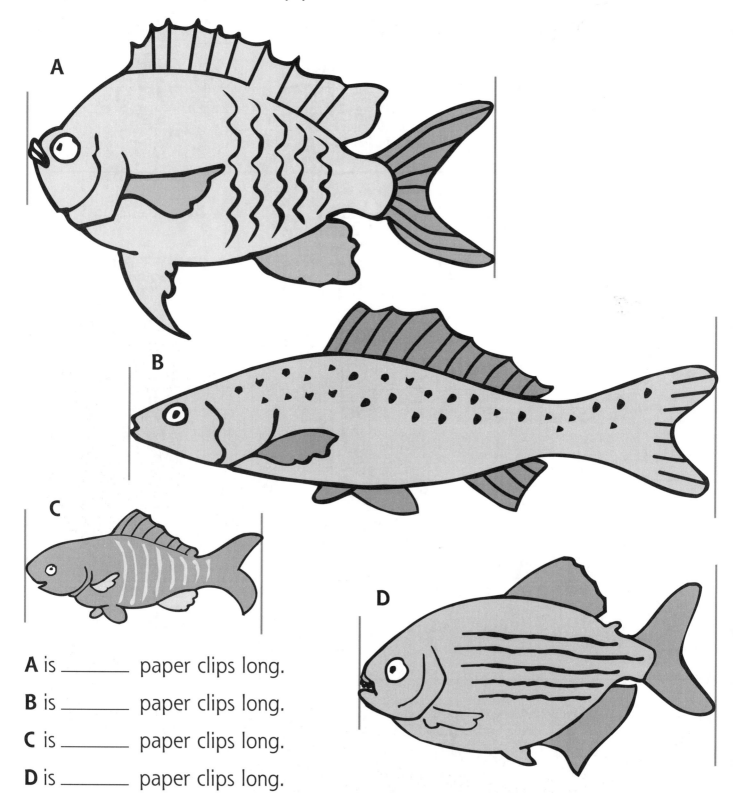

A is _____ paper clips long.

B is _____ paper clips long.

C is _____ paper clips long.

D is _____ paper clips long.

Estimate and measure the length of objects using a variety of nonstandard units

Measurement   EMC 3015 • Basic Math Skills, Grade 2 • ©2003 by Evan-Moor Corp.

Measure the Fruit

Name _____

1. Look at one paper clip. Think about how long it is.

2. Look at each piece of fruit.
   How many paper clips long or wide do you think it is?
   Write your guess on the line.

3. Measure each piece of fruit with paper clips.
   Write how long or wide it is on the line.

You will need 4 paper clips.

Fruit	Guess	Measure
banana		
apple		
kiwi		
watermelon		

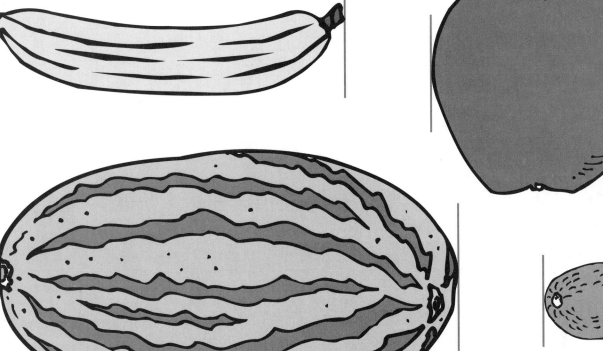

Estimate and measure the length of objects using a variety of nonstandard units

Measuring the Room

Name _____

Pick something to use as a measuring tool.
Measure these items.

My desktop is _____ wide.

My chair is _____ tall.

The bookshelf is _____ wide.

The chalkboard is _____ long.

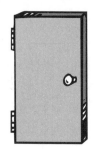

The door is _____ wide.

Estimate and measure the length of objects using a variety of nonstandard units

EMC 3015 • Basic Math Skills, Grade 2 • ©2003 by Evan-Moor Corp.

Math Test

Name _____

Fill in the circle next to the correct answer.

1. Which crayon is the longest?

Ⓐ red
Ⓑ blue
Ⓒ green
Ⓓ yellow

2. Which pencil is the shortest?

Ⓐ
Ⓑ
Ⓒ
Ⓓ

3. Which girl is the tallest?

Ⓐ   Ⓑ   Ⓒ   Ⓓ

4. Which bus is the shortest?

Ⓐ   Ⓑ   Ⓒ   Ⓓ

5. How long is the dog?

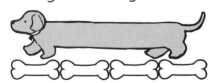

Ⓐ 6 bones long
Ⓑ 3 bones long
Ⓒ 2 bones long
Ⓓ 4 bones long

6. How long is the pencil?

Ⓐ 1 paper clip long
Ⓑ 3 paper clips long
Ⓒ 6 paper clips long
Ⓓ 10 paper clips long

7. How long is the box?

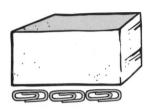

Ⓐ 7 paper clips long
Ⓑ 9 paper clips long
Ⓒ 5 paper clips long
Ⓓ 3 paper clips long

8. How long is the table?

Ⓐ 5 shoes long
Ⓑ 2 shoes long
Ⓒ 10 shoes long
Ⓓ 7 shoes long

9. How long is the fish?

Ⓐ 1 paper clip long
Ⓑ 3 paper clips long
Ⓒ 4 paper clips long
Ⓓ 10 paper clips long

10. How wide is the penny?

Ⓐ 1 paper clip wide
Ⓑ 3 paper clips wide
Ⓒ 6 paper clips wide
Ⓓ 10 paper clips wide

Estimate and measure the length of objects using a variety of nonstandard units

Who Is Winning the Race?

You will need an inch ruler to do this page.
Measure the flight path for each bumblebee.

1. ____ inches   **2.** ____ inches   **3.** ____ inches   **4.** ____ inches   **5.** ____ inches   **6.** ____ inch

Circle the bumblebee that is winning the race.

Measure the length of an object to the nearest inch

Creepy Crawly Creatures

Name _____

Help Ed measure the creepy crawly creatures in his collection.
Look at the ruler to find the length of each creature.

1.

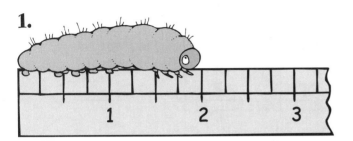

The caterpillar is _____ inches long.

2.

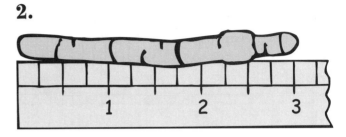

The worm is _____ inches long.

3.

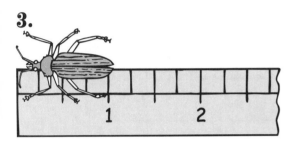

The beetle is _____ inch long.

4.

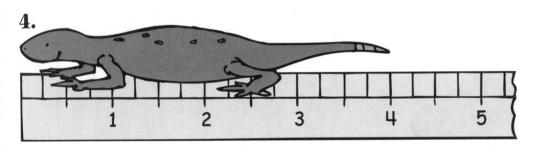

The lizard is _____ inches long.

5.

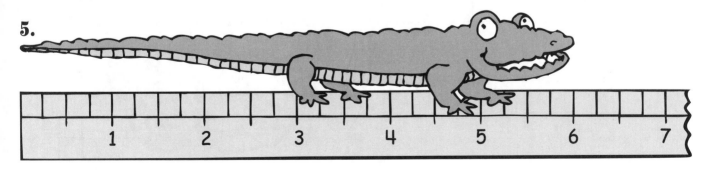

The baby crocodile is _____ inches long.

Measure the length of an object to the nearest inch

Play Ball

Name _____

What size is each item?

1.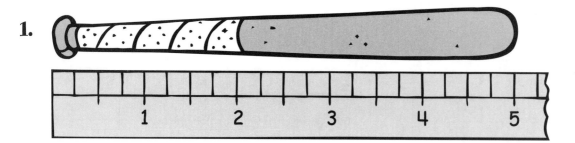

_____ inches

2. _____ inch

3. _____ inches

4.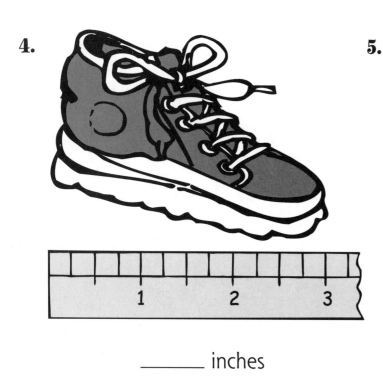

_____ inches

5. _____ inches

Measure the length of an object to the nearest inch

EMC 3015 • Basic Math Skills, Grade 2 • ©2003 by Evan-Moor Corp.

Tulip Time

Color and cut out the tulips. You will need an inch ruler to do this page.
Follow these directions for each tulip:

1. Read the number on a tulip.
2. Start at a dot.
3. Measure and draw a stem to match the number.
4. Glue the flower to the top of the stem.

Measure the length of an object to the nearest inch

Measurement

Let's Go Hunting

Name _____

You will need an inch ruler to do this page.
Find something that is about each of the sizes below.

1. 7 inches   A _____ is about 7 inches.

2. 5 inches   A _____ is about 5 inches.

3. 3 inches   A _____ is about 3 inches.

4. 10 inches   A _____ is about 10 inches.

5. 4 inches   A _____ is about 4 inches.

6. 12 inches   A _____ is about 12 inches.

Measure the length of an object to the nearest inch

EMC 3015 • Basic Math Skills, Grade 2 • ©2003 by Evan-Moor Corp.

Math Test

Fill in the circle next to the correct answer.

1. How long is it?

Ⓐ 5 inches
Ⓑ 2 inches
Ⓒ 3 inches
Ⓓ 7 inches

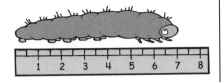

2. How long is it?

Ⓐ 2 inches
Ⓑ 6 inches
Ⓒ 3 inches
Ⓓ 4 inches

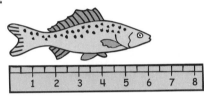

3. How long is it?

Ⓐ 8 inches
Ⓑ 6 inches
Ⓒ 4 inches
Ⓓ 12 inches

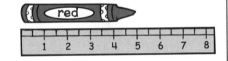

4. How long is it?

Ⓐ 2 inches
Ⓑ 4 inches
Ⓒ 1 inch
Ⓓ 5 inches

5. How wide is it?

Ⓐ 2 inches
Ⓑ 3 inches
Ⓒ 5 inches
Ⓓ 6 inches

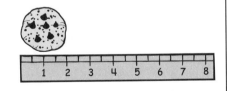

6. How wide is it?

Ⓐ 3 inches
Ⓑ 2 inches
Ⓒ 4 inches
Ⓓ 1 inch

7. How many inches are on the ruler?

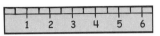

Ⓐ 2
Ⓑ 6
Ⓒ 4
Ⓓ 8

8. How many inches are on the ruler?

Ⓐ 10
Ⓑ 100
Ⓒ 25
Ⓓ 12

9. A white snake was 4 inches long. A black snake was 7 inches long. How much longer was the black snake?

Ⓐ 2 inches longer
Ⓑ 3 inches longer
Ⓒ 11 inches longer
Ⓓ 5 inches longer

10. Tina has a ribbon 12 inches long. Ann has a ribbon 5 inches long. How much longer is Tina's ribbon?

Ⓐ 6 inches longer
Ⓑ 17 inches longer
Ⓒ 7 inches longer
Ⓓ 11 inches longer

Measure the length of an object to the nearest inch

How Big Is Your Foot?

Name _____

Take off one shoe and sock.
Step onto your paper and trace around your foot.
Cut out the ruler. Measure to answer the questions.

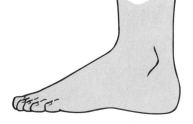

1. How long is your foot?   about _____ centimeters long

2. How wide is your foot?   about _____ centimeters wide

3. How long is your big toe?   about _____ centimeters long

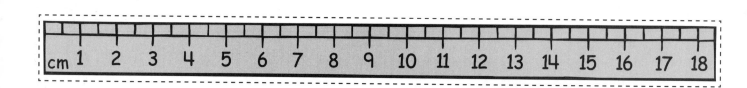

Measure the length of an object to the nearest centimeter

EMC 3015 • Basic Math Skills, Grade 2 • ©2003 by Evan-Moor Corp.

Tick, Tock, How Tall Is the Clock?

Name _____

Cut out the centimeter ruler. Help Mr. Smith measure the clocks in his shop.

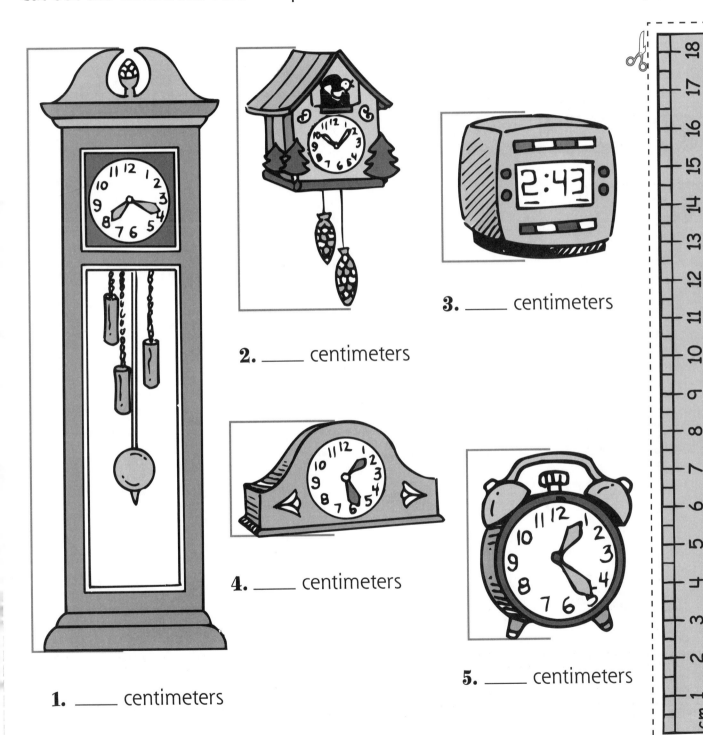

3. ____ centimeters

2. ____ centimeters

4. ____ centimeters

5. ____ centimeters

1. ____ centimeters

Measure the length of an object to the nearest centimeter

©2003 by Evan-Moor Corp. • Basic Math Skills, Grade 2 • EMC 3015

How Long Is It?

Name _____

Cut out the ruler. Measure the pictures.

1. _____ centimeters

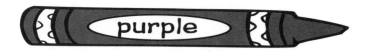

2. _____ centimeters

3. _____ centimeters

4. _____ centimeters

5. _____ centimeters

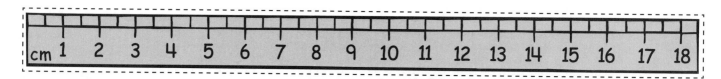

Measure the length of an object to the nearest centimeter

EMC 3015 • Basic Math Skills, Grade 2 • ©2003 by Evan-Moor Corp.

Measure and Compare

Name _____

Measure. Write the number sentence to answer the questions.

1. Look at the two insects. How much longer is the grasshopper?

_____ ◯ _____ = _____ centimeters

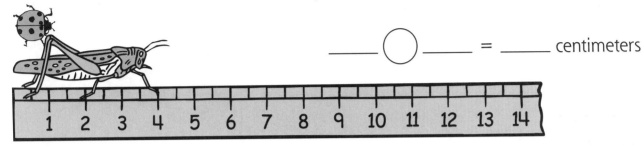

2. Look at the two worms. How much longer is the black worm?

_____ ◯ _____ = _____ centimeters

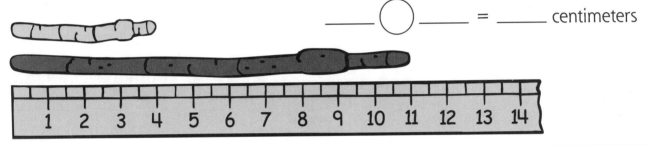

3. Look at the two lizards. How much longer is the gray lizard?

_____ ◯ _____ = _____ centimeters

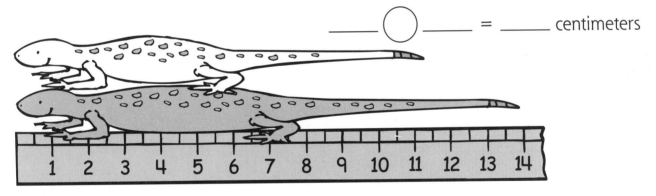

4. Look at how far these two frogs jumped. How much farther did the spotted frog jump?

_____ ◯ _____ = _____ centimeters

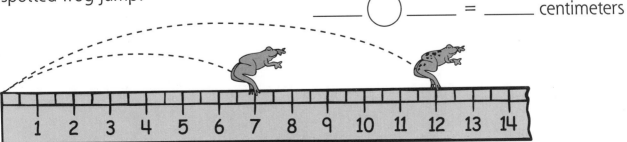

Measure the length of an object to the nearest centimeter

Centimeter Hunt

Name _____

You will need a centimeter ruler to do this page.
Find something that is about each of the sizes below.

1. 15 centimeters A _____ is about 15 centimeters.

2. 10 centimeters A _____ is about 10 centimeters.

3. 6 centimeters A _____ is about 6 centimeters.

4. 12 centimeters A _____ is about 12 centimeters.

5. 25 centimeters A _____ is about 25 centimeters.

6. 3 centimeters A _____ is about 3 centimeters.

Measure the length of an object to the nearest centimeter

EMC 3015 • Basic Math Skills, Grade 2 • ©2003 by Evan-Moor Corp.

Math Test

Name _____

Fill in the circle next to the correct answer.
Use a centimeter ruler to measure the pictures.

1. How long is it?

- Ⓐ 2 centimeters
- Ⓑ 3 centimeters
- Ⓒ 4 centimeters
- Ⓓ 5 centimeters

2. How long is it?

- Ⓐ 8 centimeters
- Ⓑ 6 centimeters
- Ⓒ 10 centimeters
- Ⓓ 12 centimeters

3. How long is it?

- Ⓐ 4 centimeters
- Ⓑ 8 centimeters
- Ⓒ 10 centimeters
- Ⓓ 6 centimeters

4. How long is it?

- Ⓐ 5 centimeters
- Ⓑ 6 centimeters
- Ⓒ 7 centimeters
- Ⓓ 8 centimeters

5. How wide is it?
- Ⓐ 4 centimeters
- Ⓑ 7 centimeters
- Ⓒ 8 centimeters
- Ⓓ 9 centimeters

6. How long is it?

- Ⓐ 1 centimeter
- Ⓑ 3 centimeters
- Ⓒ 5 centimeters
- Ⓓ 7 centimeters

7. How many centimeters are on the ruler?

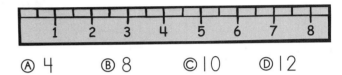

- Ⓐ 4
- Ⓑ 8
- Ⓒ 10
- Ⓓ 12

8. Which of these is true?
- Ⓐ 1 centimeter is more than 1 inch
- Ⓑ 1 inch is more than 1 centimeter
- Ⓒ 1 inch and 1 centimeter are the same
- Ⓓ 1 centimeter is almost as long as 1 inch

9. How much longer is the black ribbon?

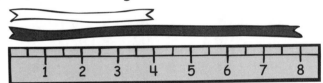

- Ⓐ 7 centimeters
- Ⓑ 15 centimeters
- Ⓒ 11 centimeters
- Ⓓ 4 centimeters

10. Ralph caught a fish 24 centimeters long.
Carlos caught a fish 12 centimeters long.
How much longer was Ralph's fish?
- Ⓐ 12 centimeters
- Ⓑ 36 centimeters
- Ⓒ 17 centimeters
- Ⓓ 26 centimeters

Measure the length of an object to the nearest centimeter

Measurement

Telling Time

Name _____

Count by 5s around the clock. From one number to the next number is five minutes.

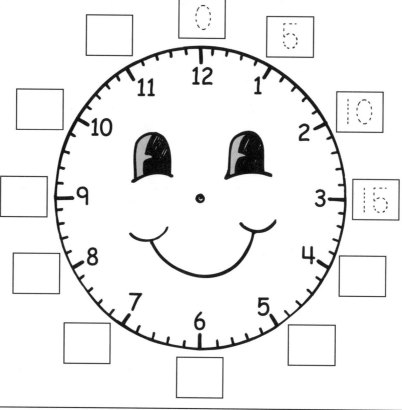

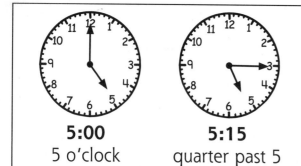

5:00	5:15	5:30	5:45
5 o'clock	quarter past 5	half past 5	quarter to 6

What time is it?

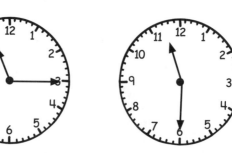

_____ : _____   _____ : _____   _____ : _____   _____ : _____

quarter to _____   quarter past _____   half past _____   _____ o'clock

Tell time to the nearest quarter-hour

EMC 3015 • Basic Math Skills, Grade 2 • ©2003 by Evan-Moor Corp.

School's Out

School is out and Gary is going home. Write the time for each clock. Color the boxes with clocks that tell the time on the hour to mark Gary's path home.

Tell time to the nearest quarter-hour

Measurement

213

Make a Match

Match each clock to the correct time.

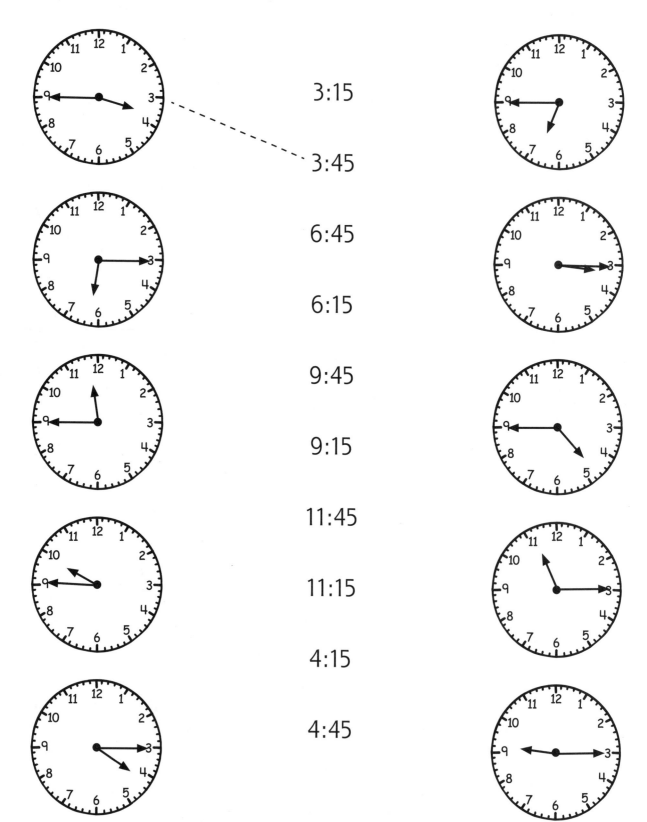

3:15

3:45

6:45

6:15

9:45

9:15

11:45

11:15

4:15

4:45

Tell time to the nearest quarter-hour

Don't Be Late!

Name _____

1. Kathy doesn't want to be late to school.
She needs to leave the house at half past 8.
Color the clock that shows when she must leave for school.

2. Zeke doesn't want to be late for his soccer game.
The game starts at 10:30.
Color the clock that shows when the game starts.

3. Amy had to be at the dentist at 11:00.
She left at 11:45.
Color the clock that shows the time she left.

Tell time to the nearest quarter-hour

Measurement

215

_____'s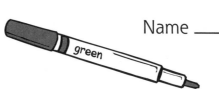

Name _____

Homework

Take this paper home. Draw the hands on the clocks. Write the times you do each thing tomorrow. Then bring the paper back to school.

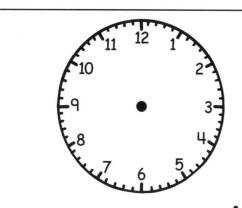

I got up. _____ :

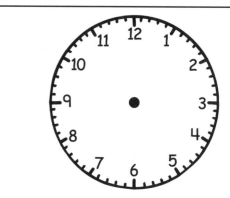

I left for school. _____ :

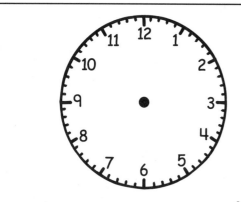

I came home. _____ :

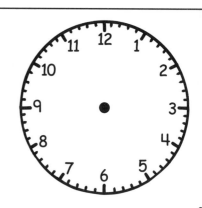

I ate dinner. _____ :

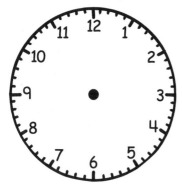

I went to bed. _____ :

Answer the questions.

1. How many hours did you play?

_____ hours

2. How many hours did you watch

television? _____ hours

3. How many hours did you sleep?

_____ hours

Tell time to the nearest quarter-hour

216 **Measurement**   EMC 3015 • Basic Math Skills, Grade 2 • ©2003 by Evan-Moor Corp.

Math Test

Fill in the circle next to the correct answer.

1. What time is it?
- Ⓐ 12:00
- Ⓑ 4:30
- Ⓒ 3:00
- Ⓓ 4:00

2. What time is it?
- Ⓐ 9:30
- Ⓑ 9:00
- Ⓒ 8:30
- Ⓓ 10:00

3. What time is it?
- Ⓐ 12:30
- Ⓑ 5:00
- Ⓒ 6:00
- Ⓓ 7:00

4. What time is it?
- Ⓐ 12:30
- Ⓑ 1:30
- Ⓒ 2:30
- Ⓓ 3:30

5. What time is it?
- Ⓐ 6:15
- Ⓑ 11:15
- Ⓒ 11:00
- Ⓓ 12:30

6. Which clock shows 2:45?

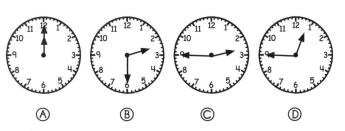

Ⓐ   Ⓑ   Ⓒ   Ⓓ

7. Which clock shows 6:15?

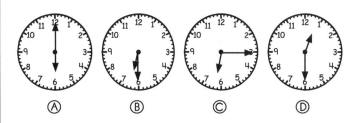

Ⓐ   Ⓑ   Ⓒ   Ⓓ

8. Angelo went to the park at 10:30. Which clock shows when he went to the park?

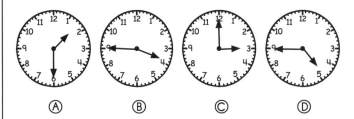

Ⓐ   Ⓑ   Ⓒ   Ⓓ

9. Tim started on his homework at 4:15. Which clock shows when he started on his homework?

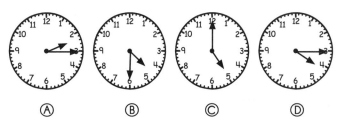

Ⓐ   Ⓑ   Ⓒ   Ⓓ

10. Which clock shows 3:45?

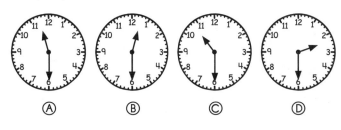

Ⓐ   Ⓑ   Ⓒ   Ⓓ

Tell time to the nearest quarter-hour

Grandma's Flower Garden

Name _____

Grandma keeps track of the time she works in her garden. Here is her record for last weekend. How much time did she spend on each task?

Weeding

   Start      Stop

How much time?

_____

Watering

   Start      Stop

How much time?

_____

Planting

   Start      Stop

How much time?

_____

Picking Flowers

   Start      Stop

How much time?

_____

Determine the duration of intervals of time in hours

EMC 3015 • Basic Math Skills, Grade 2 • ©2003 by Evan-Moor Corp.

Who Lives Here?

Name _____

Use the code to solve the riddle.

I live in a hole in the ground.
I line the hole with silk.
I sit and wait for my lunch to walk by.
What am I?

3:15–a	12:15–i	8:15–r
5:45–d	1:00–o	4:45–s
7:30–e	10:45–p	9:30–t

Read each clock. Write the time it will be **in one hour** on the line.
Then write the matching letter in the box.

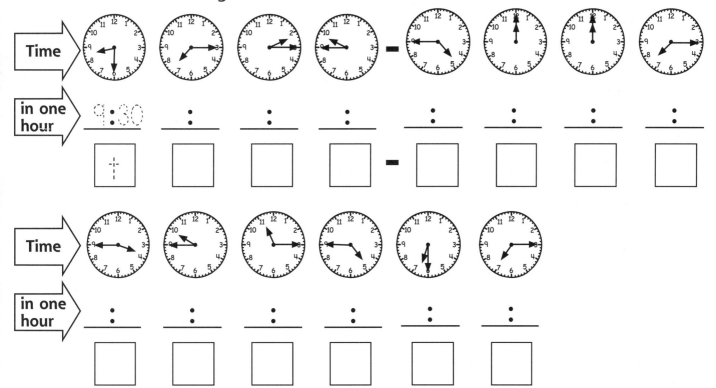

Circle my picture.

Determine the duration of intervals of time in hours

Measurement

Jeff's Jobs

Jeff's mother gave him a list of jobs to do on Saturday.
Write the time Jeff started and the time he finished each job.
Then tell how long it took him to do each job.

Job	Started	Finished	It took this long
1. Wash the car.			____ hour
2. Give the dog a bath.			____ hour
3. Clean your bedroom.			____ hours
4. Rake the lawn.			____ hour

Determine the duration of intervals of time in hours

Before and After

Name _____

Read each clock. Write the time it was 1 hour ago.
Then write the time it will be in 1 hour.

1 hour before		1 hour later
4:00		6:00
_____:_____		_____:_____
_____:_____		_____:_____
_____:_____		_____:_____
_____:_____		_____:_____
_____:_____		_____:_____
_____:_____		_____:_____

Determine the duration of intervals of time in hours

Fun at the Park

Name _____

1. Tomas went to the park at 2:00. He went home at 3:00. How long did he stay at the park?

_____ hour

2. Eli came to the park at 1:30. He left at 3:30. How long did he stay at the park?

_____ hours

3. Otto played ball at the park for 2 hours. The game started at 10:00. At what time did the game end?

_____ o'clock

Show your answer on this clock.

4. Flora went to the park at 2:00. She stayed for 3 hours. At what time did she go home?

_____ o'clock

Show your answer on this clock.

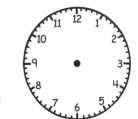

5. Cory is going to a picnic in the park. He can stay for 3 hours. If he goes to the picnic at 11:00, at what time must he go home?

_____ o'clock

Show your answer on this clock.

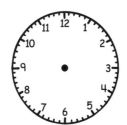

6. Mu Lan left home at 10:30. It took her one hour to get to the park. At what time did she get to the park?

_____:_____

Show your answer on this clock.

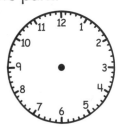

7. Write a word problem about this picture. Show the answer.

_____

_____

_____

_____:_____

Determine the duration of intervals of time in hours

EMC 3015 • Basic Math Skills, Grade 2 • ©2003 by Evan-Moor Corp.

Name _____

Fill in the circle next to the correct answer.

1. What time is it?

Ⓐ 6:00
Ⓑ 6:30
Ⓒ 9:00
Ⓓ 9:30

2. What time is it?

Ⓐ 2:00
Ⓑ 2:15
Ⓒ 2:30
Ⓓ 2:45

3. What time is it?

Ⓐ 8:15
Ⓑ 4:15
Ⓒ 4:30
Ⓓ 4:45

4. What time will it be in one hour?

Ⓐ 3:00
Ⓑ 5:00
Ⓒ 7:00
Ⓓ 9:00

5. What time will it be in one hour?

Ⓐ 10:30
Ⓑ 10:00
Ⓒ 11:00
Ⓓ 8:30

6. What time will it be in one hour?

Ⓐ 1:45
Ⓑ 2:45
Ⓒ 3:45
Ⓓ 4:45

7. What time was it one hour ago?

Ⓐ 1:00
Ⓑ 2:00
Ⓒ 4:00
Ⓓ 6:00

8. What time was it one hour ago?

Ⓐ 6:15
Ⓑ 3:15
Ⓒ 7:15
Ⓓ 4:15

9. Susan went to the park at 2:00. She stayed for 3 hours. At what time did she go home?

Ⓐ 3:00
Ⓑ 4:00
Ⓒ 5:00
Ⓓ 6:00

10. Warren went to a party at 1:30. His mother picked him up at 3:30. How long was he at the party?

Ⓐ one hour
Ⓑ two hours
Ⓒ three hours
Ⓓ four hours

Determine the duration of intervals of time in hours

Off We Go!

Name _____

Connect the months in order. Start at **January**.

• June

> There are 12
> months
> in one year.
>
> 1 - **January**
>
> 2 - **February**
>
> 3 - **March**
>
> 4 - **April**
>
> 5 - **May**
>
> 6 - **June**
>
> 7 - **July**
>
> 8 - **August**
>
> 9 - **September**
>
> 10 - **October**
>
> 11 - **November**
>
> 12 - **December**

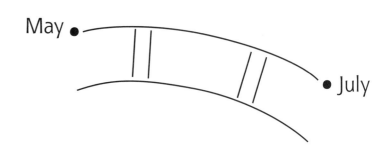

May •

• July

April •

• August

March •

• February

• October

January • • December

• November   • September

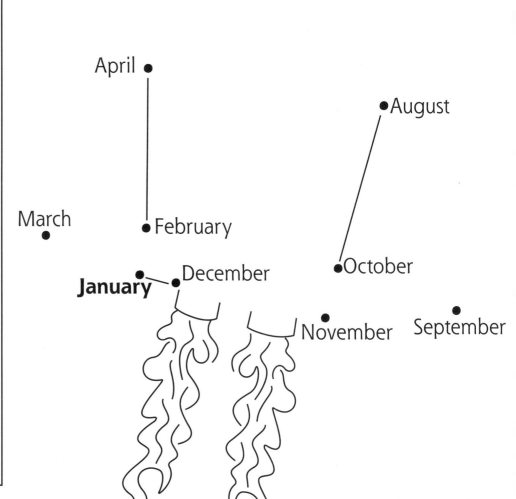

Know relationships of time (minutes in an hour, days in a month, weeks in year)

In a Minute

You will need a friend to time you and a clock with a second hand.
Guess how many times you can do each of these things in **1 minute**.

	My Guess	**The number of times I did it.**
1. Sing Happy Birthday.		
2. Hop on one foot.		
3. Write the alphabet.		

Now list all of the things you do in **5 minutes**.

Time I started. [:]

Things I did:

_____

_____

_____

_____

_____

Time I finished. [:]

Know relationships of time (minutes in an hour, days in a month, weeks in year)

How Many Days?

Name _____

Use the chart to find the answers.

Month	Days	Month	Days
January	31	July	31
February	28	August	31
March	31	September	30
April	30	October	31
May	31	November	30
June	30	December	31

1. How many months have 31 days? _____ months

2. Which month has the fewest number of days? _____

How many days does it have? _____ days

3. Which four months have 30 days?

_____ _____ _____ _____

4. Circle your birthday month in red.

How many days are there in that month? _____ days

Know relationships of time (minutes in an hour, days in a month, weeks in year)

EMC 3015 • Basic Math Skills, Grade 2 • ©2003 by Evan-Moor Corp.

Count Around the Clock

Name _____

Each line on the clock stands for one minute.
Write the numbers around the clock.

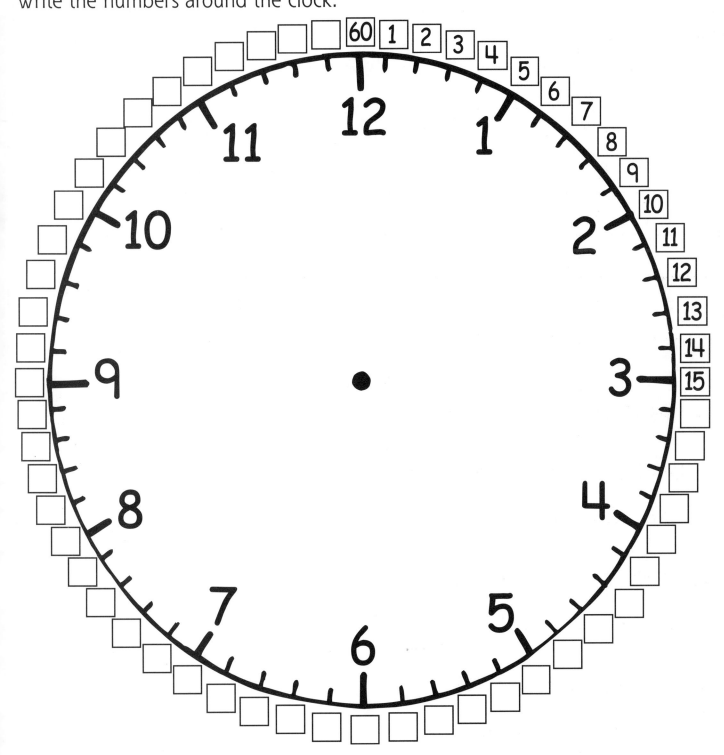

There are _____ minutes in one hour. The minute hand goes around
the clock one time in an hour. There are 24 hours in one day.

Know relationships of time (minutes in an hour, days in a month, weeks in year)

Measurement

It's About Time

Name _____

Read the chart. Answer the questions.

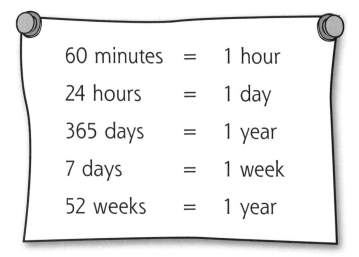

60 minutes	=	1 hour
24 hours	=	1 day
365 days	=	1 year
7 days	=	1 week
52 weeks	=	1 year

1. How many hours are there in one day? _____ hours

2. How many hours are there in two days? _____ hours

3. How many days are there in one week? _____ days

4. How many days are there in five weeks? _____ days

5. Write two ways to name one year.

_____   _____

Match the numbers.

1 year   60 minutes

1 day   7 days

1 week   365 days

1 hour   24 hours

Know relationships of time (minutes in an hour, days in a month, weeks in year)

EMC 3015 • Basic Math Skills, Grade 2 • ©2003 by Evan-Moor Corp.

Name _____

Fill in the circle next to the correct answer.

1. Find the number of days in one week.

Ⓐ 5
Ⓑ 7
Ⓒ 24
Ⓓ 30

2. Find the number of days in most months.

Ⓐ 14
Ⓑ 22
Ⓒ 24
Ⓓ 31

3. Find the number of days in one year.

Ⓐ 356
Ⓑ 365
Ⓒ 653
Ⓓ 536

4. Find the number of months in one year.

Ⓐ 10
Ⓑ 11
Ⓒ 12
Ⓓ 13

5. Which day comes next?
Tuesday, Wednesday, _____

Ⓐ Saturday
Ⓑ Friday
Ⓒ Thursday
Ⓓ Sunday

6. Which day comes next?
Friday, Saturday, _____

Ⓐ Monday
Ⓑ Thursday
Ⓒ Tuesday
Ⓓ Sunday

7. Which is the first month of the year?

Ⓐ January
Ⓑ December
Ⓒ June
Ⓓ March

8. Which is the last month of the year?

Ⓐ January
Ⓑ December
Ⓒ June
Ⓓ March

9. How many minutes are there in one hour?

Ⓐ 30
Ⓑ 40
Ⓒ 50
Ⓓ 60

10. How many hours are there in one day?

Ⓐ 12
Ⓑ 24
Ⓒ 30
Ⓓ 365

Know relationships of time (minutes in an hour, days in a month, weeks in year)

Data Analysis & Probability

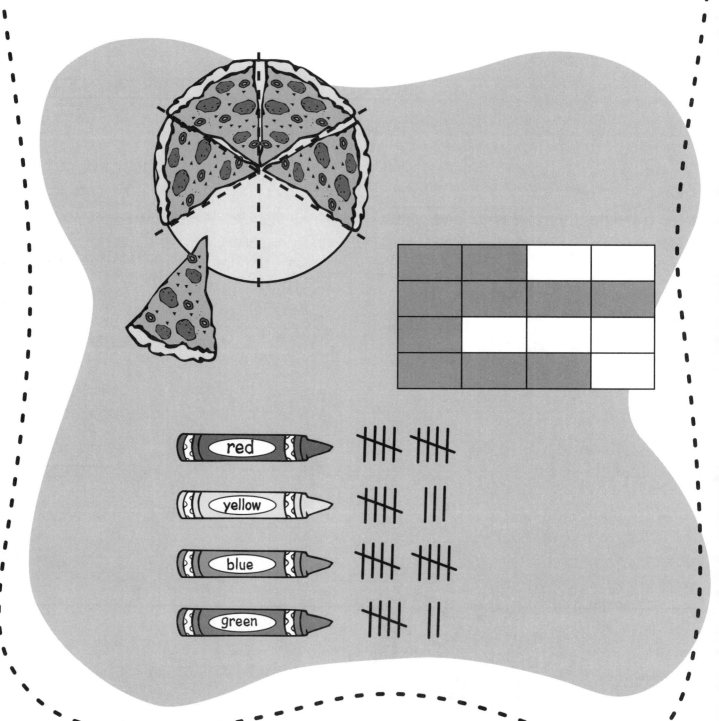

Bug Hunt

Name _____

Teddy went on a bug hunt. Look at the graph to see what he found.

	1	2	3	4	5	6	7
ladybug	🐞	🐞	🐞				
butterfly	🦋	🦋	🦋	🦋	🦋		
grasshopper	🦗	🦗					
bee	🐝	🐝	🐝				
ant	🐜	🐜	🐜	🐜	🐜	🐜	🐜
dragonfly	🪰						

Use the graph to answer the questions.

1. Which insect did Teddy see the most? How many did he see?

_____

2. Which insect did Teddy see the least? How many did he see?

_____

3. How many more butterflies than bees did Teddy see?

Show the number sentence.

_____ – _____ = _____

4. How many ants and ladybugs did Teddy see?

Show the number sentence.

_____ + _____ = _____

5. How many more ants than bees did Teddy see?

Show the number sentence.

_____ – _____ = _____

6. Write a new question about the graph.

_____

_____

_____

What is the answer to your question?

_____

Ask and answer questions related to data representations

Pizza Party

Carlos, Anna, and Kim love pizza.
Look at the pictures to see how many slices of pizza they ate.

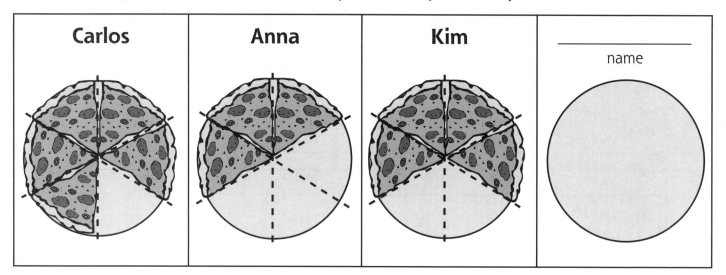

| Carlos | Anna | Kim | _____
name |

Use the pictures to answer the questions.

1. Who ate the most slices of pizza?   _____

2. Who ate the fewest slices of pizza?   _____

3. How many more slices did Anna eat than Kim?
   Show the number sentence.

   _____ $\bigcirc$ _____ = _____

4. How many pieces of pizza did the children eat in all?
   Show the number sentence.

   _____ $\bigcirc$ _____ $\bigcirc$ _____ = _____

5. Write your name in the last box.
   Show how many slices of pizza you can eat.

   How much more or less can you eat than Carlos?   _____ slices

Ask and answer questions related to data representations

Ready, Set, Go!

Name ____________________

Six contestants had a race.
Their times are shown on the chart.

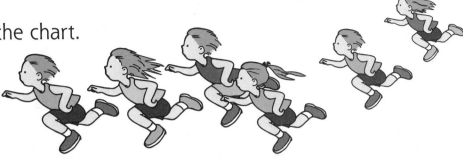

Name	Time
Arnold	9 minutes
Martha	5 minutes
Kisha	7 minutes
Paul	8 minutes
Angela	4 minutes
Ali	6 minutes

Use the chart to answer the questions.

1. Who won the race? ____________________
2. Who came in last? ____________________
3. Who came in second? ____________________
4. Who finished one minute before Ali? ____________________
5. How many minutes faster was Martha than Paul? ____________________

Write a new question about this chart.

____

____

What is the answer to your question? ____________________

Ask and answer questions related to data representations

How Much Does It Weigh? Name _____

Look at the chart. Then answer the questions.

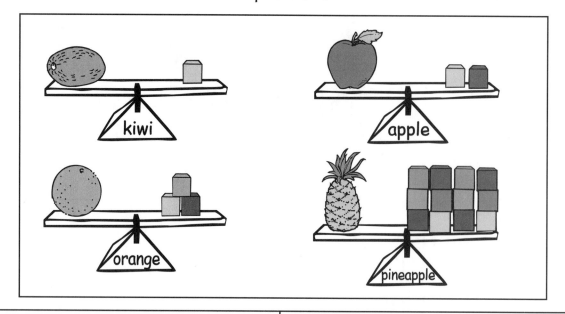

1. What weighs the most? pineapple How much does it weigh? 12 blocks	**2.** What weighs the least? _____ How much does it weigh? _____ block
3. How much do the orange and the apple weigh together? _____ blocks	**4.** How much will 3 apples weigh? _____ blocks
5. How much more does the pineapple weigh than the orange? _____ blocks more	**6.** Write a new question about this chart. _____ _____ What is the answer to your question? _____

Ask and answer questions related to data representations

Data Analysis & Probability   EMC 3015 • Basic Math Skills, Grade 2 • ©2003 by Evan-Moor Corp.

Find the Missing Numbers

Name _____

Use the multiplication chart to help you answer the questions.

2 x 1 = 2	3 x 1 = 3	4 x 1 = 4	5 x 1 = 5
2 x 2 = 4	3 x 2 = 6	4 x 2 = 8	5 x 2 = 10
2 x 3 = 6	3 x 3 = 9	4 x 3 = 12	5 x 3 = 15
2 x 4 = 8	3 x 4 = 12	4 x 4 = 16	5 x 4 = 20
2 x 5 = 10	3 x 5 = 15	4 x 5 = 20	5 x 5 = 25
2 x 6 = 12	3 x 6 = 18	4 x 6 = 24	5 x 6 = 30
2 x 7 = 14	3 x 7 = 21	4 x 7 = 28	5 x 7 = 35
2 x 8 = 16	3 x 8 = 24	4 x 8 = 32	5 x 8 = 40
2 x 9 = 18	3 x 9 = 27	4 x 9 = 36	5 x 9 = 45

1. Fill in the missing numbers.

5 x ____ = 10   3 x ____ = 21   5 x ____ = 25

____ x 3 = 9   ____ x 8 = 16   ____ x 4 = 8

2. Find two number sentences that equal 15.

____ x ____ = 15   ____ x ____ = 15

3. Find two number sentences that equal 24.

____ x ____ = 24   ____ x ____ = 24

4. Find two more number sentences that equal the same amount. Write them here.

____ x ____ = ____   ____ x ____ = ____

Ask and answer questions related to data representations

Name _____

Math Test

Fill in the circle next to the correct answer.

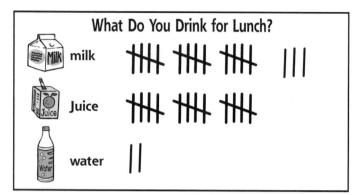

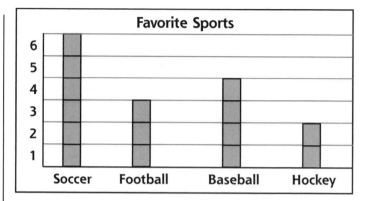

1. Look at the tally chart. How many children drink milk for lunch?
   - Ⓐ 2
   - Ⓑ 18
   - Ⓒ 15
   - Ⓓ 12

2. How many children drink juice for lunch?
   - Ⓐ 8
   - Ⓑ 12
   - Ⓒ 15
   - Ⓓ 5

3. What do the fewest children drink for lunch?
   - Ⓐ milk   Ⓑ juice   Ⓒ soda   Ⓓ water

4. How many children drink milk and water in all?
   - Ⓐ 18
   - Ⓑ 20
   - Ⓒ 33
   - Ⓓ 35

5. How many more children drink milk than juice?
   - Ⓐ 3   Ⓒ 5
   - Ⓑ 4   Ⓓ 6

6. Look at the graph. What is it about?
   - Ⓐ balls
   - Ⓑ sports
   - Ⓒ teams
   - Ⓓ toys

7. Which sport is liked least of all?
   - Ⓐ hockey
   - Ⓑ baseball
   - Ⓒ football
   - Ⓓ soccer

8. Which sport is liked most of all?
   - Ⓐ hockey
   - Ⓑ baseball
   - Ⓒ football
   - Ⓓ soccer

9. How many more like soccer than football?
   - Ⓐ 2
   - Ⓑ 3
   - Ⓒ 4
   - Ⓓ 5

10. How many more like baseball than hockey?
   - Ⓐ 2
   - Ⓑ 3
   - Ⓒ 4
   - Ⓓ 5

Ask and answer questions related to data representations

Data Analysis & Probability   EMC 3015 • Basic Math Skills, Grade 2 • ©2003 by Evan-Moor Corp.

Old Mac Donald's Farm

Name _____

Count the animals.
Color one square for each animal you count.

Record numerical data in systematic ways, keeping track of what has been counted

Data Analysis & Probability

Here Comes the Circus Parade

Name _____

We saw these things in the circus parade.

1	band
8	dogs
3	funny cars
5	elephants
12	clowns
10	horses

Label the graph. Color in boxes to show the information on the chart.

	1	2	3	4	5	6	7	8	9	10	11	12
___ band ___	▓											
_____												
_____												
_____												
_____												
_____												

Record numerical data in systematic ways, keeping track of what has been counted

Data Analysis & Probability   EMC 3015 • Basic Math Skills, Grade 2 • ©2003 by Evan-Moor Corp.

Camp-Out

Mr. Gomez asked his students, "Have you ever slept outside in a tent?"
The students wrote their names on the list below. Use the information to
make a picture graph.

**Have you ever slept
outside in a tent?**

Yes	No
Ben	Carl
Ramon	Beth
Blanca	Frank
Carol	Jared
Annie	Raul
Tori	Chen
	Ann

Draw one ⛺ for each name.

Yes	
No	

Use the graph to answer the questions.

1. How many children answered the question? _____

2. Did more children answer **yes** or **no**? _____

How many more? _____

3. Have you ever slept outside in a tent? _____

Write your name on the list. Then add one ⛺ on the graph.

Record numerical data in systematic ways, keeping track of what has been counted

How Many Fruits and Vegetables?

Name _____

Color one part of the graph for each fruit and vegetable.

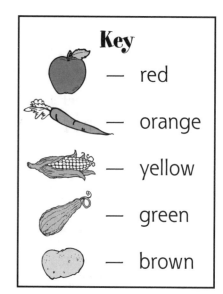

Key

— red

— orange

— yellow

— green

— brown

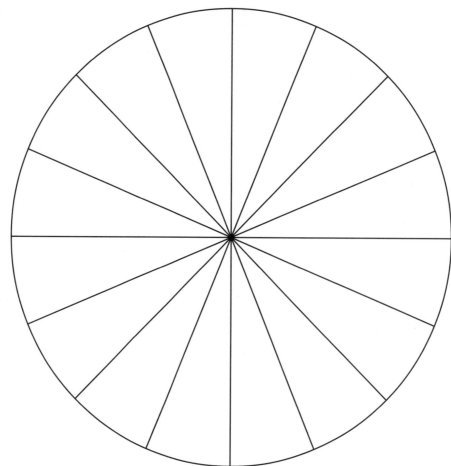

Record numerical data in systematic ways, keeping track of what has been counted

Happy Birthday!

Name _____

Ask 15 children, "When is your birthday?"

Make a tally mark in the correct space to show how many children had birthdays each month.

January	
February	
March	
April	
May	
June	
July	
August	
September	
October	
November	
December	

Record numerical data in systematic ways, keeping track of what has been counted

Name _____

Fill in the circle next to the correct answer.

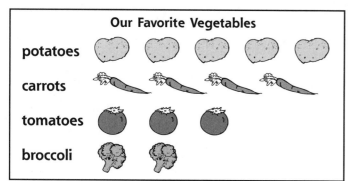

Our Favorite Vegetables

potatoes

carrots

tomatoes

broccoli

1. What is the tally chart about?
   Ⓐ fruits   © vegetables
   Ⓑ drinks   Ⓓ sweets

2. Look at the graph. How many people like broccoli the best?
   Ⓐ 3
   Ⓑ 4
   © 2
   Ⓓ 7

3. How many people like potatoes and carrots in all?
   Ⓐ 7
   Ⓑ 9
   © 11
   Ⓓ 12

4. Which vegetable is liked most of all?
   Ⓐ tomatoes   © potatoes
   Ⓑ carrots   Ⓓ broccoli

5. How many more people like carrots than tomatoes?
   Ⓐ 1
   Ⓑ 2
   © 5
   Ⓓ 7

6. Look at the graph. What is it about?
   Ⓐ fun at school
   Ⓑ fun in the backyard
   © fun at camp
   Ⓓ fun at the pool

7. Which do campers like least?
   Ⓐ to swim   © to ride horses
   Ⓑ to hike   Ⓓ to fish

8. Which do campers like most?
   Ⓐ to swim
   Ⓑ to hike
   © to ride horses
   Ⓓ to fish

9. How many more campers like to swim than to fish?
   Ⓐ 3
   Ⓑ 5
   © 7
   Ⓓ 9

10. How many more campers like to ride horses than to hike?
   Ⓐ 1
   Ⓑ 2
   © 3
   Ⓓ 4

Record numerical data in systematic ways, keeping track of what has been counted

Data Analysis & Probability

EMC 3015 • Basic Math Skills, Grade 2 • ©2003 by Evan-Moor Corp.

Family Favorites

Name _____

Margaret asked her family, "What is your favorite food?"
She marked each food that a person liked.

	Pizza	Hamburger	Taco	Stir-Fry	Steak
Mother	X			X	X
Father	X		X		X
Ernesto	X	X	X		
Kelsey	X	X		X	
Blanca	X	X	X		

Use the chart to complete this graph.

My Family's Favorite Foods

6					
5					
4					
3					
2					
1					
	Pizza	Hamburger	Taco	Stir-Fry	Steak

Represent the same data set in more than one way

Data Analysis & Probability

Shells

Mark, Tim, Susan, and Mary went to the beach.
They found shells on the beach.

Complete the tally.

Name	Number of Shells	Tally
Mark	6	卌 l
Tim	10	
Susan	8	
Mary	12	

Draw shells on the graph to show how many shells were found.

Mark	
Tim	
Susan	
Mary	

Represent the same data set in more than one way

EMC 3015 • Basic Math Skills, Grade 2 • ©2003 by Evan-Moor Corp.

Picking Flowers

Name _____

Draw the number of flowers. Then make tally marks to show how many of each kind you drew.

	Draw Here	Tally Marks
6  🌼		
10  🌹		
3  🌸		
12  🌺		

Now color one space on the graph for each flower.

	1	2	3	4	5	6	7	8	9	10	11	12
🌼												
🌹												
🌸												
🌺												

Represent the same data set in more than one way

Colors

Tony asked first-graders, "What is your favorite color?"
He made a picture chart to show their answers.

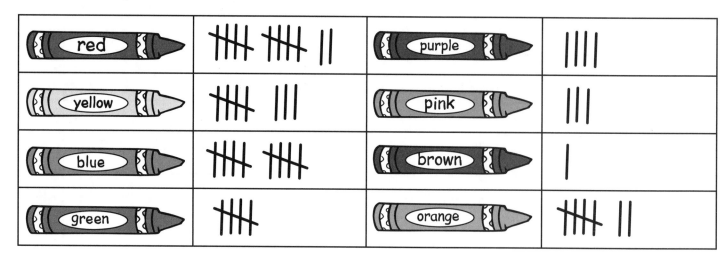

Show the information on this graph. Color one space for each mark.

	red	yellow	blue	green	purple	pink	brown	orange
14								
13								
12								
11								
10								
9								
8								
7								
6								
5								
4								
3								
2								
1								

Represent the same data set in more than one way

Funny Stories— Scary Stories

Name _____

Ask 12 people, "Which do you like better—funny stories or scary stories?"
Write each name under the answer.

Funny	Scary

Now color one section for each answer.

Funny — green
Scary — red

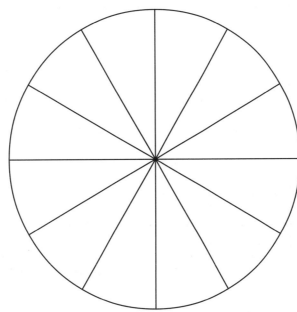

Represent the same data set in more than one way

Data Analysis & Probability

Name _____

Fill in the circle next to the correct answer.

How Many Peanuts?

Jill   Bob   Lee   Jerry   Ann

Kisha's Toys

3 dolls   4 bears   1 bicycle

2 games   2 kites

1. What does this graph show?
   Ⓐ how many marbles they have
   Ⓑ how many peanuts they have
   Ⓒ how many boys like nuts
   Ⓓ how many girls like nuts

2. How do you record numbers on a tally chart?
   Ⓐ draw a picture for each object
   Ⓑ color a box for each object
   Ⓒ make one mark for each object
   Ⓓ color part of a circle for each object

3. Mark the boxes that would be on a graph showing Jill's peanuts.
   Ⓐ
   Ⓑ
   Ⓒ
   Ⓓ

4. Mark the boxes that would be on a graph showing Jerry's peanuts.
   Ⓐ
   Ⓑ
   Ⓒ
   Ⓓ

5. How many more boxes would you mark to show Lee's peanuts than Bob's?
   Ⓐ 1   Ⓑ 2   Ⓒ 6   Ⓓ 8

6. What does this chart tell about?
   Ⓐ Kisha's friends
   Ⓑ Kisha's pets
   Ⓒ Kisha's toys
   Ⓓ Kisha's shoes

7. How many more bears than kites does Kisha have?
   Ⓐ 1   Ⓑ 2   Ⓒ 3   Ⓓ 4

8. Mark the pictures that would be on a graph showing Kisha's dolls.
   Ⓐ   Ⓒ
   Ⓑ   Ⓓ

9. Mark the pictures that would be on a graph showing Kisha's kites.
   Ⓐ   Ⓒ
   Ⓑ    Ⓓ

10. Mark the pictures that would be on a graph showing Kisha's bears.
   Ⓐ   Ⓒ
   Ⓑ    Ⓓ

Represent the same data set in more than one way

Data Analysis & Probability   EMC 3015 • Basic Math Skills, Grade 2 • ©2003 by Evan-Moor Corp.

Ben's Crayons

Name _____

Color the crayons.

Answer the questions.

1. If Ben chooses one crayon without looking,
   which color is he MOST likely to choose?   _____

   Tell why. _____

   _____

2. If Ben chooses one crayon without looking,
   which color is he LEAST likely to choose?   _____

   Tell why. _____

   _____

3. If Ben chooses one crayon without looking,
   which color is IMPOSSIBLE to choose?   _____

   Tell why. _____

   _____

Explore probability

In the Cookie Jar

Name _____

Maurice chooses one cookie without looking. What is the chance he will get each of these cookies? Circle one:

1.

sugar cookie

Most likely   **Least likely**   **Impossible**

Tell why. _____

_____

2.

sugar wafer

Most likely   **Least likely**   **Impossible**

Tell why. _____

_____

3.

chocolate cookie

Most likely   **Least likely**   **Impossible**

Tell why. _____

_____

Explore probability

EMC 3015 • Basic Math Skills, Grade 2 • ©2003 by Evan-Moor Corp.

Which Color Will Tina Pick?

Name _____

Color the gumdrops.

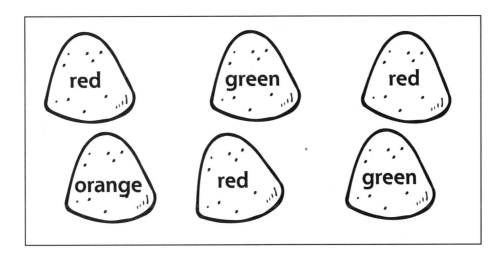

Tina will pick one gumdrop without looking.
Color the gumdrops to show the answers.

1. Show all the colors Tina can choose.

2. Show 2 colors that are IMPOSSIBLE to choose.

3. Show the color Tina is MOST likely to choose.

4. Show the color she is LEAST likely to choose.

Explore probability

Data Analysis & Probability

Spin the Wheel

Timmy used a spinner wheel to make his chart.
Look at Timmy's chart. Then answer the questions.

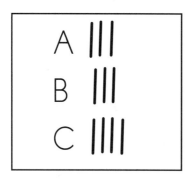

1. Which spinner did Timmy most likely use? Circle it.

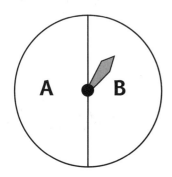 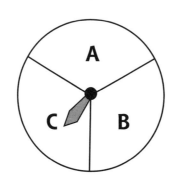 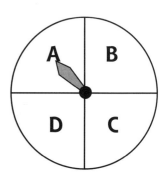

2. Why did you choose this answer?

_____

_____

3. Look at the chart below. Then draw the spinner that was most likely used.

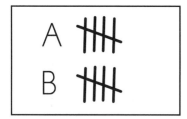 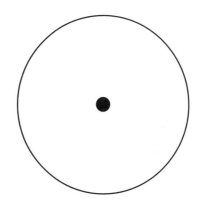

Explore probability

EMC 3015 • Basic Math Skills, Grade 2 • ©2003 by Evan-Moor Corp.

Puppy

Cut out the letters. Put them facedown on your desk. Mix up the letters. Pick one and record the letter. Return it to the desk facedown, mix again, and pick a card. Do this 10 times.

I picked this letter.

1. _____   6. _____

2. _____   7. _____

3. _____   8. _____

4. _____   9. _____

5. _____   10. _____

1. How many P's did you pick? _____

2. How many U's did you pick? _____

3. How many Y's did you pick? _____

4. Guess how many P's you would get if you did it 10 more times. _____

Do it 10 more times.

5. How many P's did you pick? _____

Compare your results with a friend.

Explore probability

Data Analysis & Probability

Name _____

Fill in the circle next to the correct answer.

Math Test

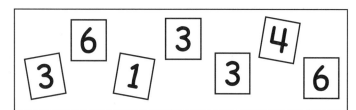

1. Which number is MOST likely to be picked without looking?

| 1 | 3 | 4 | 6 |
| Ⓐ | Ⓑ | Ⓒ | Ⓓ |

2. Which number is LEAST likely to be picked without looking?

| 1 | 3 | 4 | 6 |
| Ⓐ | Ⓑ | Ⓒ | Ⓓ |

3. Which number is IMPOSSIBLE to pick without looking?

| 6 | 1 | 3 | 0 |
| Ⓐ | Ⓑ | Ⓒ | Ⓓ |

4. If one object is chosen without looking, what is the chance it will be a ball?

Ⓐ certain
Ⓑ most likely
Ⓒ least likely
Ⓓ impossible

5. If one object is chosen without looking, what is the chance it will be a toy car?

Ⓐ certain
Ⓑ most likely
Ⓒ least likely
Ⓓ impossible

6. A white can is _____ to be picked without looking.

Ⓐ certain   Ⓒ least likely
Ⓑ most likely   Ⓓ impossible

7. A black can is _____ to be picked without looking.

Ⓐ certain   Ⓒ least likely
Ⓑ most likely   Ⓓ impossible

8. Which are equally likely to be picked without looking?

Ⓐ white and gray   Ⓒ black and striped
Ⓑ gray and black   Ⓓ striped and gray

9. Which spinner could have been used to make this chart?

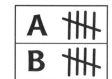

Ⓐ   Ⓑ   Ⓒ   Ⓓ

10. Which spinner could have been used to make this chart?

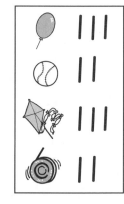

Ⓐ   Ⓒ

Ⓑ   Ⓓ

Explore probability

Data Analysis & Probability   EMC 3015 • Basic Math Skills, Grade 2 • ©2003 by Evan-Moor Corp.

Resources

Name _____

Math Test Page _____

1. Ⓐ Ⓑ Ⓒ Ⓓ   6. Ⓐ Ⓑ Ⓒ Ⓓ

2. Ⓐ Ⓑ Ⓒ Ⓓ   7. Ⓐ Ⓑ Ⓒ Ⓓ

3. Ⓐ Ⓑ Ⓒ Ⓓ   8. Ⓐ Ⓑ Ⓒ Ⓓ

4. Ⓐ Ⓑ Ⓒ Ⓓ   9. Ⓐ Ⓑ Ⓒ Ⓓ

5. Ⓐ Ⓑ Ⓒ Ⓓ   10. Ⓐ Ⓑ Ⓒ Ⓓ

Name _____

Time: _____   Number Correct: _____

4 +2	2 +5	3 +4	5 +5	8 +2	7 +3	4 +5	3 +6
4 +3	2 +8	8 +0	6 +1	1 +8	2 +6	6 +4	0 +7
3 +7	5 +2	6 +3	8 +1	2 +4	4 +6	1 +6	10 +0
2 +7	5 +4	7 +2	3 +5	6 +2	1 +9	3 +3	6 +0

- -

Name _____

Time: _____   Number Correct: _____

6 +1	2 +8	3 +4	4 +2	1 +9	6 +0	5 +4	7 +2
2 +7	3 +3	6 +2	2 +6	0 +7	7 +3	3 +6	10 +0
5 +2	8 +1	4 +6	3 +5	4 +5	8 +2	6 +4	1 +8
1 +6	2 +4	6 +3	3 +7	2 +5	4 +3	5 +5	8 +0

Name _____

Time: _____   Number Correct: _____

10 −4	9 −9	6 −4	8 −7	9 −3	8 −5	10 −8	8 −0
6 −2	8 −4	10 −5	7 −3	8 −3	6 −5	10 −1	10 −10
8 −6	6 −3	7 −7	9 −5	7 −4	8 −1	6 −6	7 −1
10 −6	8 −2	10 −9	4 −2	9 −8	7 −2	6 −1	10 −7

- -

Name _____

Time: _____   Number Correct: _____

8 −4	10 −10	7 −6	6 −6	8 −5	7 −1	6 −2	10 −1
6 −1	8 −6	10 −7	6 −3	10 −4	9 −9	8 −2	10 −9
9 −5	7 −2	9 −8	7 −7	6 −4	10 −6	8 −7	9 −3
8 −0	7 −4	10 −8	8 −1	6 −5	7 −3	8 −3	10 −5

Name _____

Time: _____   Number Correct: _____

9	6	2	7	10	0	9	7
−0	+1	+8	−5	−2	+7	−1	−3

8	5	7	10	8	2	3	10
−4	+4	+3	−5	−8	+6	+6	−5

3	6	8	6	6	6	8	9
+3	+2	−3	−5	−3	+4	−4	−8

7	8	7	10	3	4	9	6
+2	−6	−3	−1	+4	+2	−7	−2

- -

Name _____

Time: _____   Number Correct: _____

10	5	6	7	10	8	2	10
−3	+5	−0	+3	−9	−5	+4	−8

8	10	6	8	6	8	9	6
+0	−4	−4	+2	+4	−7	−3	+3

8	4	9	2	2	10	1	10
−2	+5	−4	+5	+6	−10	+6	−6

5	7	4	3	10	4	9	3
+2	−2	+6	+5	−0	+3	−6	+6

Time: _____   Number Correct: _____

9 +1	3 +8	7 +4	8 +7	2 +9	6 +6	2 +8	6 +7
4 +6	3 +9	4 +9	8 +6	9 +6	7 +7	6 +4	9 +2
6 +9	7 +6	8 +5	7 +8	4 +7	9 +3	5 +8	9 +4
5 +9	7 +5	6 +8	5 +6	5 +5	4 +8	5 +7	6 +5

- -

Time: _____   Number Correct: _____

8 +5	7 +6	6 +9	9 +6	6 +7	4 +9	9 +3	5 +9
8 +7	6 +4	9 +2	4 +6	3 +9	7 +7	2 +9	6 +6
2 +8	8 +6	4 +7	5 +5	7 +8	4 +8	5 +7	6 +5
3 +8	7 +4	9 +1	6 +8	5 +6	9 +4	7 +5	5 +8

Name _____

Time: _____   Number Correct: _____

14	11	13	10	10	15	15	12
−7	−4	−5	−8	−9	−6	−8	−9

12	11	10	12	14	11	10	11
−3	−7	−3	−6	−9	−2	−5	−3

13	12	11	12	14	12	15	11
−8	−4	−8	−7	−8	−5	−7	−6

14	15	12	11	14	13	15	10
−0	−9	−8	−5	−6	−9	−15	−7

- -

Name _____

Time: _____   Number Correct: _____

14	13	10	12	15	15	10	12
−7	−9	−8	−9	−6	−8	−3	−6

11	12	13	11	14	12	11	15
−8	−4	−8	−2	−8	−7	−3	−15

15	14	12	11	10	10	12	11
−7	−9	−5	−6	−5	−9	−3	−7

15	12	10	15	11	13	14	13
−9	−8	−7	−7	−5	−7	−6	−5

Name _____

Time: _____   Number Correct: _____

9 +6	7 +5	15 −6	13 −5	2 +8	9 +1	12 −8	7 +6
11 −9	5 +7	8 +4	13 −7	11 −4	12 −3	3 +8	5 +6
14 −7	7 +4	9 +3	14 −5	10 −9	7 +3	13 −4	5 +5
8 +7	10 −5	11 −7	8 +5	14 −9	4 +6	6 +5	10 −4

- -

Name _____

Time: _____   Number Correct: _____

2 +9	10 −6	8 +3	12 −7	6 +9	13 −6	6 +7	10 −8
4 +9	11 −3	9 +4	3 +9	14 −6	9 +2	12 −5	15 −15
14 −8	15 −9	11 −2	8 +6	3 +7	12 −4	6 +8	15 −7
11 −6	5 +8	9 +5	6 +6	4 +8	11 −5	12 −9	13 −8

Name _____

Time: _____   Number Correct: _____

6 +6	8 +4	7 +8	6 +5	3 +9	8 +9	6 +7	9 +6
7 +4	8 +7	5 +9	5 +7	3 +8	4 +7	10 +4	8 +5
7 +9	8 +3	9 +5	9 +9	5 +6	6 +9	8 +8	6 +8
9 +8	9 +4	2 +9	4 +8	9 +3	5 +8	10 +1	15 +0

- -

Name _____

Time: _____   Number Correct: _____

2 +9	8 +8	9 +5	7 +8	8 +3	7 +4	8 +7	13 +0
8 +5	6 +6	9 +3	10 +4	6 +8	9 +9	6 +7	3 +9
6 +5	7 +9	8 +9	7 +7	5 +6	9 +4	8 +8	7 +5
9 +6	8 +4	4 +7	4 +8	6 +9	9 +8	8 +7	10 +6

    EMC 3015 • Practice Basic Math Skills, Grade 2 • ©2003 by Evan-Moor Corp.

Name _____

Time: _____   Number Correct: _____

12	17	16	15	13	11	15	15
−3	−9	−7	−8	−6	−2	−7	−0

14	15	13	14	12	13	14	13
−8	−9	−5	−9	−9	−8	−7	−9

13	12	17	14	16	12	15	11
−7	−6	−8	−5	−8	−8	−6	−4

13	11	18	14	11	16	14	18
−4	−7	−9	−6	−6	−9	−6	−18

Name _____

Time: _____   Number Correct: _____

13	12	11	14	16	18	15	11
−4	−9	−7	−6	−7	−9	−8	−2

13	17	15	17	14	14	12	14
−7	−8	−6	−9	−7	−9	−6	−5

13	12	16	14	14	13	11	15
−9	−0	−9	−8	−4	−5	−6	−9

13	12	15	13	16	11	12	16
−8	−3	−7	−6	−8	−4	−8	−16

Name _____

Time: _____   Number Correct: _____

12	13	6	11	7	9	11	11
−4	−6	+8	−9	+6	+7	−8	−3

6	15	8	12	10	12	8	4
+9	−8	+4	−9	+4	−7	+6	+9

7	7	16	8	3	5	13	12
+5	+8	−7	+8	+9	+6	−8	−6

11	17	9	6	13	16	14	10
−5	−7	+2	+5	−7	−9	−9	+8

- -

Name _____

Time: _____   Number Correct: _____

9	15	14	17	13	5	14	15
+8	−9	−7	−8	−4	+8	−5	−6

13	16	3	7	15	18	12	14
−5	−7	+9	+9	−7	−9	−8	+0

8	14	11	12	17	9	8	16
+3	−6	−7	−3	−9	+3	+5	−8

3	6	9	5	7	4	7	12
+8	+7	+9	+6	+9	+7	+8	−6

EMC 3015 • Practice Basic Math Skills, Grade 2 • ©2003 by Evan-Moor Corp.

Name _____

Time: _____   Number Correct: _____

1 ×2	2 ×5	7 ×2	4 ×2	5 ×8	1 ×5	3 ×5	3 ×2
9 ×5	7 ×5	4 ×5	2 ×0	5 ×6	5 ×7	2 ×8	5 ×0
5 ×2	9 ×2	6 ×2	8 ×5	5 ×4	2 ×4	2 ×1	2 ×6
6 ×5	8 ×2	5 ×5	2 ×2	5 ×9	2 ×3	2 ×9	5 ×1

- -

Name _____

Time: _____   Number Correct: _____

6 ×2	5 ×4	5 ×2	2 ×5	9 ×2	2 ×3	2 ×8	5 ×1
4 ×5	8 ×5	1 ×5	1 ×2	2 ×1	7 ×2	3 ×5	2 ×9
2 ×2	9 ×5	2 ×6	4 ×2	6 ×5	8 ×2	5 ×3	5 ×9
3 ×2	2 ×4	5 ×6	7 ×5	5 ×7	5 ×5	5 ×8	2 ×7

Name _____

Time: _____   Number Correct: _____

1 ×2	10 ×6	3 ×5	6 ×5	5 ×2	10 ×2	5 ×8	10 ×9
2 ×2	10 ×3	2 ×5	9 ×5	7 ×2	10 ×8	2 ×4	5 ×7
3 ×2	4 ×5	10 ×7	1 ×5	8 ×2	10 ×1	5 ×3	6 ×2
4 ×2	5 ×5	8 ×5	10 ×4	2 ×6	7 ×5	10 ×5	9 ×2

- -

Name _____

Time: _____   Number Correct: _____

1 ×5	8 ×2	10 ×1	9 ×5	7 ×2	10 ×8	1 ×2	10 ×6
4 ×2	7 ×5	2 ×2	10 ×3	2 ×5	10 ×4	2 ×6	5 ×7
3 ×2	4 ×5	10 ×7	3 ×5	2 ×6	5 ×3	6 ×5	5 ×2
10 ×2	8 ×5	6 ×2	2 ×4	5 ×5	5 ×8	10 ×5	9 ×2

Math Timed Tests–Class Record Sheet

Student Names												
1 + 0–10												
2 + 0–10												
3 – 0–10												
4 – 0–10												
5 +/– 0–10												
6 +/– 0–10												
7 + 10–15												
8 + 10–15												
9 – 10–15												
10 – 10–15												
11 +/– 10–15												
12 +/– 10–15												
13 + 11–18												
14 + 11–18												
15 – 11–18												
16 – 11–18												
17 +/– 11–18												
18 +/– 11–18												
19 x 2s, 5s												
20 x 2s, 5s												
21 x 2s, 5s, 10s												
22 x 2s, 5s, 10s												

Name _____

Math Test Page _____

1. Ⓐ Ⓑ Ⓒ Ⓓ   6. Ⓐ Ⓑ Ⓒ Ⓓ

2. Ⓐ Ⓑ Ⓒ Ⓓ   7. Ⓐ Ⓑ Ⓒ Ⓓ

3. Ⓐ Ⓑ Ⓒ Ⓓ   8. Ⓐ Ⓑ Ⓒ Ⓓ

4. Ⓐ Ⓑ Ⓒ Ⓓ   9. Ⓐ Ⓑ Ⓒ Ⓓ

5. Ⓐ Ⓑ Ⓒ Ⓓ   10. Ⓐ Ⓑ Ⓒ Ⓓ

Name _____

Math Test Page _____

1. Ⓐ Ⓑ Ⓒ Ⓓ   6. Ⓐ Ⓑ Ⓒ Ⓓ

2. Ⓐ Ⓑ Ⓒ Ⓓ   7. Ⓐ Ⓑ Ⓒ Ⓓ

3. Ⓐ Ⓑ Ⓒ Ⓓ   8. Ⓐ Ⓑ Ⓒ Ⓓ

4. Ⓐ Ⓑ Ⓒ Ⓓ   9. Ⓐ Ⓑ Ⓒ Ⓓ

5. Ⓐ Ⓑ Ⓒ Ⓓ   10. Ⓐ Ⓑ Ⓒ Ⓓ

Name _____

Math Test Page _____

1. Ⓐ Ⓑ Ⓒ Ⓓ   6. Ⓐ Ⓑ Ⓒ Ⓓ

2. Ⓐ Ⓑ Ⓒ Ⓓ   7. Ⓐ Ⓑ Ⓒ Ⓓ

3. Ⓐ Ⓑ Ⓒ Ⓓ   8. Ⓐ Ⓑ Ⓒ Ⓓ

4. Ⓐ Ⓑ Ⓒ Ⓓ   9. Ⓐ Ⓑ Ⓒ Ⓓ

5. Ⓐ Ⓑ Ⓒ Ⓓ   10. Ⓐ Ⓑ Ⓒ Ⓓ

Name _____

Math Test Page _____

1. Ⓐ Ⓑ Ⓒ Ⓓ   6. Ⓐ Ⓑ Ⓒ Ⓓ

2. Ⓐ Ⓑ Ⓒ Ⓓ   7. Ⓐ Ⓑ Ⓒ Ⓓ

3. Ⓐ Ⓑ Ⓒ Ⓓ   8. Ⓐ Ⓑ Ⓒ Ⓓ

4. Ⓐ Ⓑ Ⓒ Ⓓ   9. Ⓐ Ⓑ Ⓒ Ⓓ

5. Ⓐ Ⓑ Ⓒ Ⓓ   10. Ⓐ Ⓑ Ⓒ Ⓓ

EMC 3015 • Basic Math Skills, Grade 2 • ©2003 by Evan-Moor Corp.

Awards

Math Whiz

_____
name

is a Math Super Star because

_____

_____

Keep up the Good Work!

You're doing better!

_____
name

is ready for the next timed test.

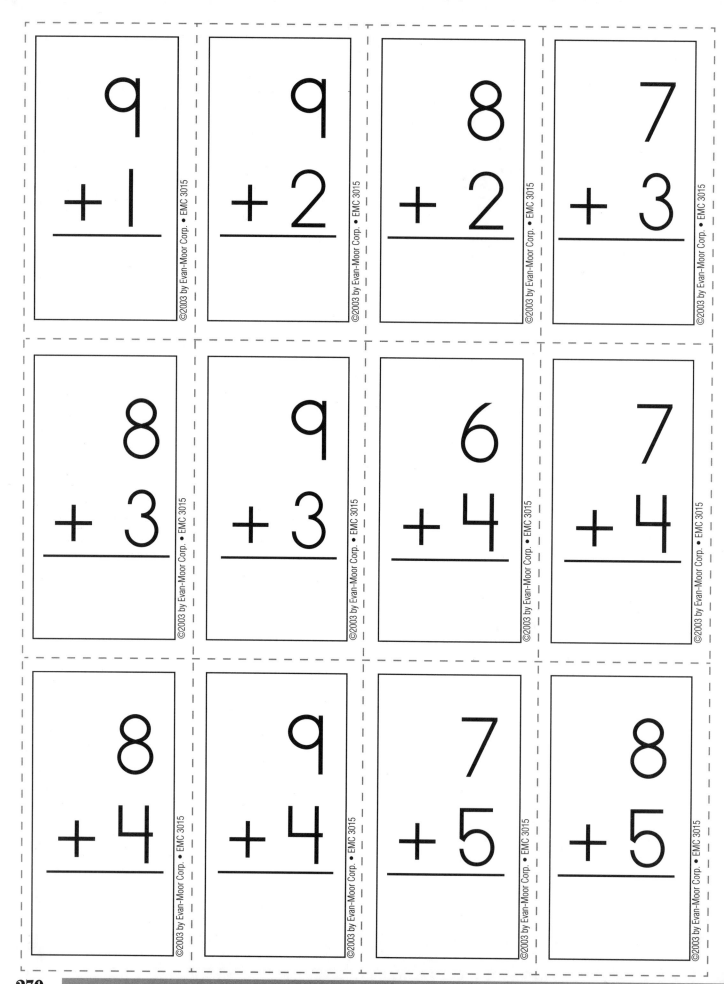

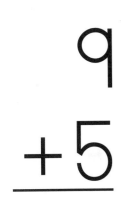

$$\begin{array}{r} 9 \\ +5 \\ \hline \end{array}$$

©2003 by Evan-Moor Corp. • EMC 3015

$$\begin{array}{r} 8 \\ +6 \\ \hline \end{array}$$

©2003 by Evan-Moor Corp. • EMC 3015

$$\begin{array}{r} 5 \\ +5 \\ \hline \end{array}$$

©2003 by Evan-Moor Corp. • EMC 3015

$$\begin{array}{r} 6 \\ +5 \\ \hline \end{array}$$

©2003 by Evan-Moor Corp. • EMC 3015

$$\begin{array}{r} 4 \\ +6 \\ \hline \end{array}$$

©2003 by Evan-Moor Corp. • EMC 3015

$$\begin{array}{r} 5 \\ +6 \\ \hline \end{array}$$

©2003 by Evan-Moor Corp. • EMC 3015

$$\begin{array}{r} 6 \\ +6 \\ \hline \end{array}$$

©2003 by Evan-Moor Corp. • EMC 3015

$$\begin{array}{r} 7 \\ +6 \\ \hline \end{array}$$

©2003 by Evan-Moor Corp. • EMC 3015

$$\begin{array}{r} 9 \\ +6 \\ \hline \end{array}$$

©2003 by Evan-Moor Corp. • EMC 3015

$$\begin{array}{r} 7 \\ +7 \\ \hline \end{array}$$

©2003 by Evan-Moor Corp. • EMC 3015

$$\begin{array}{r} 6 \\ +7 \\ \hline \end{array}$$

©2003 by Evan-Moor Corp. • EMC 3015

$$\begin{array}{r} 8 \\ +7 \\ \hline \end{array}$$

©2003 by Evan-Moor Corp. • EMC 3015

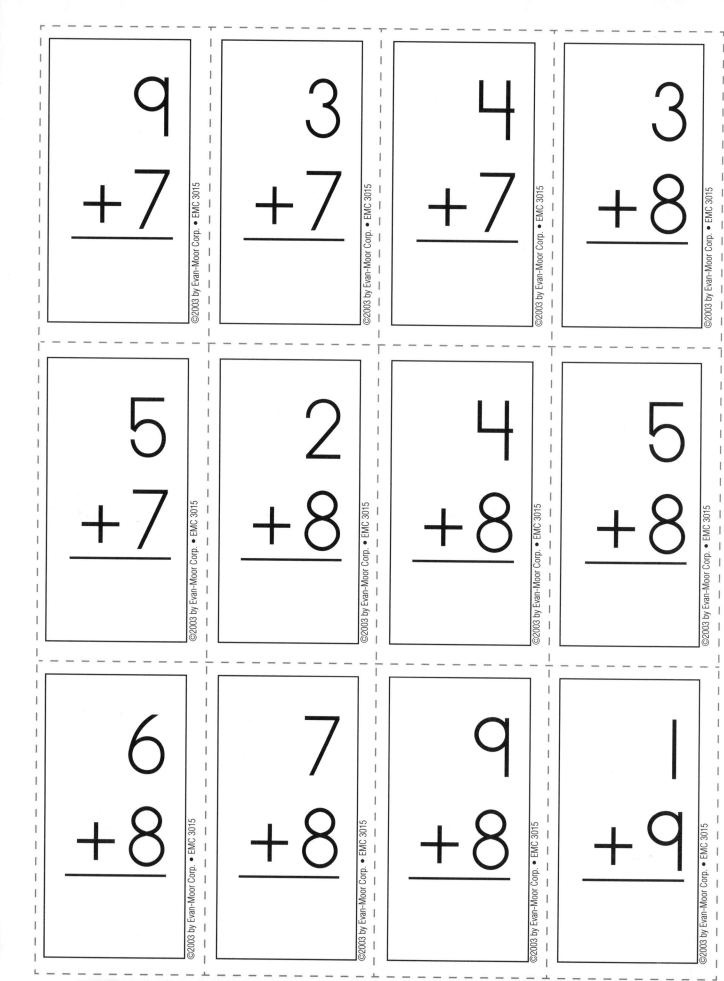

$$\begin{array}{r} 9 \\ +7 \\ \hline \end{array}$$

$$\begin{array}{r} 3 \\ +7 \\ \hline \end{array}$$

$$\begin{array}{r} 4 \\ +7 \\ \hline \end{array}$$

$$\begin{array}{r} 3 \\ +8 \\ \hline \end{array}$$

$$\begin{array}{r} 5 \\ +7 \\ \hline \end{array}$$

$$\begin{array}{r} 2 \\ +8 \\ \hline \end{array}$$

$$\begin{array}{r} 4 \\ +8 \\ \hline \end{array}$$

$$\begin{array}{r} 5 \\ +8 \\ \hline \end{array}$$

$$\begin{array}{r} 6 \\ +8 \\ \hline \end{array}$$

$$\begin{array}{r} 7 \\ +8 \\ \hline \end{array}$$

$$\begin{array}{r} 9 \\ +8 \\ \hline \end{array}$$

$$\begin{array}{r} 1 \\ +9 \\ \hline \end{array}$$

©2003 by Evan-Moor Corp. • EMC 3015

$$\begin{array}{r} 2 \\ +\,9 \\ \hline \end{array}$$ ©2003 by Evan-Moor Corp. • EMC 3015

$$\begin{array}{r} 3 \\ +\,9 \\ \hline \end{array}$$ ©2003 by Evan-Moor Corp. • EMC 3015

$$\begin{array}{r} 4 \\ +\,9 \\ \hline \end{array}$$ ©2003 by Evan-Moor Corp. • EMC 3015

$$\begin{array}{r} 5 \\ +\,9 \\ \hline \end{array}$$ ©2003 by Evan-Moor Corp. • EMC 3015

$$\begin{array}{r} 6 \\ +\,9 \\ \hline \end{array}$$ ©2003 by Evan-Moor Corp. • EMC 3015

$$\begin{array}{r} 7 \\ +\,9 \\ \hline \end{array}$$ ©2003 by Evan-Moor Corp. • EMC 3015

$$\begin{array}{r} 8 \\ +\,9 \\ \hline \end{array}$$ ©2003 by Evan-Moor Corp. • EMC 3015

$$\begin{array}{r} 9 \\ +\,9 \\ \hline \end{array}$$ ©2003 by Evan-Moor Corp. • EMC 3015

$$\begin{array}{r} 10 \\ +\,5 \\ \hline \end{array}$$ ©2003 by Evan-Moor Corp. • EMC 3015

$$\begin{array}{r} 10 \\ +\,0 \\ \hline \end{array}$$ ©2003 by Evan-Moor Corp. • EMC 3015

$$\begin{array}{r} 10 \\ +\,9 \\ \hline \end{array}$$ ©2003 by Evan-Moor Corp. • EMC 3015

$$\begin{array}{r} 10 \\ +\,10 \\ \hline \end{array}$$ ©2003 by Evan-Moor Corp. • EMC 3015

18	17	16	15
$-\ 9$	$-\ 9$	$-\ 9$	$-\ 9$

14	13	12	11
$-\ 9$	$-\ 9$	$-\ 9$	$-\ 9$

10	17	16	15
$-\ 9$	$-\ 8$	$-\ 8$	$-\ 8$

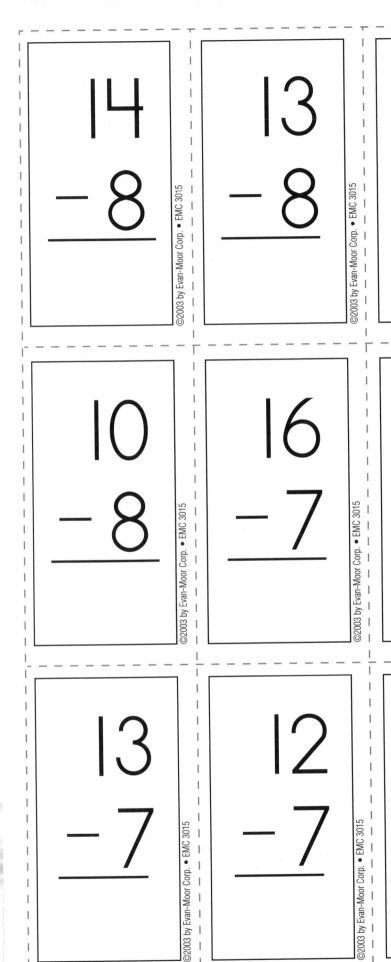

14
− 8
———
©2003 by Evan-Moor Corp. • EMC 3015

13
− 8
———
©2003 by Evan-Moor Corp. • EMC 3015

12
− 8
———
©2003 by Evan-Moor Corp. • EMC 3015

11
− 8
———
©2003 by Evan-Moor Corp. • EMC 3015

10
− 8
———
©2003 by Evan-Moor Corp. • EMC 3015

16
− 7
———
©2003 by Evan-Moor Corp. • EMC 3015

15
− 7
———
©2003 by Evan-Moor Corp. • EMC 3015

14
− 7
———
©2003 by Evan-Moor Corp. • EMC 3015

13
− 7
———
©2003 by Evan-Moor Corp. • EMC 3015

12
− 7
———
©2003 by Evan-Moor Corp. • EMC 3015

11
− 7
———
©2003 by Evan-Moor Corp. • EMC 3015

10
− 7
———
©2003 by Evan-Moor Corp. • EMC 3015

15	14	13	12
− 6	− 6	− 6	− 6

11	10	14	13
− 6	− 6	− 5	− 5

12	11	10	13
− 5	− 5	− 5	− 4

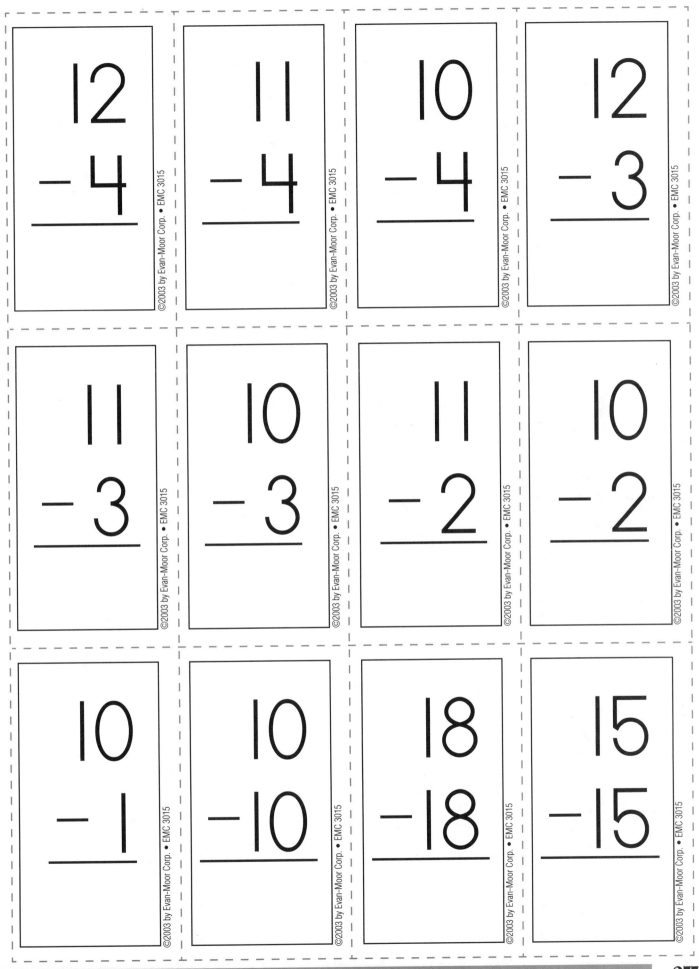

Practice Cards

$$\begin{array}{r} 1 \\ \times 2 \\ \hline \end{array}$$

$$\begin{array}{r} 2 \\ \times 2 \\ \hline \end{array}$$

$$\begin{array}{r} 3 \\ \times 2 \\ \hline \end{array}$$

$$\begin{array}{r} 4 \\ \times 2 \\ \hline \end{array}$$

$$\begin{array}{r} 5 \\ \times 2 \\ \hline \end{array}$$

$$\begin{array}{r} 6 \\ \times 2 \\ \hline \end{array}$$

$$\begin{array}{r} 7 \\ \times 2 \\ \hline \end{array}$$

$$\begin{array}{r} 8 \\ \times 2 \\ \hline \end{array}$$

$$\begin{array}{r} 9 \\ \times 2 \\ \hline \end{array}$$

$$\begin{array}{r} 1 \\ \times 5 \\ \hline \end{array}$$

$$\begin{array}{r} 2 \\ \times 5 \\ \hline \end{array}$$

$$\begin{array}{r} 3 \\ \times 5 \\ \hline \end{array}$$

$$\begin{array}{r} 4 \\ \times 5 \\ \hline \end{array}$$

$$\begin{array}{r} 5 \\ \times 5 \\ \hline \end{array}$$

$$\begin{array}{r} 6 \\ \times 5 \\ \hline \end{array}$$

$$\begin{array}{r} 7 \\ \times 5 \\ \hline \end{array}$$

$$\begin{array}{r} 8 \\ \times 5 \\ \hline \end{array}$$

$$\begin{array}{r} 9 \\ \times 5 \\ \hline \end{array}$$

$$\begin{array}{r} 10 \\ \times 3 \\ \hline \end{array}$$

$$\begin{array}{r} 10 \\ \times 4 \\ \hline \end{array}$$

$$\begin{array}{r} 10 \\ \times 5 \\ \hline \end{array}$$

$$\begin{array}{r} 10 \\ \times 6 \\ \hline \end{array}$$

$$\begin{array}{r} 10 \\ \times 7 \\ \hline \end{array}$$

$$\begin{array}{r} 10 \\ \times 8 \\ \hline \end{array}$$

Answer Key

Number & Operations

Page 5

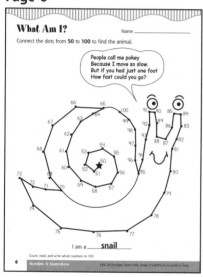

100 Puzzle Name _____

1	2	3	4	5	6	7	8	9	10
11	12	13	14	15	16	17	18	19	20
21	22	23	24	25	26	27	28	29	30
31	32	33	34	35	36	37	38	39	40
41	42	43	44	45	46	47	48	49	50
51	52	53	54	55	56	57	58	59	60
61	62	63	64	65	66	67	68	69	70
71	72	73	74	75	76	77	78	79	80
81	82	83	84	85	86	87	88	89	90
91	92	93	94	95	96	97	98	99	100

Count, read, and write whole numbers to 100

Page 6

What Am I? Name _____

Connect the dots from **50** to **100** to find the animal.

People call me pokey
Because I move so slow.
But if you had just one foot
How fast could you go?

I am a __snail__

Count, read, and write whole numbers to 100

Page 7

In-between	After	Before
50 <u>51</u> 52	37 <u>38</u>	<u>66</u> 67
26 <u>27</u> 28	69 <u>70</u>	<u>36</u> 37
82 <u>83</u> 84	56 <u>57</u>	<u>53</u> 54
37 <u>38</u> 39	30 <u>31</u>	<u>48</u> 49
29 <u>30</u> 31	49 <u>50</u>	<u>18</u> 19
42 <u>43</u> 44	57 <u>58</u>	<u>69</u> 70
39 <u>40</u> 41	70 <u>71</u>	<u>87</u> 88
68 <u>69</u> 70	89 <u>90</u>	<u>68</u> 69
59 <u>60</u> 61	53 <u>54</u>	<u>19</u> 20
92 <u>93</u> 94	19 <u>20</u>	<u>99</u> 100

Page 8

1. 11, 12, 13, 14, 15, 16
2. 30, 40, 50, 60, 70, 80
3. 77, 78, 79, 80, 81, 82
4. 52, 53, 54, 55, 56, 57
5. 16, 27, 35, 44, 59, 68
6. 57, 63, 76, 82, 98, 100

Page 9

1. 60 paper clips
2. 35 crayons
3. Answers will vary.

Page 10

1. D
2. B
3. D
4. C
5. D
6. A
7. D
8. A
9. B
10. C

Page 11

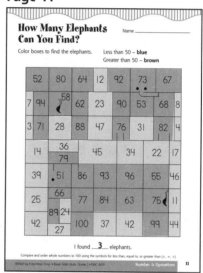

How Many Elephants Can You Find? Name _____

Color boxes to find the elephants.   Less than 50 – **blue**
Greater than 50 – **brown**

I found __3__ elephants.

Compare and order whole numbers to 100 using the symbols for less than, equal to, or greater than (<, =, >)

Page 12

1. 12 > 8
2. 15 > 10
3. 36 > 29
4. 27 < 75
5. 30 = 30
6. 41 > 26
7. 74 < 75
8. 88 > 59
9. 65 < 95
10. 46 > 32

Page 13

1. Jamal > Tyrone
2. Arthur < Max
3. Sara > Miyeko
4. Sara + Miyeko < Max
5. Tyrone < Mieyko + Arthur
6. Miyeko + Tyrone > Arthur

EMC 3015 • Basic Math Skills, Grade 2 • ©2003 by Evan-Moor Corp.

Page 14

1. 3 < 8   9 > 4   7 > 5
2. 40 > 20   50 > 20   60 > 30
3. 46 > 26   62 > 32   28 > 18
4. 63 < 68   49 = 49   32 < 37
5. 59 < 61   27 < 32   44 < 63
6. 95 > 67   83 > 69   72 < 91

41   59   68   72

Page 15

Answers will vary.

Page 16

1. D	6. B
2. D	7. C
3. C	8. D
4. B	9. A
5. A	10. C

Page 17

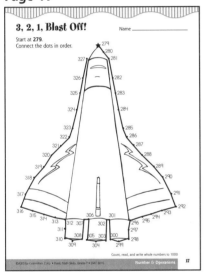

3, 2, 1, Blast Off!

Start at 279.
Connect the dots in order.

Page 18

100   200   300
400   500   600
700   800   900   1,000

100   <u>200</u>   300   <u>400</u>
700   <u>800</u>   900   <u>1,000</u>
400   <u>500</u>   500   <u>600</u>
200   <u>300</u>   800   <u>900</u>
600   <u>700</u>

Page 19

100	110	120	130	140	150	160	170	180	190	
200	210	220	230	240	250	260	270	280	290	
300	310	320	330	340	350	360	370	380	390	
400	410	420	430	440	450	460	470	480	490	
500	510	520	530	540	550	560	570	580	590	
600	610	620	630	640	650	660	670	680	690	
700	710	720	730	740	750	760	770	780	790	
800	810	820	830	840	850	860	870	880	890	
900	910	920	930	940	950	960	970	980	990	1,000

200	201	202	203	204	205	206	207	208	209
450	451	452	453	454	455	456	457	458	459
893	894	895	896	897	898	899	900	901	902

Page 20

1. 134 <u>135</u> 136	11. 515 <u>516</u> 517
2. 301 <u>302</u> 303	12. 222 <u>223</u> 224
3. 645 <u>646</u> 647	13. 715 <u>716</u> 717
4. 578 <u>579</u> 580	14. 600 <u>601</u> 602
5. 832 <u>833</u> 834	15. 256 <u>257</u> 258
6. 327 <u>328</u> 329	16. 483 <u>484</u> 485
7. 161 <u>162</u> 163	17. 720 <u>721</u> 722
8. 929 <u>930</u> 931	18. 900 <u>901</u> 902
9. 499 <u>500</u> 501	19. 199 <u>200</u> 201
10. 800 <u>801</u> 802	20. 998 <u>999</u> 1,000

Page 21

126	247	369
484	500	692
718	835	991

Page 22

1. D	6. A
2. B	7. B
3. D	8. A
4. C	9. D
5. D	10. C

Page 23

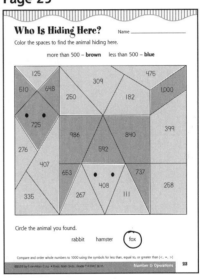

Who Is Hiding Here?

Color the spaces to find the animal hiding here.

more than 500 – **brown**   less than 500 – **blue**

Circle the animal you found.

rabbit   hamster   (fox)

Page 24

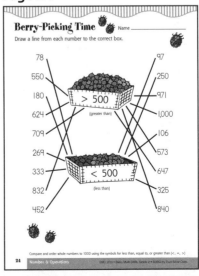

Berry-Picking Time

Draw a line from each number to the correct box.

Page 25

1. 15 < 50
2. 100 > 20
3. 96 < 250
4. 419 > 82

5. 76 < 79   100 > 80   112 < 115
6. 99 < 100   200 < 201   190 > 180
7. 342 < 399   410 > 400   777 > 766
8. 450 > 449   305 < 315   942 < 952
9. 700 < 800   580 > 570   191 < 911

Page 26

1. 90 = 90   400 > 40   200 > 100
2. 600 < 800   806 > 622   160 < 176
3. 243 < 460   329 < 519   999 > 781
4. 404 = 404   580 > 315   191 < 570
5. 708 > 449   952 > 800   315 < 911
6. 405 < 952   257 = 257   1,000 > 900
7. 9 − 0 = 5 + 4
8. 10 − 5 = 2 + 3
9. 2 + 8 > 5 + 3
10. 10 − 6 > 8 − 7

Page 27

1. 125 < 195   Hamid
2. 150 < 190   Kimiko and Yoshi
3. 298 > 295   Scott
4. 999 > 895   Elm Street School
5. 315 < 453
6. 247 = 247
7. Answers will vary.

Page 28

1. D   6. B
2. C   7. C
3. B   8. D
4. D   9. A
5. A   10. B

Page 29

1. 100 + 20 + 6 = 126 chickens
2. 300 + 10 + 9 = 319 chickens
3. 500 + 30 + 3 = 533 chickens
4. 200 + 70 + 4 = 274 chickens

Page 30

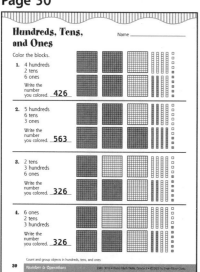

Page 31

1. 1 hundred 5 tens 6 ones, 156
2. 3 hundreds 4 tens 2 ones, 342
3. 2 hundreds 1 ten 9 ones, 219
4. 6 hundreds 3 tens 5 ones, 635

Page 32

1. 235   2. 324
3. 252   4. 468
5. 129   6. 603

Page 33

239

183

305

251

330

1. Domingo   4. Yoshi
2. Jacob   5. Alice
3. Tanisha

Page 34

1. C   6. B
2. B   7. B
3. C   8. C
4. C   9. A
5. D   10. D

Page 35

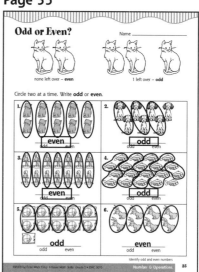

Page 36

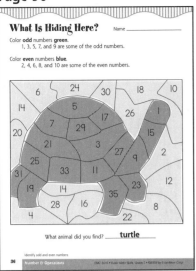

What Is Hiding Here? Name _____

Color **odd** numbers **green**.
1, 3, 5, 7, and 9 are some of the odd numbers.

Color **even** numbers **blue**.
2, 4, 6, 8, and 10 are some of the even numbers.

What animal did you find? **turtle**

Page 37

Boxed: 0 2 4 6 8 10 12

Circled: 1 3 5 7 9 11

0	2	4	6	8
10	12	14	16	18
20	22	24	26	28
30				

1	3	5	7	9
11	13	15	17	19
21	23	25	27	29

Page 38

Circled: 17 9 25 23 29

Boxed: 6 8 12 14 30

50 52 54 56 58 60
66 68 70 72 74 76

79 81 83 85 87 89
51 53 55 57 59 61

Page 39

Answers will vary.

Page 40

1. A	6. D
2. D	7. C
3. B	8. B
4. D	9. A
5. C	10. D

Page 41

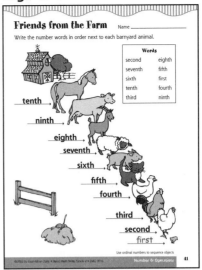

Friends from the Farm Name _____

Write the number words in order next to each barnyard animal.

Words
second, eighth, seventh, fifth, sixth, first, tenth, fourth, third, ninth

tenth
ninth
eighth
seventh
sixth
fifth
fourth
third
second
first

Page 42

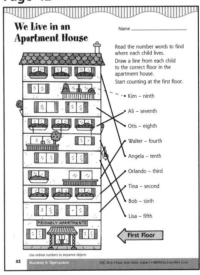

We Live in an Apartment House Name _____

Read the number words to find where each child lives.

Draw a line from each child to the correct floor in the apartment house. Start counting at the first floor.

- Kim – ninth
- Ali – seventh
- Otis – eighth
- Walter – fourth
- Angela – tenth
- Orlando – third
- Tina – second
- Bob – sixth
- Lisa – fifth

First Floor

Page 43

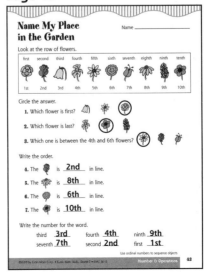

Name My Place in the Garden Name _____

Look at the row of flowers.

first, second, third, fourth, fifth, sixth, seventh, eighth, ninth, tenth
1st, 2nd, 3rd, 4th, 5th, 6th, 7th, 8th, 9th, 10th

Circle the answer.

1. Which flower is first?
2. Which flower is last?
3. Which one is between the 4th and 6th flowers?

Write the order.

4. The 🌹 is **2nd** in line.
5. The 🌼 is **8th** in line.
6. The 🌻 is **6th** in line.
7. The 🌺 is **10th** in line.

Write the number for the word.

third **3rd**   fourth **4th**   ninth **9th**
seventh **7th**   second **2nd**   first **1st**

Page 44

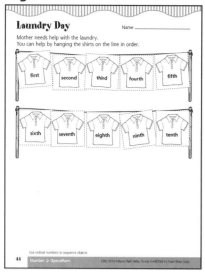

Page 45

Answers will vary.

Page 46

1. D
2. C
3. C
4. A
5. B
6. C
7. B
8. C
9. B
10. C

Page 47

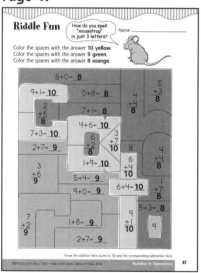

Page 48

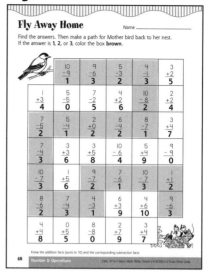

Page 49

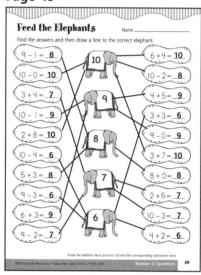

Page 50

1. 3	1	8	3	4	3	4	10
2. 6	10	2	10	5	0	9	7
3. 4	5	9	10	7	6	9	3
4. 5	1	6	2	8	6	6	4
5. 7	6	9	2	8	2	9	10

Page 51

1. 9 pumpkins, add
2. 4 baskets of beans, subtract
3. 8 carrots, add
4. 9 heads of cabbage, add
5. 4 ears of corn, subtract
6. 6 vegetables, add
7. Answers will vary.

Page 52

1. B
2. C
3. D
4. D
5. D
6. C
7. C
8. D
9. B
10. C

Page 53

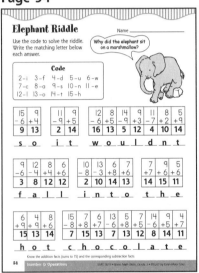

Page 54

Page 55

1. 12   9   9   11   9   ~~15~~
2. 12   3   11 ~~15~~ ~~15~~ 4   11 12
3. 8   5   4 ~~15~~ 12 7   8 13
4. 7   8 ~~15~~ ~~15~~ 11 5   7 14
5. 6 14 ~~15~~ 6   12 3   8   9
6.   ~~15~~ 14 14 7   5   6

Page 56

1. 4 (13) 10 12 9 (13) 6 5
2. (14) 11 15 8 10 (14) 7 3
3. 15 6 (7) 9 13 (7) 14 4
5. 6 5 (13) 11 8 15 (13) 4

Page 57

1. 15 − 6 = 9
   9 more small rocks
2. 4 + 9 = 13
   13 baseball cards
3. 15 − 9 = 6
   6 more stickers
4. 4 + 6 = 10
   10 stamps
5. 7 + 8 = 15
   15 children
6. 11 − 3 = 8
   8 model cars
7. Answers will vary.

Page 58

1. B   6. A
2. D   7. C
3. C   8. D
4. A   9. D
5. C   10. B

Page 59

1. 8 doughnuts   2. 2 pies   3. 5 cupcakes
4. 3 gingerbread   5. 6 chocolate   6. 0 sugar
   boys   cookies   cookies
7. 8 sold   8. 12 sold
9. 3 sold   10. 4 sold
11. 8 sold   12. 8 sold

Page 60

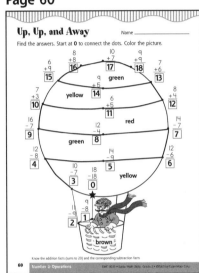

Page 61

1. 18 14 7 6 13 7 4 10
2. 13 9 8 14 8 12 6 11
3. 16 9 9 14 9 9 16 12
4. 8 12 6 15 13 7 6 12
5. 6 17 10 13 11 16 13 14

Page 62

Add 9	Add 8	Add 7
18	16	12
14	13	14
17	15	16
16	17	11
13	14	15
15	12	13

Subtract 9	Subtract 8	Subtract 7
9	9	4
5	4	7
7	7	5
4	6	9
6	5	8
8	8	6

Page 63

1. 5 animals, add
2. 13 carrot bits, add
3. 10 boys, subtract
4. 6 cans of food, add
5. 6 more children, subtract
6. 8 had more pets, subtract
7. Answers will vary.

Page 64

1. D
2. C
3. B
4. C
5. C
6. B
7. A
8. C
9. D
10. C

Page 65

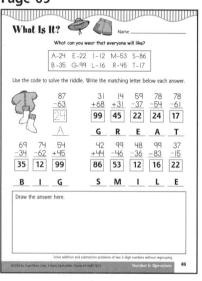

Page 66

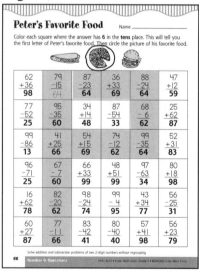

Page 67

1.	–	+	+
2.	–	–	+
3.	–	–	+
4.	+	–	–
5.	+	–	–
6.	+	–	–
7.	–	+	–
8.	+	+	+
9.	+	–	+
10.	+	–	+

Page 68

Page 69

1. 38 marbles
   26 + 12 = 38
2. 12 more marbles
   48 – 36 = 12
3. 69 marbles
   23 + 23 + 23 = 69
4. 59 marbles
   35 + 24 = 59
5. 14 more small marbles
   38 – 24 = 14
6. less
   12 + 15 = 27
7. Answers will vary.

Page 70

1. C
2. A
3. B
4. D
5. C
6. B
7. A
8. D
9. B
10. D

EMC 3015 • Basic Math Skills, Grade 2 • ©2003 by Evan-Moor Corp.

Page 71

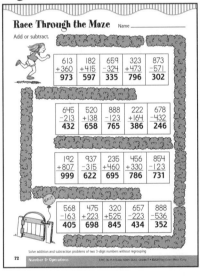

Riddle Time

When is an old car like a baby?

412–a	378–h	897–l	779–r
129–e	303–t	339–n	999–s
	768–t	533–w	

Use the code to solve the riddle. Write the matching letter below each answer.

433 +100 **533**	226 +152 **378**	659 −530 **129**	126 +213 **339**		828 −525 **303**	645 +123 **768**
w	h	e	n		i	t

699 −321 **378**	646 −234 **412**	594 +405 **999**		879 −467 **412**
h	a	s		a

274 +505 **779**	202 +210 **412**	999 −231 **768**	263 +505 **768**	684 +213 **897**	739 −610 **129**
r	a	t	t	l	e

Solve addition and subtraction problems of two 3-digit numbers without regrouping

Page 72

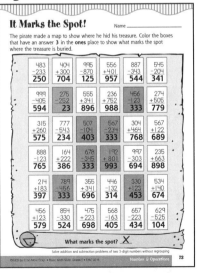

Race Through the Maze

Add or subtract.

613 +360 **973**	182 +415 **597**	659 −324 **335**	323 +473 **796**	873 −571 **302**
645 −213 **432**	520 +138 **658**	888 −123 **765**	222 +164 **386**	678 −432 **246**
192 +807 **999**	937 −315 **622**	235 +460 **695**	456 +330 **786**	854 −123 **731**
568 −163 **405**	475 +223 **698**	320 +525 **845**	657 −223 **434**	888 −536 **352**

Solve addition and subtraction problems of two 3-digit numbers without regrouping

Page 73

It Marks the Spot!

The pirate made a map to show where he hid his treasure. Color the boxes that have an answer **3** in the **ones** place to show what marks the spot where the treasure is buried.

483 −233 **250**	404 +300 **704**	995 −870 **125**	556 +401 **957**	887 −343 **544**	545 −204 **341**
999 −405 **594**	275 −252 **23**	555 +341 **896**	236 +752 **988**	456 −123 **333**	274 +505 **779**
315 +260 **575**	777 −543 **234**	507 −104 **403**	567 −234 **333**	304 +464 **768**	567 +122 **689**
888 −123 **765**	164 +222 **386**	678 −345 **333**	192 +801 **993**	997 −303 **694**	235 +663 **898**
214 +183 **397**	789 −456 **333**	355 +341 **696**	446 −132 **314**	330 +123 **453**	534 +140 **674**
456 +123 **579**	854 −330 **524**	475 +223 **698**	568 −163 **405**	657 −223 **434**	629 −525 **104**

What marks the spot? **X**

Solve addition and subtraction problems of two 3-digit numbers without regrouping

Page 74

224	331	778	332	598
955	877	80	531	324
487	599	17	242	596
402	399	612	826	320

Page 75

1. $7.40   2. $2.65   3. $8.14
4. $5.53   5. $9.30   6. Answers will vary.

Page 76

1. C   6. A
2. D   7. C
3. C   8. C
4. B   9. B
5. B   10. A

Page 77

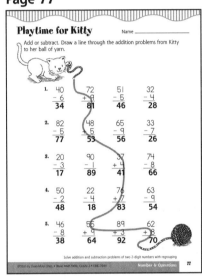

Playtime for Kitty

Add or subtract. Draw a line through the addition problems from Kitty to her ball of yarn.

1. 40 −6 **34**   72 +9 **81**   51 −5 **46**   32 −4 **28**
2. 82 −5 **77**   48 +5 **53**   65 −9 **56**   33 −7 **26**
3. 20 −3 **17**   90 −1 **89**   37 +4 **41**   74 −8 **66**
4. 50 −2 **48**   22 −4 **18**   76 +7 **83**   63 −9 **54**
5. 46 −8 **38**   55 +9 **64**   89 +3 **92**   62 +8 **70**

Solve addition and subtraction problems of two 2-digit numbers with regrouping

Page 78

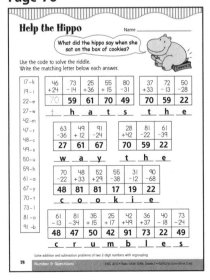

Help the Hippo

What did the hippo say when she sat on the box of cookies?

Use the code to solve the riddle. Write the matching letter below each answer.

17–k	19–i	22–e	27–w	42–m	47–r	48–c	49–s	50–u	59–h	61–a	67–y	70–t	73–l	81–o	91–b

46 +24 **70**	73 −14 **59**	25 +36 **61**	55 +15 **70**	80 −31 **49**		37 +33 **70**	72 −13 **59**	50 −28 **22**
h	a	t	s		t	h	e

63 −36 **27**	49 +12 **61**	91 −24 **67**		28 +42 **70**	81 −22 **59**	61 −39 **22**
w	a	y		t	h	e

70 −22 **48**	48 +33 **81**	52 +29 **81**	55 −38 **17**	31 −12 **19**	90 −68 **22**
c	o	o	k	i	e

61 −13 **48**	81 −34 **47**	35 +15 **50**	25 +17 **42**	42 +49 **91**	36 +37 **73**	40 −18 **22**	73 −24 **49**
c	r	u	m	b	l	e	s

Solve addition and subtraction problems of two 2-digit numbers with regrouping

Page 79

81	63	30	48	96	38	85	21
14	45	12	5	57	49	27	38

Page 80

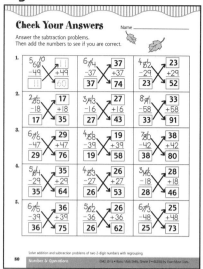

Check Your Answers

Answer the subtraction problems.
Then add the numbers to see if you are correct.

Solve addition and subtraction problems of two 2-digit numbers with regrouping

Page 81

1. 95 miles
2. 66 miles
3. 29 miles
4. Answers will vary.

Page 82

1. C   6. B
2. B   7. A
3. A   8. D
4. C   9. C
5. C   10. D

Page 83

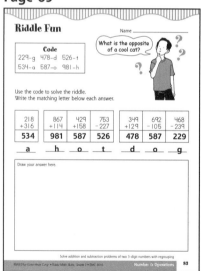

Riddle Fun

Code
229-g   478-d   526-t
534-a   587-o   981-h

What is the opposite of a cool cat?

Use the code to solve the riddle.
Write the matching letter below each answer.

218 +316	867 +114	429 +158	753 -227		349 +129	692 -105	468 -239
534	**981**	**587**	**526**		**478**	**587**	**229**
a	h	o	t		d	o	g

Draw your answer here.

Solve addition and subtraction problems of two 3-digit numbers with regrouping

Page 84

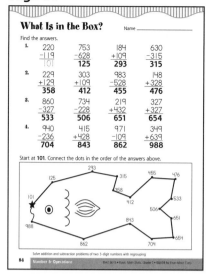

What Is in the Box?

Find the answers.

1. 220 -119 **101**   753 -628 **125**   184 +109 **293**   630 -315 **315**
2. 229 +129 **358**   303 +109 **412**   983 -528 **455**   148 +328 **476**
3. 860 -327 **533**   734 -228 **506**   219 +432 **651**   327 +327 **654**
4. 940 -236 **704**   415 +428 **843**   971 -109 **862**   349 +639 **988**

Start at **101**. Connect the dots in the order of the answers above.

Solve addition and subtraction problems of two 3-digit numbers with regrouping

Page 85

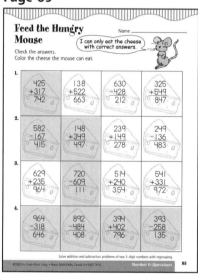

Feed the Hungry Mouse

I can only eat the cheese with correct answers.

Check the answers.
Color the cheese the mouse can eat.

1. 425 +317 **742**   138 +522 **663**   630 -428 **212**   325 +549 **847**
2. 582 -167 **415**   148 +349 **497**   239 +149 **278**   249 -136 **483**
3. 629 +235 **964**   720 -609 **111**   514 +240 **354**   541 +331 **972**
4. 964 -318 **646**   892 -484 **408**   394 +402 **796**   393 -258 **135**

Solve addition and subtraction problems of two 3-digit numbers with regrouping

Page 86

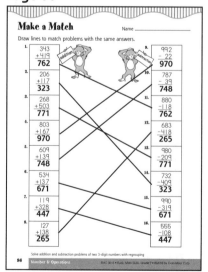

Make a Match

Draw lines to match problems with the same answers.

1. 343 +419 **762**
2. 206 +117 **323**
3. 268 +503 **771**
4. 803 +167 **970**
5. 609 +139 **748**
6. 534 +137 **671**
7. 119 +328 **447**
8. 127 +138 **265**

9. 992 -22 **970**
10. 787 -39 **748**
11. 880 -118 **762**
12. 683 -418 **265**
13. 980 -209 **771**
14. 732 -409 **323**
15. 990 -319 **671**
16. 555 -108 **447**

Solve addition and subtraction problems of two 3-digit numbers with regrouping

EMC 3015 • Basic Math Skills, Grade 2 • ©2003 by Evan-Moor Corp.

Page 87

1. $3.92
2. $8.17
3. $3.81
4. $1.18
5. $1.23
6. $4.28
7. Answers will vary.

Page 88

1. B
2. D
3. C
4. D
5. B
6. B
7. A
8. B
9. D
10. C

Page 89

Page 90

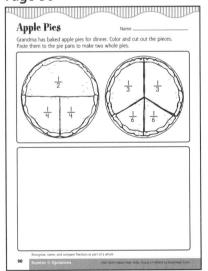

Page 91

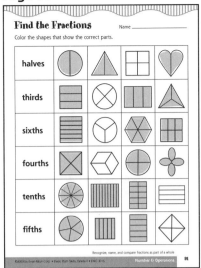

Page 92

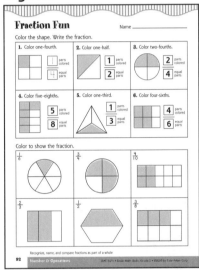

Page 93

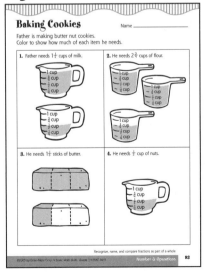

Page 94

1. D
2. B
3. D
4. C
5. C
6. D
7. A
8. C
9. D
10. C

Page 95

1. 6 berries in each bowl
2. 4 berries in each bowl

Page 96

1. 1 colored ladybug
2. 4 colored ladybugs
3. 2 colored ladybugs
4. 3 colored ladybugs
5. 6 colored ladybugs
6. 4 colored ladybugs

Numbers 2 & 6 should be circled.

Page 97

1. 2 colored octopuses
2. 1 colored sea star
3. 1 colored fish
4. 3 colored crabs
5. 4 colored hermit crabs
6. 5 colored snails

Page 98

$\frac{1}{2}$ $\frac{1}{3}$ $\frac{1}{5}$

$\frac{1}{2}$ $\frac{1}{4}$ $\frac{1}{3}$

$\frac{2}{3}$ $\frac{4}{8}$ $\frac{1}{12}$

Page 99

1. 3 cookies colored
2. 6 balls colored
3. 4 mice colored
4. 6 cookies in each bag
5. 1 apple in one basket, 2 apples in the other basket
6. 4 goldfish in big bowl, 2 goldfish in each small bowl

Page 100

1. B
2. C
3. A
4. D
5. A
6. C
7. C
8. D
9. C
10. B

Page 101

Page 102

The coins circled will vary, but must equal the cost.
1. 65¢
2. 70¢
3. 90¢

Page 103

1. 10   20   21   22   23   23¢
2. 10   20   30   40   50   50¢
3. 10   20   30   35   40   40¢
4. 25   50   60   65   66   66¢
5. 25   50   75   80   81   82   82¢
6. 25   30   35   40   41   42   42¢
7. Otis
8. Tanya

Page 104

1. circle 1 nickel and 1 penny
2. circle 1 nickel and 1 dime
3. circle 2 pennies
4. circle 3 pennies
5. circle 1 nickel

Page 105

1. yes 15¢ > 14¢
2. yes 18¢ = 18¢
3. no 14¢ < 16¢
4. no 18¢ < 20¢
5. no 10¢ < 12¢
6. yes 25¢ = 25¢
7. Answers will vary.

Page 106

1. B
2. C
3. C
4. D
5. C
6. B
7. D
8. C
9. B
10. C

Page 107

Making One Dollar

There are 100 pennies or 100¢ in $1.00.
Count to find out how many other coins equal $1.00.

Count nickels.	$ .05	$ .10	$ .15	$ .20	$ .25
	$ .30	$ .35	$ .40	$ .45	$ .50
	$ .55	$ .60	$ .65	$ .70	$ .75
	$ .80	$ .85	$ .90	$ .95	$ 1.00
	$ .10	$ .20	$ .30	$ .40	$ .50
	$ .60	$ .70	$ .80	$ .90	$ 1.00
	$ .25	$ .50	$ .75	$ 1.00	
	$ .50	$ 1.00			

How many   in $1.00? 20   How many   in $1.00? 4

How many   in $1.00? 10   How many   in $1.00? 2

Page 108

ice-cream cone	$0.15
wagon	$1.40
star	$0.80
clown	$0.65
house	$1.80
kite	$0.40

Page 109

Answers will vary, but must equal the correct amount.

Page 110

Page 111

1. $1.16
2. $1.65
3. $1.75
4. $2.55
5. $3.95

Page 112

1. D   6. A
2. C   7. C
3. C   8. B
4. D   9. B
5. D   10. B

Page 113

5	10	15	20	25	30	35	40	45	50
55	60	65	70	75	80	85	90	95	

10	20	30	40	50	60	70	80	90

2	4	6	8	10	12	14	16	18

Page 114

Page 115

Page 116

Written answers will vary, but must be logical.
1. 8 legs, counted by 2s
2. 30 legs, counted by 10s
3. 45 legs, counted by 5s

Page 117

Pictures will vary, but must represent the problem.
1. 30 ears of corn
2. 40 tomatoes
3. 16 squash
4. Answers will vary.

Page 118

1. D   6. C
3. A   7. D
3. B   8. C
4. A   9. A
5. C   10. D

Page 119

1. 2 + 2 + 2 = 6
   3 twos = 6
2. 5 + 5 = 10
   2 fives = 10
3. 2 + 2 + 2 + 2 + 2 + 2 = 12
   6 twos = 12
4. 5 + 5 + 5 = 15
   3 fives = 15

Page 120

1. 1 3 3   2. 3 5 15
3. 2 4 8   4. 5 2 10

Page 121

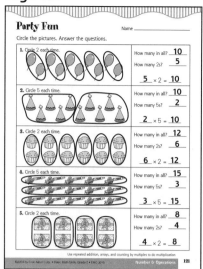

Page 122

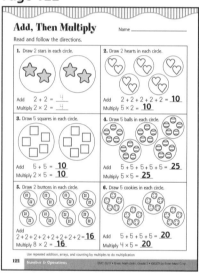

Page 123

1. 5 + 5 + 5 = 15   3 x 5 = 15
2. 5 + 5 + 5 + 5 + 5 = 25   5 x 5 = 25
3. 10 + 10 + 10 = 30   3 x 10 = 30
4. 2 + 2 + 2 + 2 + 2 + 2 = 12   6 x 2 = 12
5. Answers will vary.

Page 124

1. B   6. D
2. C   7. C
3. C   8. C
4. C   9. D
5. D   10. A

Page 125

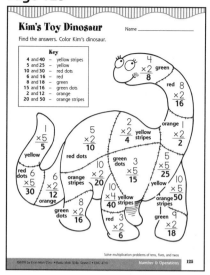

Page 126

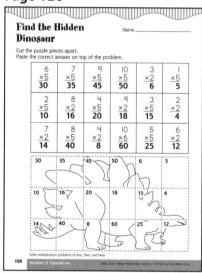

Page 127

0   2   4   6   8   10 12 14 16 18
6   4   16 0   10
8   2   12 14 18

0   5   10 15 20 25 30 35 40 45
25 10 45 15 35
0   20 40 5   30

0   10 20 30 40 50 60 70 80 90
30 10 50 0   80
40 20 90 70 60

EMC 3015 • Basic Math Skills, Grade 2 • ©2003 by Evan-Moor Corp.

Page 128

Page 134

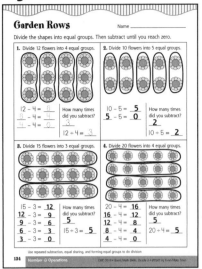

Page 129

X	2	5	10
1	2	5	10
2	4	10	20
3	6	15	30
4	8	20	40
5	10	25	50
6	12	30	60
7	14	35	70
8	16	40	80
9	18	45	90
10	20	50	100

Page 135

1. 5 fish
   $25 \div 5 = 5$
2. 9 tadpoles
   $45 \div 5 = 9$
3. 10 flowers
   $20 \div 2 = 10$

Page 136

1. C	6. C
2. A	7. C
3. A	8. B
4. B	9. A
5. C	10. A

Algebra

Page 138

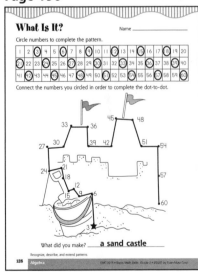

Page 130

1. D	6. C
2. A	7. B
3. C	8. D
4. B	9. A
5. A	10. D

Page 131

1. 3 sets of 2, 2 bananas
2. 4 sets of 3, 3 ears of corn
3. 2 sets of 4, 4 bundles of hay
4. 4 sets of 5, 5 fish

Page 132

Circles will vary, but must show the correct amount in each.
1. 4 in each group
2. 4 in each group
3. 8 in each group
4. 4 in each group
5. 12 in each group
6. 6 in each group

Page 133

1. 2 groups, 4 in each group
2. 4 groups, 2 in each group
3. 3 groups, 3 in each group
4. 8 groups, 2 in each group
5. 2 groups, 4 in each group, 1 left over
6. 3 groups, 3 in each group, 1 left over

Page 139

first ladder	second ladder	third ladder
12	17	27
14	15	24
16	13	21
18	11	18
20	9	15
22	7	9
24	5	6
26	3	3
28	1	

Page 140

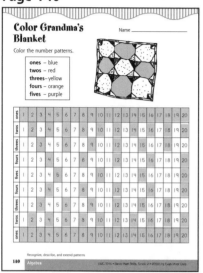

Page 141

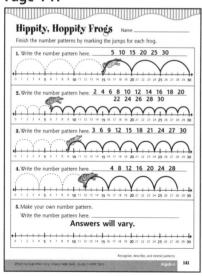

Page 142

1. 1   3   5   7   9   11   13   15
   rule +2

2. 15   13   11   9   7   5   3   1
   rule − 2

3. 1   6   5   10   9   14   13   18   17   22   21
   rule +5, − 1

Page 143

1. C   6. C
2. B   7. A
3. B   8. D
4. C   9. A
5. B   10. B

Page 144

1. 3 more
   1 + 3 = 4

2. 4 more
   2 + 4 = 6

3. 9 more
   1 + 9 = 10

4. 4 more
   3 + 4 = 7

Page 145

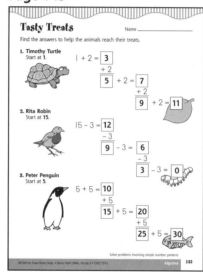

Page 146

Page 147

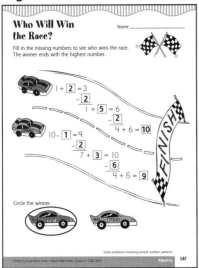

Page 148

1. 5 more
   7 + 5 = 12
2. 6 more
   9 + 6 = 15
3. 4 eggs
   12 − 8 = 4
4. 6 more
   3 + 6 = 9
5. Answers will vary.

Page 149

1. C
2. B
3. C
4. B
5. B
6. A
7. D
8. C
9. D
10. B

Page 150

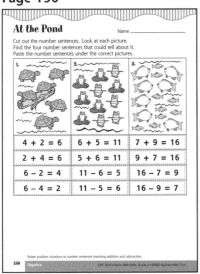

Page 151

1. 12 − 2 = 10
2. 12 − 8 = 4
3. 12 − 6 = 6
4. 12 − 3 = 9
5. 12 − 5 = 7
6. 12 − 7 = 5

Page 152

1. 9¢ + 3¢ = 12¢
2. 9¢ + 7¢ = 16¢
3. 8¢ + 9¢ = 17¢
4. 6¢ + 9¢ = 15¢
5. 10¢ + 10¢ = 20¢
6. 40¢ + 20¢ = 60¢
7. 30¢ + 30¢ = 60¢
8. 70¢ + 20¢ = 90¢

Page 153

Answers will vary, but should be logical.

Page 154

Answers will vary, but must reflect the stated task.

Page 155

1. D
2. B
3. A
4. B
5. C
6. B
7. B
8. C
9. D
10. D

Page 156

1. 6	6	8. 13	13
2. 12	12	9. 13	13
3. 14	14	10. 17	17
4. 15	15	11. 17	17
5. 13	13	12. 12	12
6. 12	12	13. 10	10
7. 22	22	14. 100	100
15. 10	10	18. 8	8
16. 30	30	19. 40	40
17. 6	6	20. 50	50

Page 157

1. 3 + 5 = 8   1 + 7 = 8
2. 11 + 2 = 13   6 + 7 = 13
3. 11 + 4 = 15   6 + 9 = 15
4. 10 + 5 = 15   7 + 8 = 15
5. 4 + 8 = 12   2 + 10 = 12
6. 14 + 5 = 19   9 + 10 = 19
7. 12 + 0 = 12   4 + 8 = 12
8. 4 x 5 = 20   2 x 10 = 20

Page 158

Written answers will vary, but must accurately explain the process the student followed.

1. 16
2. 12
3. 17
4. 13
5. 13
6. 18

Page 159

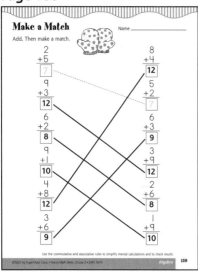

Make a Match

Add. Then make a match.

Name _____

2 +5 **7**	8 +4 **12**
9 +3 **12**	5 +2 **7**
6 +2 **8**	6 +3 **9**
9 +1 **10**	3 +9 **12**
4 +8 **12**	2 +6 **8**
3 +6 **9**	1 +9 **10**

Use the commutative and associative rules to simplify mental calculations and to check results

©2003 by Evan-Moor Corp. • Basic Math Skills, Grade 2 • EMC 3015   Algebra   159

Page 160

1. 6¢ + 10¢ = 16¢   1¢ + 15¢ = 16¢
2. 11¢ + 1¢ = 12¢   1¢ + 11¢ = 12¢
3. 5¢ + 30¢ = 35¢   30¢ + 5¢ = 35¢
4. 10¢ + 10¢ = 20¢
   5¢ + 15¢ = 20¢
5. 26¢ + 1¢ = 27¢
   25¢ + 2¢ = 27¢
6. 5¢ + 35¢ = 40¢
   15¢ + 25¢ = 40¢
7. 25¢ + 30¢ = 55¢
   30¢ + 25¢ = 55¢

Page 161

1. C   6. A
2. B   7. C
3. C   8. D
4. B   9. D
5. C   10. C

Geometry

Page 163

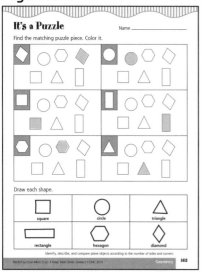

It's a Puzzle

Name _____

Find the matching puzzle piece. Color it.

Draw each shape.

square	circle	triangle
rectangle	hexagon	diamond

Identify, describe, and compare plane objects according to the number of sides and corners

©2003 by Evan-Moor Corp. • Basic Math Skills, Grade 2 • EMC 3015   Geometry   163

Page 164

an alarm clock

Page 165

1. square   2. triangle
   4 sides   3 sides
   4 corners   3 corners
3. circle   4. hexagon
   0 sides   6 sides
   0 corners   6 corners
5. rectangle   6. pentagon
   4 sides   5 sides
   4 corners   5 corners
7. 6 sides   8. 5 sides   9. 7 sides
   6 corners   5 corners   7 corners

Page 166

1–4. Pictures will vary, but must accurately reflect the description.

5. Answers will vary, but must explain that the shapes are alike because they have the same number of sides and corners, and different because their sides sare different lengths.

Page 167

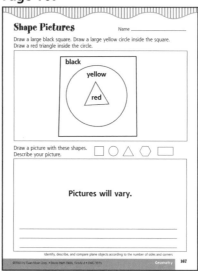

Shape Pictures

Name _____

Draw a large black square. Draw a large yellow circle inside the square. Draw a red triangle inside the circle.

black
yellow
red

Draw a picture with these shapes. Describe your picture.

Pictures will vary.

Identify, describe, and compare plane objects according to the number of sides and corners

©2003 by Evan-Moor Corp. • Basic Math Skills, Grade 2 • EMC 3015   Geometry   167

Page 168

1. C   6. C
2. A   7. A
3. B   8. C
4. D   9. A
5. B   10. C

Page 169

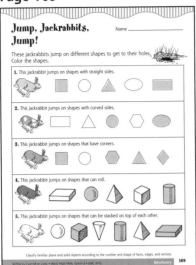

Page 170

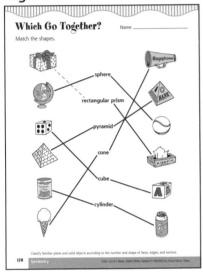

Page 171

sphere	cube	rectangular prism
globe	jack-in-the-box	gift box
soccer ball	crate	book
cone	**cylinder**	**pyramid**
ice-cream cone	can	rooftop
clown hat	glass	pyramid

Page 172

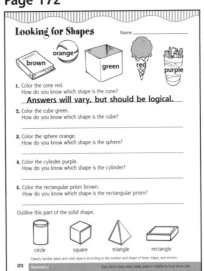

Page 173

Answers will vary.

Page 174

1. D	6. C
2. A	7. D
3. C	8. B
4. D	9. C
5. C	10. D

Page 175

yes

Page 176

Page 177

bone - yes
bear - yes
sneaker - no
hamburger - yes
baseball glove - no
rope - no

Page 178

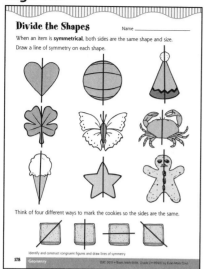

Page 179

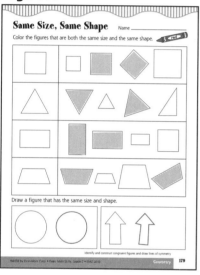

Page 180

1. C
2. C
3. D
4. C
5. B

6. A
7. D
8. B
9. C
10. B

Page 181

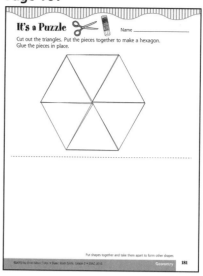

Page 182

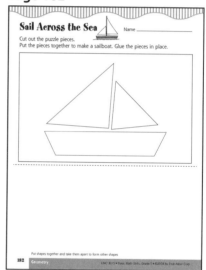

Page 183

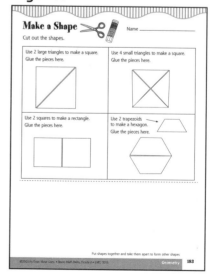

EMC 3015 • Basic Math Skills, Grade 2 • ©2003 by Evan-Moor Corp.

Page 184

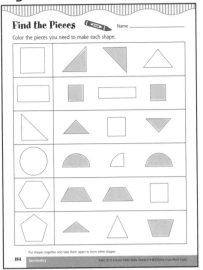

Page 185

Answers will vary, but must accurately reflect the task.

Page 186

1. C
2. B
3. A
4. C
5. B

6. C
7. A
8. C
9. B
10. C

Page 187

1. 36
2. 50
3. 20
4. 30
5. dog

Page 188

1. 24
3. 27
5. 22

2. 24
4. 27
6. 34

Page 189

1. 18
3. 37

2. 30
4. 30

Numbers 2 and 4 should be circled.

Page 190

1. 16
3. 24
5. 21

2. 21
4. 12
6. 12

Page 191

1. 20 inches
3. 20 feet
5. Answers will vary.

2. 24 inches
4. 50 centimeters

Page 192

1. C
2. C
3. D
4. D
5. B

6. C
7. C
8. C
9. D
10. A

Measurement

Page 194

dog bed - 5 bones
dish - 2 bones
rope toy - 3 bones
leash - 7 bones
dog sweater - 4 bones

Page 195

1. 5 hats tall
2. 6 hats tall
3. 2 hats tall
4. 3 hats tall
5. 1 hat tall
6. 4 hats tall

Page 196

A 4
B 5
C 2
D 3

Page 197

Guesses will vary.
banana 3
apple 2
kiwi 1
watermelon 4

Page 198

Answers will vary.

Page 199

1. D
2. B
3. A
4. C
5. D

6. C
7. D
8. A
9. B
10. A

Page 200

1. 3 inches
2. 4 inches
3. 2 inches
4. 5 inches
5. 4 inches
6. 1 inch

Number 4 bee should be circled.

Page 201

1. 2 inches
2. 3 inches
3. 1 inch
4. 4 inches
5. 6 inches

Page 202

1. 5 inches
2. 1 inch
3. 2 inches
4. 3 inches
5. 4 inches

Page 203

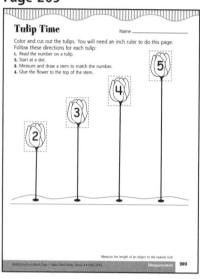

Page 204

Answers will vary.

Page 205

1. D
2. C
3. B
4. D
5. A

6. D
7. B
8. D
9. B
10. C

Page 206

Answers will vary.

Page 207

1. 16 centimeters
2. 7 centimeters
3. 4 centimeters
4. 3 centimeters
5. 5 centimeters

Page 208

1. 15 centimeters
2. 9 centimeters
3. 5 centimeters
4. 12 centimeters
5. 4 centimeters

Page 209

1. 4 – 1 = 3 centimeters
2. 11 – 4 = 7 centimeters
3. 14 – 11 = 3 centimeters
4. 12 – 7 = 5 centimeters

Page 210

Answers will vary.

Page 211

1. B
2. A
3. D
4. C
5. A

6. C
7. B
8. B
9. D
10. A

Page 212

0 5 10 15 20 25 30 35 40 45 50 55

11:45   11:15   11:30   11:00

quarter to 12   quarter past 11   half past 11   11 o'clock

Page 213

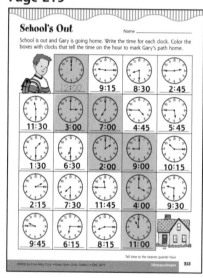

Page 214

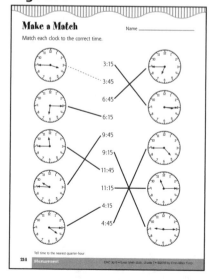

EMC 3015 • Basic Math Skills, Grade 2 • ©2003 by Evan-Moor Corp.

Page 215
1. Color first clock. 2. Color third clock. 3. Color third clock.

Page 216
Answers will vary.

Page 217
1. D
2. A
3. C
4. A
5. B

6. C
7. C
8. C
9. D
10. B

Page 218
weeding - 3 hours
watering - 1 hour
planting - 2 hours
picking flowers - 4 hours

Page 219
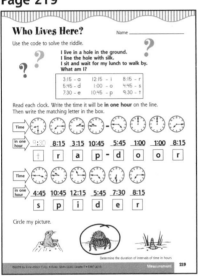

Page 220
1. 1 hour   2. 1 hour   3. 2 hours   4. 1 hour

Page 221
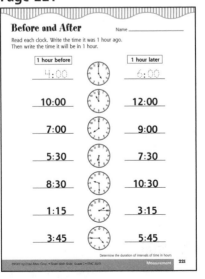

Page 222
1. 1 hour
3. 12 o'clock
5. 2 o'clock
7. Answers will vary.

2. 2 hours
4. 5 o'clock
6. 11:30

Page 223
1. D
2. B
3. D
4. C
5. A

6. C
7. B
8. D
9. C
10. B

Page 224
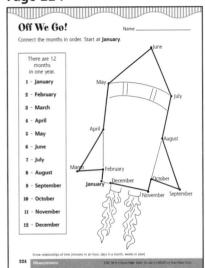

Page 225
Answers will vary.

Page 226
1. 7 months
2. February, 28 days
3. April, June, September, November
4. Answers will vary.

Page 227
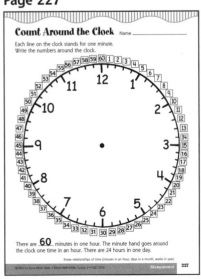

Page 228

1. 24 hours
2. 48 hours
3. 7 days
4. 35 days
5. 52 weeks, 365 days

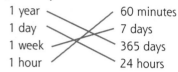

1 year — 24 hours
1 day — 365 days
1 week — 7 days
1 hour — 60 minutes

Page 229

1. B
2. D
3. B
4. C
5. C

6. D
7. A
8. B
9. D
10. B

Data Analysis & Probability

Page 231

1. ants   7
3. 5 − 3 = 2
5. 7 − 3 = 4

2. dragonfly 1
4. 7 + 3 = 10
6. Answers will vary.

Page 232

1. Anna
2. Carlos
3. 3 − 2 = 1
4. 1 + 3 + 2 = 6
5. Answers will vary.

Page 233

1. Angela
2. Arnold
3. Martha
4. Martha
5. 3 minutes
Answers will vary.

Page 234

1. pineapple 12 blocks
3. 5 blocks
5. 9 blocks more

2. kiwi   1 block
4. 6 blocks
6. Answers will vary.

Page 235

1. 5 x 2 = 10   3 x 7 = 21   5 x 5 = 25
   3 x 3 = 9   2 x 8 = 16   2 x 4 = 8
2. 3 x 5 = 15   5 x 3 = 15
3. 3 x 8 = 24   4 x 6 = 24
4. Answers will vary.

Page 236

1. B
2. C
3. D
4. B
5. A

6. B
7. A
8. D
9. B
10. A

Page 237

Page 238

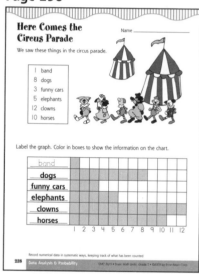

Page 239

yes < 6 tents drawn >

no < 7 tents drawn >

1. 13
2. no, 1 more
3. Answers will vary.

Page 240

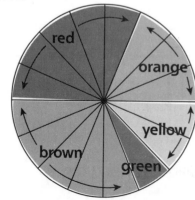

Page 241

Answers will vary.

Page 242

1. C
2. C
3. B
4. C
5. A

6. C
7. B
8. A
9. A
10. B

Page 243

My Family's Favorite Foods

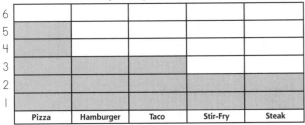

Page 244

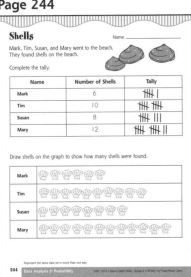

Page 245

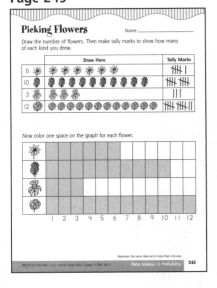

Page 246

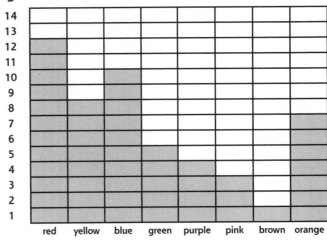

Page 247

Answers will vary.

Page 248

1. B
2. C
3. A
4. B
5. D

6. C
7. B
8. B
9. A
10. C

Page 249

1. red—there are more reds than any other color
2. purple—there is only one purple
3. Answers will vary, but cannot be red, green, blue, or purple.

Page 250

1. most likely—there are more sugar cookies than any other kind
2. impossible—there aren't any sugar wafers in the cookie jar
3. least likely—there are only 2 chocolate cookies in the jar

Page 251

1. red, green, orange
2. Answers will vary, but cannot be red, green, or orange.
3. red
4. orange

Page 252

1.

2. There are three letters on the chart and three letters on the spinner.

3.

Page 253

Answers will vary.

Page 254

1. B
2. A
3. D
4. A
5. D

6. B
7. C
8. D
9. C
10. B

Timed Tests

Page 256   Test 1

6 7 7 10 10 10 9 9
7 10 8 7 9 8 10 7
10 7 9 9 6 10 7 10
9 9 9 8 8 10 6 6

Test 2

7 10 7 6 10 6 9 9
9 6 8 8 7 10 9 10
7 9 10 8 9 10 10 9
7 6 9 10 7 7 10 8

Page 257   Test 3

6 0 2 1 6 3 2 8
4 4 5 4 5 1 9 0
2 3 0 4 3 7 0 6
4 6 1 2 1 5 5 3

Test 4

4 0 1 0 3 6 4 9
5 2 3 3 6 0 6 1
4 5 1 0 2 4 1 6
8 3 2 7 1 4 5 5

Page 258   Test 5

9 7 10 2 8 7 8 4
4 9 10 5 0 8 9 5
6 8 5 1 3 10 4 1
9 2 4 9 7 6 2 4

Test 6

7 10 6 10 1 3 6 2
8 6 2 10 10 1 6 9
6 9 5 7 8 0 7 4
7 5 10 8 10 7 3 9

Page 259   Test 7

10 11 11 15 11 12 10 13
10 12 13 14 15 14 10 11
15 13 13 15 11 12 13 13
14 12 14 11 10 12 12 11

Test 8

13 13 15 15 13 13 12 14
15 10 11 10 12 14 11 12
10 14 11 10 15 12 12 11
11 11 10 14 11 13 12 13

Page 260   Test 9

7 7 8 2 1 9 7 3
9 4 7 6 5 9 5 8
5 8 3 5 6 7 8 5
14 6 4 6 8 4 0 3

Test 10

7 4 2 3 9 7 7 6
3 8 5 9 6 5 8 0
8 5 7 5 5 1 9 4
6 4 3 8 6 6 8 8

Page 261   Test 11

15 12 9 8 10 10 4 13
2 12 12 6 7 9 11 11
7 11 12 9 1 10 9 10
15 5 4 13 5 10 11 6

Test 12

11 4 11 5 15 7 13 2
13 8 13 12 8 11 7 0
6 6 9 14 10 8 14 8
5 13 14 12 12 6 3 5

Page 262   Test 13

12 12 15 11 12 17 13 15
11 15 14 12 11 11 14 13
16 11 14 18 11 15 16 14
17 13 11 12 12 13 11 15

Test 14

11 16 14 15 11 11 15 13
13 12 12 14 14 18 13 12
11 16 17 14 11 13 16 12
15 12 11 12 15 17 15 16

Page 263   Test 15

9 8 9 7 7 9 8 15
6 6 8 5 3 5 7 4
6 6 9 9 8 4 9 7
9 4 9 8 5 7 8 0

Test 16

9 3 4 8 9 9 7 9
6 9 9 8 7 5 6 9
4 12 7 6 10 8 5 6
5 9 8 7 8 7 4 0

Page 264   Test 17

8 7 14 2 13 16 3 8
15 7 12 3 14 5 14 13
12 15 9 16 12 11 5 6
6 10 11 11 6 7 5 18

Test 18

17 6 7 9 9 13 9 9
8 9 12 16 8 9 4 14
11 8 4 9 8 12 13 8
11 13 18 11 16 11 15 6

Page 265   Test 19

2 10 14 8 40 5 15 6
45 35 20 0 30 35 16 0
10 18 12 40 20 8 2 12
30 16 25 4 45 6 18 5

Test 20

12 20 10 10 18 6 16 5
20 40 5 2 2 14 15 18
4 45 12 8 30 16 15 45
6 8 30 35 35 25 40 14

Page 266   Test 21

2 60 15 30 10 20 40 90
4 30 10 45 14 80 8 35
6 20 70 5 16 10 15 12
8 25 40 40 12 35 50 18

Test 22

5 16 10 45 14 80 2 60
8 35 4 30 10 40 12 35
6 20 70 15 12 15 30 10
20 40 12 8 25 40 50 18

EMC 3015 • Basic Math Skills, Grade 2 • ©2003 by Evan-Moor Corp.